Cirencester before Corinium

Excavations at Kingshill North, Cirencester, Gloucestershire

by Edward Biddulph and Ken Welsh

with a major contribution by David Mullin

Other contributions by

Leigh Allen, Paul Booth, Carl Champness, Sharon Clough, John Cotter, Jane Evans, R A Ixer, Lynne Keys, Angela Lamb, Rebecca Nicholson, Cynthia Poole, Fiona Roe, Ian Scott, Lena Strid, Ruth Shaffrey, Wendy Smith, Dan Stansbie, Roger Taylor, Jane Timby, Helen Webb and Alistair Zochowski

Illustrated by

Hannah Kennedy, Mark Littlewood, Daniel Bashford, Magdalena Wachnik and Sarah Lucas

Oxford Archaeology
Thames Valley Landscapes Monograph No. 34
2011

The publication of this volume was generously funded by Robert Hitchens Ltd

Published for Oxford Archaeology by Oxford University School of Archaeology as part of the
Thames Valley Landscapes Monograph series

Designed by Oxford Archaeology Graphics Office

Edited by Ian Scott

This book is part of a series of monographs about the Thames Valley Landscapes which can be bought
from all good bookshops and internet bookshops

For more information visit http://thehumanjourney.net/

Figures 1, 43 and 44 contain Ordnance Survey data © Crown copyright and database right 2011

Front cover: Beaker from grave and ring-ditch group, 8454 (photograph and drawing by Magdalena Wachnik)

Back cover: Dog skeleton from Middle Iron Age pit 8851

ISBN 978-1-905905-22-5

Typeset by Production Line, Oxford
Printed in Great Britain by Information Press, Eynsham, Oxfordshire

Contents

CHAPTER 6: ENVIRONMENTAL EVIDENCE

CHPTER 7: DISCUSSION

List of Figures

Summary

An excavation by Oxford Archaeology in 2008 at Kingshill North, to the north-east of Cirencester, Gloucestershire, uncovered evidence for prehistoric occupation. The earliest evidence comprised storage pits dating to the late Neolithic period. Some of the features contained Grooved Ware pottery decorated with exceptionally rare 'lattice lozenge' motifs, pig bones suggestive of feasting, bone pins and awls, worked flint imported from some distance, and fragments of Cornish axe heads. The pit groups point to a community able to mobilise a wide range of resources and dispose of them in a highly visible way. The fieldwork uncovered two Beaker burials, one enclosed by a ring-ditch. The isotopes from the individuals indicate that they were not local; one individual came from the chalklands of eastern or southern England, the other was from a more south-westerly chalkland region. As such they fit within an emerging picture of population mobility. Another inhumation grave, dated to the middle Bronze Age, was also recorded. More storage pits were dug during the middle Iron Age. These were filled with domestic waste, but there was evidence of structured deposits in the form of crow or rook and dog burials. The late Iron Age settlement comprised a sequence of ditches which formed boundaries or enclosures and surrounded structures and pits. These were set within a pastoral landscape and areas of grassland and meadows. Three human burials, all interred in ditches, were also recorded. The settlement was within the territory of the Dobunni, whose centre was at nearby Bagendon, but the inhabitants of Kingshill North did not benefit materially from the proximity, and their focus remained local. The settlement was abandoned by the late 1st century AD, before or coincident with the establishment of the Roman town of Corinium Dobunnorum, although agricultural activity continued to a limited extent through the Roman period, and there was a single cremation burial dated between the late 1st and mid 3rd century AD. The medieval and post-medieval periods were represented by an agricultural landscape of field boundaries and drainage features.

Acknowledgements

The authors are indebted to Robert Hitchens Ltd for funding the archaeological fieldwork, post-excavation programme and publication. The work was commissioned by CgMs Consulting, and thanks are owed to Myk Flitcroft of CgMs for ensuring that the project proceeded smoothly. The authors are also grateful to Charles Parry and Jan Wills of Gloucestershire County Council Archaeology Service for their support.

The fieldwork was directed by Vix Hughes and was managed by Ken Welsh. The post-excavation project was managed by Edward Biddulph. Support was provided by Leigh Allen (finds management), Paul Backhouse and Sarah Lucas (graphics management), Matt Bradley (geomatics management), Louise Loe (burials management), Rebecca Nicholson (environmental management), Nicola Scott (archives management), and Alex Smith (project monitoring). Victoria Wilkinson digitised the site plans, and Mark Littlewood drafted the GIS-based report figures. Finds were drawn or photographed by Daniel Bashford, Sarah Lucas, Jane Timby and Magdalena Wachnik. Hannah Kennedy drafted additional drawings, with some preliminary work by Georgina Slater, and prepared final versions of all the figures. The authors are grateful to Jane Randle for permission to reproduce the aerial photograph shown in Figure 3.

Oxford Archaeology would like to thank the following for their significant contribution to the project during and after fieldwork: Gary Baddeley, Robert Bailey, Robin Bashford, Claire Burke, Nathan Chichen, Liz Collinson, Martyn Cooper, Geraldine Crann, Jodie Ford, Andrew Frudd, Fiona Gordon, Anthony Haskins, Sarah Hopes, Nate Jepson, Trevor Jose, Mike Kershaw, Neil Lambert, Paul Leader, Robin Maggs, Ben McAndrew, Hefin Meara, Andrea Paylor, Kay Proctor, Chris Reese, Christopher Richardson, Jennifer Salter, Mark Sycamore, Rowena Tucker, Robert Tutt, Matthew Weightman, and Victoria Wilkinson. David Mullin is indebted to Ann Woodward for her expert guidance on the earlier prehistoric pottery. The report was edited for publication by Ian Scott. The authors are especially grateful to Charles Parry, Myk Flitcroft and Neil Holbrook for reading and commenting on the text. Any errors, however, remain the responsibility of the authors alone.

Chapter 1: Introduction

Project background (Fig. 1)

Oxford Archaeology (OA) was commissioned by CgMs Consulting on behalf of Robert Hitchins Ltd to undertake a programme of archaeological works to mitigate the impact of residential development on land at Kingshill North, Cirencester. Fieldwork was carried out in order to comply with a condition attached to planning permission granted by Cotswold District Council (application ref: 07/00748/OUT). The work was carried out between April and August 2008 in line with a written scheme of investigation (OA 2008) prepared by OA and agreed with Cotswold District Council and its archaeological advisers.

The Kingshill North development is located to the north-east of Cirencester and centred on grid reference SP 0365 0250 (Fig. 1). The site is bounded by Burford Road to the north, London Road to the south, the gardens of existing housing to the west, and the A417/419 Trunk road to the east. The excavation area was on the western side of the development site and measured 5.8 ha (Figs 2 and 3). The site was under arable cultivation, except for the northern area, which comprised disused allotments and an early-modern waste disposal site. The waste disposal site was not subject to archaeological mitigation. A watching brief was maintained at the site after the main excavation stage.

Fieldwork methodology (Fig. 4)

Topsoil and overburden were removed by mechanical excavator using a toothless ditching bucket under constant archaeological supervision. Mechanical excavation ceased at either undisturbed natural deposits or when archaeological features were identified. The nature of these deposits was assessed by hand excavation. The spoil heaps and exposed features were scanned for metal finds by a competent metal-detectorist using suitable equipment. OA staff were trained as detectorists and therefore the work was done under archaeological conditions.

Data-capture for site plans was by a combination of EDM and GPS. Data-capture for site plans was, as standard, capable of reproduction at a scale of 1:100; more complex features or areas of complex archaeological remains were recorded at greater resolution (for reproduction at 1:10, 1:20, or 1:50 as necessary). The sections of excavated archaeological features were recorded by measured drawing at an appropriate scale (1:10). Spot heights and levels of individual features were recorded relative to Ordnance Datum (OD).

All features and deposits were issued with unique context numbers, and context recording was carried out in accordance with established OA practice (Wilkinson 1992). The environmental sampling strategy included the routine sampling of undisturbed, securely dated deposits for the retrieval and assessment of the preservation conditions and potential for analysis of all biological remains. The sampling strategy included a programme of sampling and assessment for charred plant macrofossils, molluscs, animal and human bone. All environmental work was undertaken in accordance with current English Heritage guidelines.

All artefacts were treated in accordance with United Kingdom Institute for Conservation of Historic and Artistic Works (Archaeology Section) guidelines (Watkinson and Neal 1998). All registered finds were processed and packaged according to standards of good practice. In accordance with current English Heritage guidelines, all iron objects, a selection of non-ferrous artefacts (including all coins) and a sample of any industrial debris relating to metallurgy were submitted for X-radiography and stabilisation where appropriate.

The human remains (and articulated animal remains) were cleaned with minimal disturbance prior to recording and removal. Investigation and excavation of human remains were undertaken by, or under the supervision of, suitably experienced specialist staff and in accordance with IFA guidelines.

Geology and topography (Fig. 5)

The Kingshill North site is located close to the junction of the Cotswolds dip slope and the flat lands of the upper Thames valley (see Fig. 25). The River Churn, which flows roughly from north to south through Cirencester and into the Thames near Cricklade about 13 km away, is at its closest point *c* 800 m south-west of Kingshill North. The site is highest in the north and plateaus at an elevation of 130 m OD (Fig. 5). The site slopes downwards to the east, south, and west, so that the contours of the slope form an arc across the southern part of the site. The slope begins gently with a gradient of about 1-in-26, or 0.04, but becomes steeper towards the southern edge of excavation, increasing in its gradient to 1-in-10, or 0.1. The southernmost tip of the site lies at a height of *c* 115 m OD. The local geology is highly variable over a relatively small area and consisted of bands of Forest Marble Limestone, White Limestone Formation and Signet Member, all of which date to the Bathonian Age in

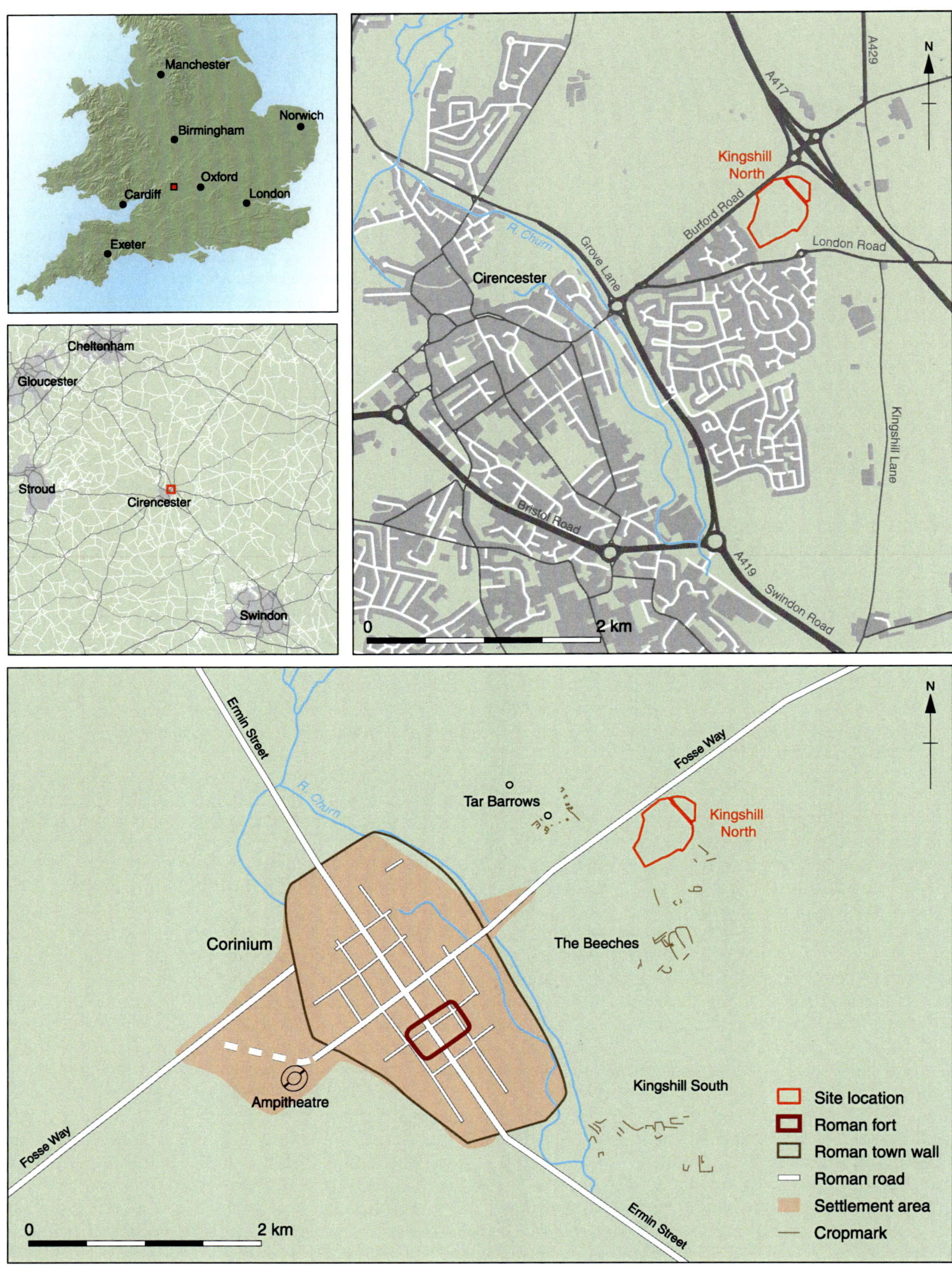

Fig. 1   *Site location and archaeological background*

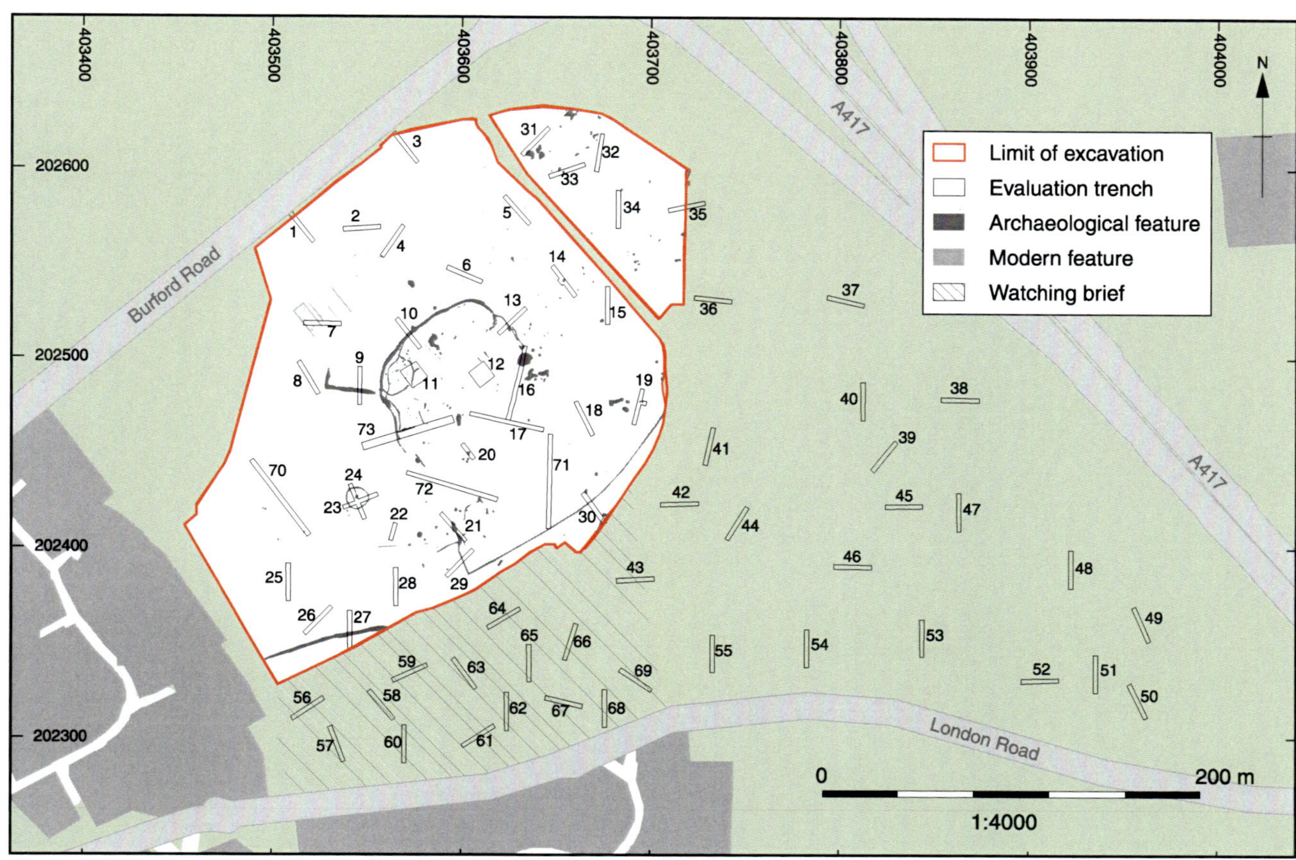

Fig. 2   *Areas of investigation*

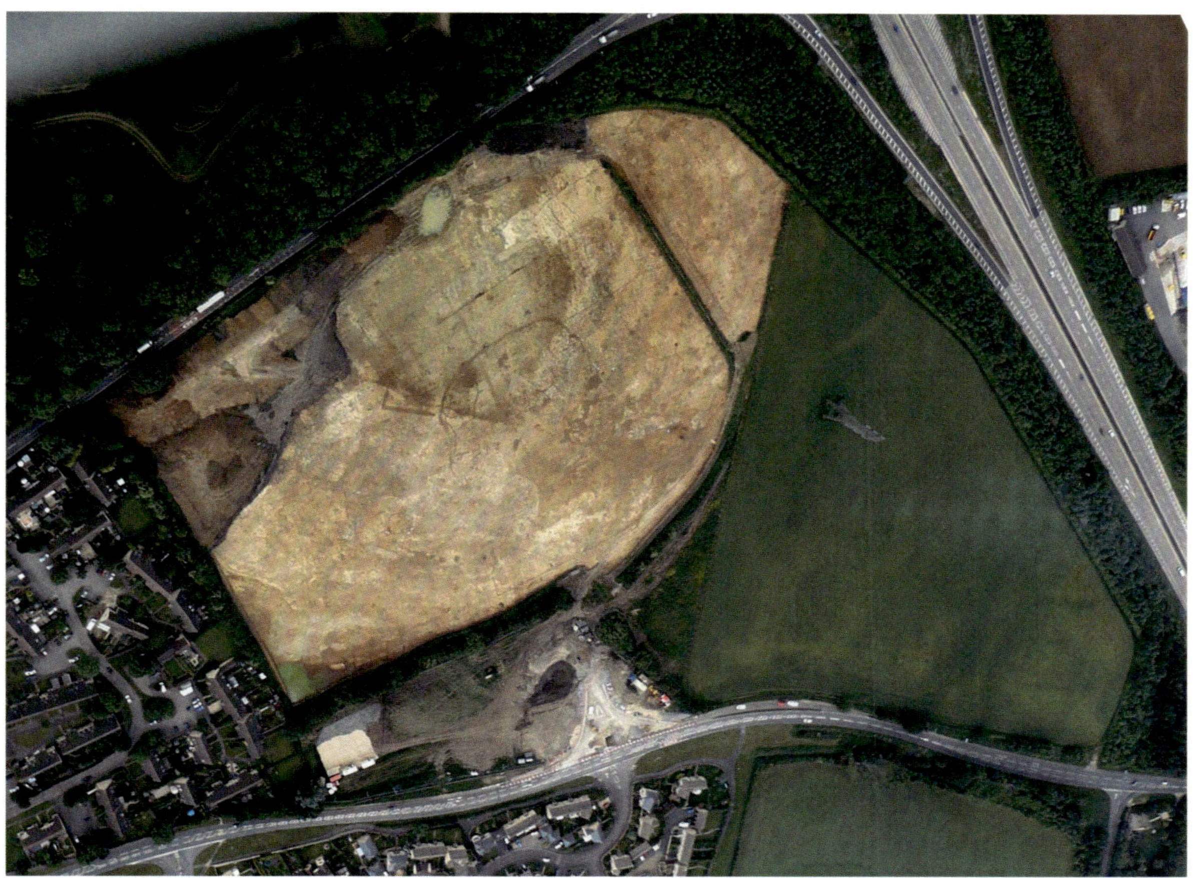

Fig. 3   *Aerial view of the site (image courtesy of Jane Randle)*

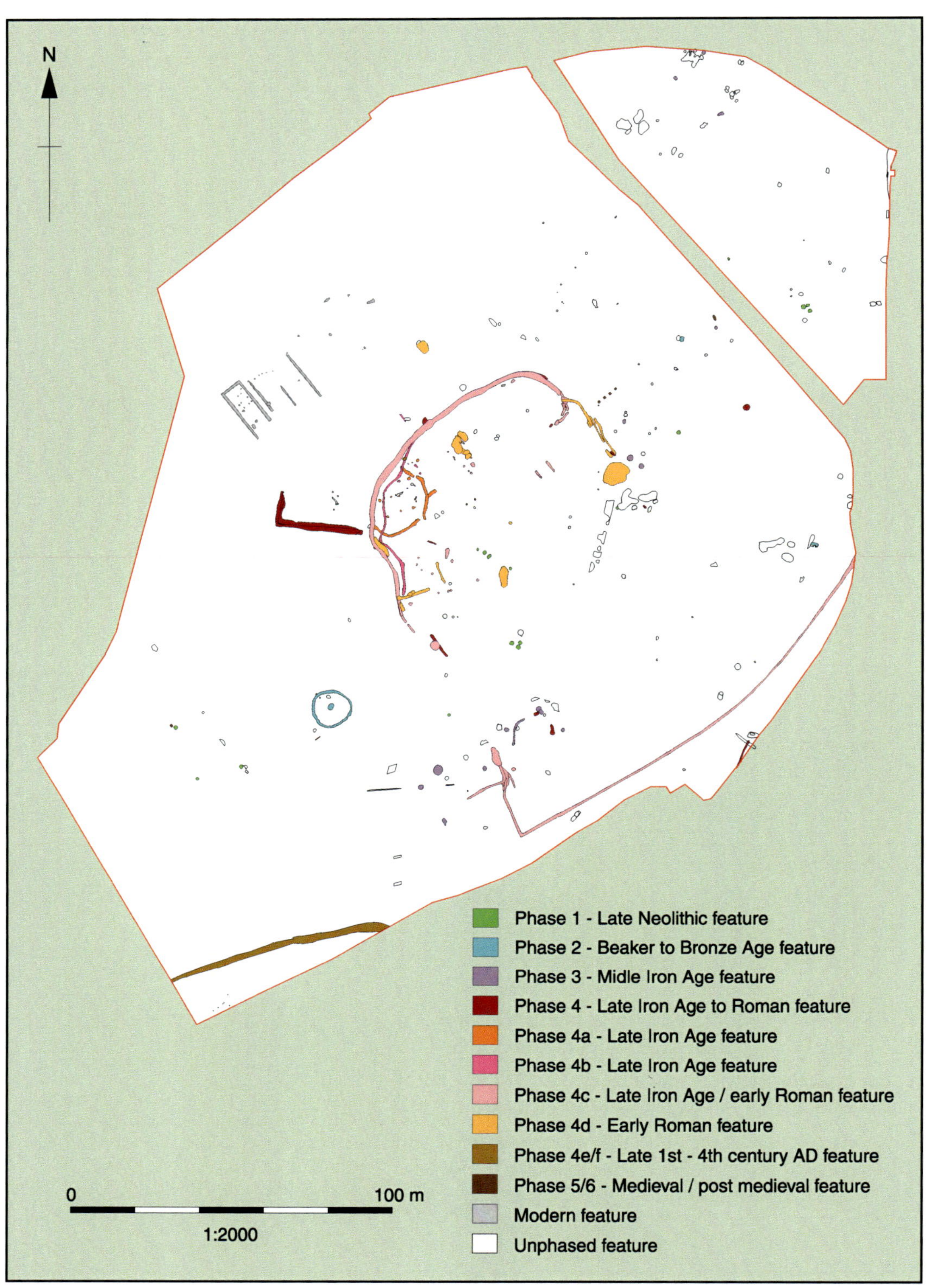

Fig. 4 Plan of all excavated features, showing phasing

the Jurassic Period. Derivative fine loamy, clayey soils of the Elmton 2 association and loose fossiliferous limestone or cornbrash overlie the solid geology.

Archaeological and historical background (Figs 1 and 44)

The archaeological potential of the Kingshill North development site was evaluated through desk-based assessment (JSAC 2001; 2005), geophysical survey (GSB Prospection 2000; 2006) and trial trenching (OA 2006). At least two round barrows, known as the Tar Barrows, survive on the north side of Burford Road and are protected as Scheduled Monuments (County number 268). Two further possible barrows are recorded by the county Historic Environment Records (HER) database. One is located on the north of the Burford Road (HER 2096), while the other (HER 2125) is located northwest of Whiteway Farm, *c* 2.5 km from the development area. A survey by the Royal Commission on Historical Monuments (England) revealed potential ditches showing as cropmarks immediately southeast of the development site on the edge of London Road. More cropmarks, identified as enclosures, were recorded some 500 m south of the Kingshill North at the Beeches. Another concentration of enclosures was detected *c* 1 km south of those (Leech 1977, 7).

In 1999, archaeological work in advance of residential development at the Beeches provided an opportunity for some of the cropmarks to be investigated (Fig. 1). The fieldwork revealed significant

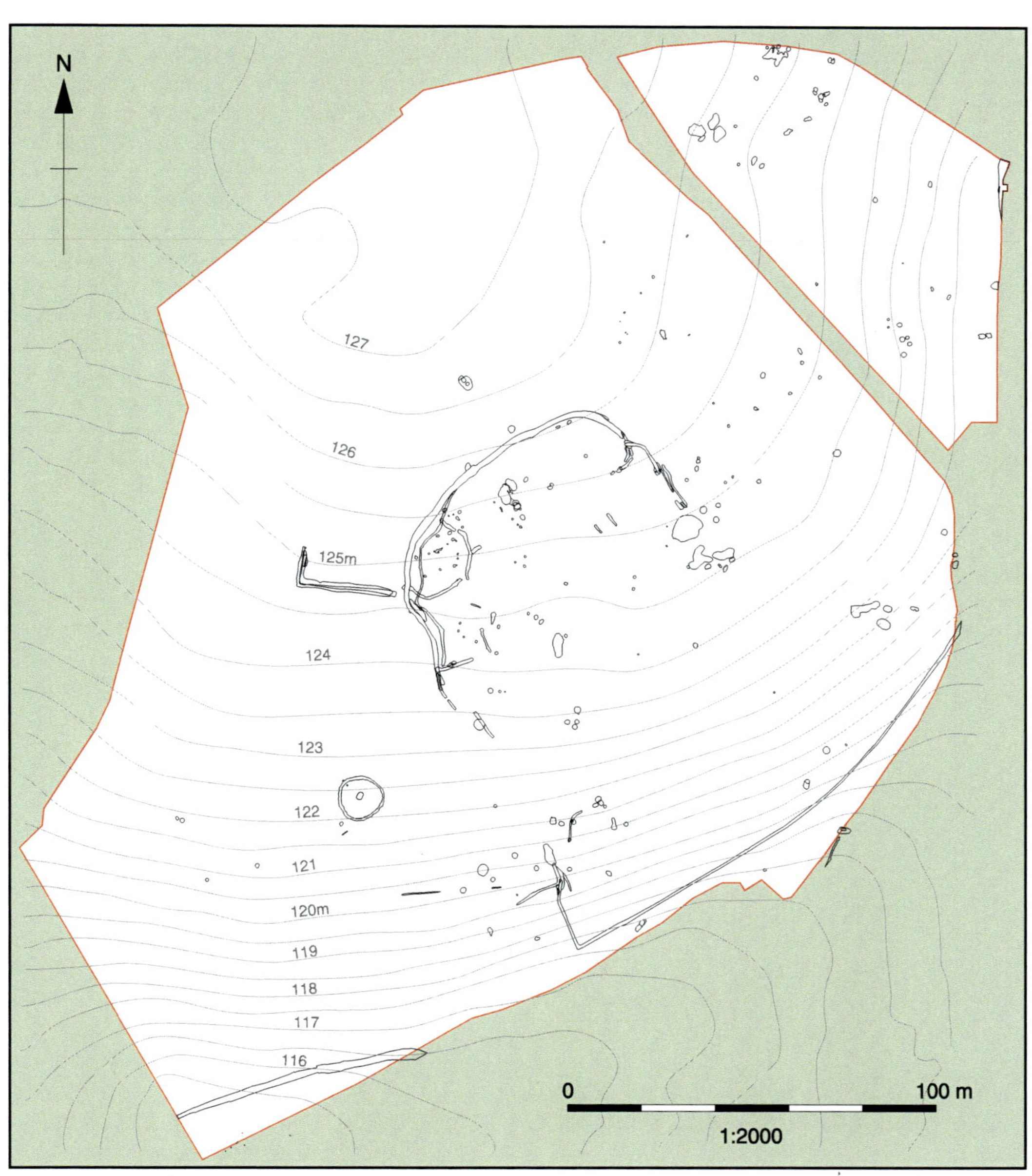

Fig. 5 Topography of Kingshill North

evidence of prehistoric activity on the site (Young 2001). Two excavation areas were examined in detail, one containing an enclosure and postholes dating to the middle Bronze Age, the other containing a ditched enclosure dating to the early Iron Age (HER 17205; Young 2001). The cropmarks further south were investigated in excavations at Kingshill South to the south-east of Cirencester on the town's ring-road (Fig. 1). The work uncovered shallow ditches that were attributed to the 1st, and possibly the 2nd, century AD (Reece 1990, 39-40). Further excavations in that area by Oxford Archaeology revealed a ditch dated to the Neolithic period by Grooved Ware pottery, early Roman enclosures and boundary ditches (possibly forming part of the archaeology discovered by Reece), and a villa-like building and associated apsidal structure assigned to the mid and late Roman periods (Ken Welsh, pers. comm.).

An evaluation in 2006 by OA (Fig. 2) uncovered remains of a crouched human burial associated with Beaker pottery (recorded as 1402, see below). Another burial, associated with a ring ditch, was identified but remained unexcavated until the excavation (8588). A third burial, a supine human inhumation (1905) was recorded further east. The fieldwork also identified a number of features in the central part of the site that could be broadly dated to the later Iron Age, including a large oval enclosure, gullies and structural features. These were all re-examined during the subsequent excavation.

The Iron Age activity at Kingshill North was part of a regional settlement pattern that included enclosures at Middle Duntisbourne and Dunstisbourne Grove (Mudd *et al.* 1999b, 95), pits at Stratton (Wymark 2003), and an earthwork complex at Bagendon and related enclosure at Ditches (Trow *et al.* 2009) (Fig. 44). Further south, the extensive archaeological landscape down the River Churn and more widely within the Upper Thames Valley is also of enormous relevance to Kingshill North. The prehistoric and Roman settlements at Cotswold

Community (Powell *et al.* 2010), Claydon Pike (Miles *et al.* 2007), Ashton Keynes (Powell *et al.* 2008) and Latton Lands (Powell *et al.* 2009) provide key points of comparison.

Roman Cirencester (*Corinium*) was established first in the Churn valley as a fort in the mid 1st century AD, before developing into a town after *c* AD 75 (Wacher and McWhirr 1982) (Fig. 1). The town replaced the Bagendon/Ditches complex as a regional centre, but a villa was maintained at Ditches until the 3rd century (Trow *et al.* 2009, 45-6). The extra-mural area to the north-east of the town saw little activity and formed part of the rural landscape (Holbrook 2008a, 138).

Cirencester was re-established as a major centre in Gloucestershire by the time of Domesday (1086) and was one of only four Gloucestershire towns recorded as having a market at that time, although there may have been more. A small medieval settlement existed in the area around Norcote Farm, *c* 500 metres east of the development site. The post-medieval period saw the Burford Road, Akeman Street and London Road develop as turnpikes. By the early 19th century, an area of parkland, Hare Bushes, had been established. It was bounded to the south by Burford Road and around much of the perimeter had belt planting typical of later 18th-century 'naturalistic' parkland layouts.

The local geology lent itself to lime production. Evidence of this is contained in the local field name 'Lime Kiln Ground' (HER 9822). Limestone may also have been extracted for building stone or road making, and the south-easternmost part of the development area is shown on some earlier maps as 'Quarry Forestal'. During the early part of this century the north-western part of the proposed development area was used as a rubbish pit, presumably after quarrying for limestone, although this has not been identified on early OS maps. Geotechnical test pitting in connection with the development has identified the extent of this quarried area.

Chapter 2: Archaeological Description

Phase 1 – Late Neolithic, *c* 3000-2400 BC (Figs 6-9)

Evidence of Neolithic activity was confined to pits dug across the southern half of the site (Fig. 6). Eighteen pits have been dated to this phase by various means, including radiocarbon dating and a range of artefactual material (Table 1). The features were small and oval in plan and measured on average 1.14 m long, 0.91 m wide and 0.3 m deep. The pits varied in terms of profile but generally conformed to three broad types (Figs 7-9). Most were flat-based and steep-sided. These were relatively shallow (up to 0.25 m deep), but did include deeper examples; pit 9144, which cut similarly-profiled pit 9164, was 0.5 m deep (Fig. 9). Other pits were concave or U-shaped. All were dug through the natural cornbrash sediment, although where the admixture of small limestone nodules, silt and sand gave way to limestone bedrock, the pits tended to be more irregular, with stepped sides and uneven bases.

The pits were filled by silty or clay deposits that contained the remnants of burning from hearths and the like in the form of charcoal and burnt limestone. Most features contained two fills, but single fills and as many as four deposits were recorded. Where there was more than one fill, the bottom deposit tended to contain a higher proportion of cornbrash material, though it also held artefacts. That many of the fills contained objects of human activity suggests that the fills were formed primarily through deliberate deposition, perhaps from the clearance of near-by cooking or flint-knapping areas, rather than through natural silting. The pits contained a varied assemblage of finds that included Grooved Ware pottery, flint scrapers, bone pins, stone axe heads, antler fragments, and cattle and pig bone.

Though distributed widely in the southern half of the excavation area, the pits form at least four groups, each consisting of three or four features. These groupings do not appear to be chronologically significant, as radiocarbon determinations reveal no great differences in the periods of deposition. A nutshell fragment from pit 9100 (Fig. 8),

Table 1: Artefactual and dating evidence from Neolithic pits

Group	Pit	Pottery (sherds)	Flint (no.)	Animal Bone	Charred plant remains	Other	Radiocarbon date
8103	8058	21	14	pig, cattle, deer, goat	--	antler x2, bone pin tip	
	8100	--	72	pig, cattle, deer, sheep/goat	hazelnut shells	pierced stone, antler x2, hammerstone, axe flake	2863 to 2673 cal BC
	8064	286	80	pig, cattle, sheep/goat, deer	hazelnut shells, cereal grain	antler x1, bone ?spatula, bone pins x2	2856 to 2571 cal BC
9103	8813	59	505	pig, cattle, deer, horse, sheep/goat, ?aurochs	hazelnut shells	complete stone axe, bone pins x5, worked bone, antler x1	
	8930	3	145	pig, cattle, deer	charcoal	antler x3	
	9100	98	202	pig, cattle, sheep/goat, aurochs, deer	hazelnut shells, tuber, ?cereal, crab apple	bone pins x3, antler x1	3261 to 2922 cal BC (context 9101) 2859 to 2500 cal BC (context 9102)
n/a	8721	--	--	sheep/goat	--	no finds	
n/a	8708	--	--	--	charcoal	no finds	
n/a	8714	--	--	--	--	no finds	
n/a	8738	--	8	pig, cattle, deer	hazelnut shells	antler x1	
n/a	8164	17	81	pig	not sampled	--	
n/a	8392	69	117	pig, cattle, sheep/goat, deer, dog	hazelnut shells, ?tuber	--	
n/a	8455	305	136	pig, cattle, sheep/goat, dog	hazelnut shells	stone axe fragment	
n/a	8928	29	170	pig, cattle, sheep/goat	--	axe fragments x2, polished pebble	
n/a	9063	--	1	pig, cattle, sheep/goat, horse	--	--	
n/a	9096	144	84	pig, cattle, deer, sheep/goat	hazelnut shells, ?cereal	antler x4, hammerstone	2886 to 2665 cal BC
n/a	9144/ 9164	30	11	pig, cattle, deer, sheep/goat	not sampled	antler x2	

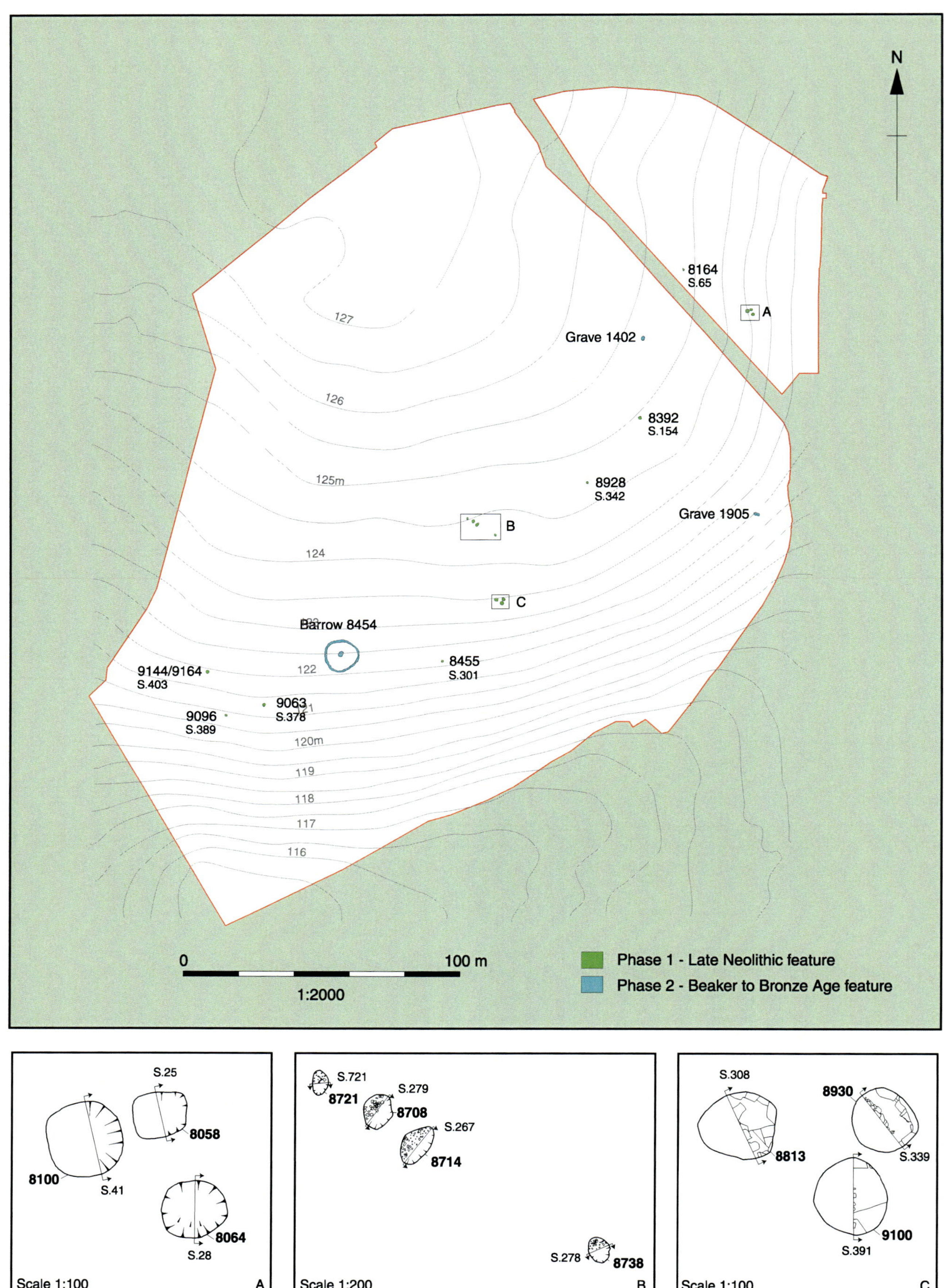

Fig. 6   Phase 1 and 2. Late Neolithic and Bronze Age activity

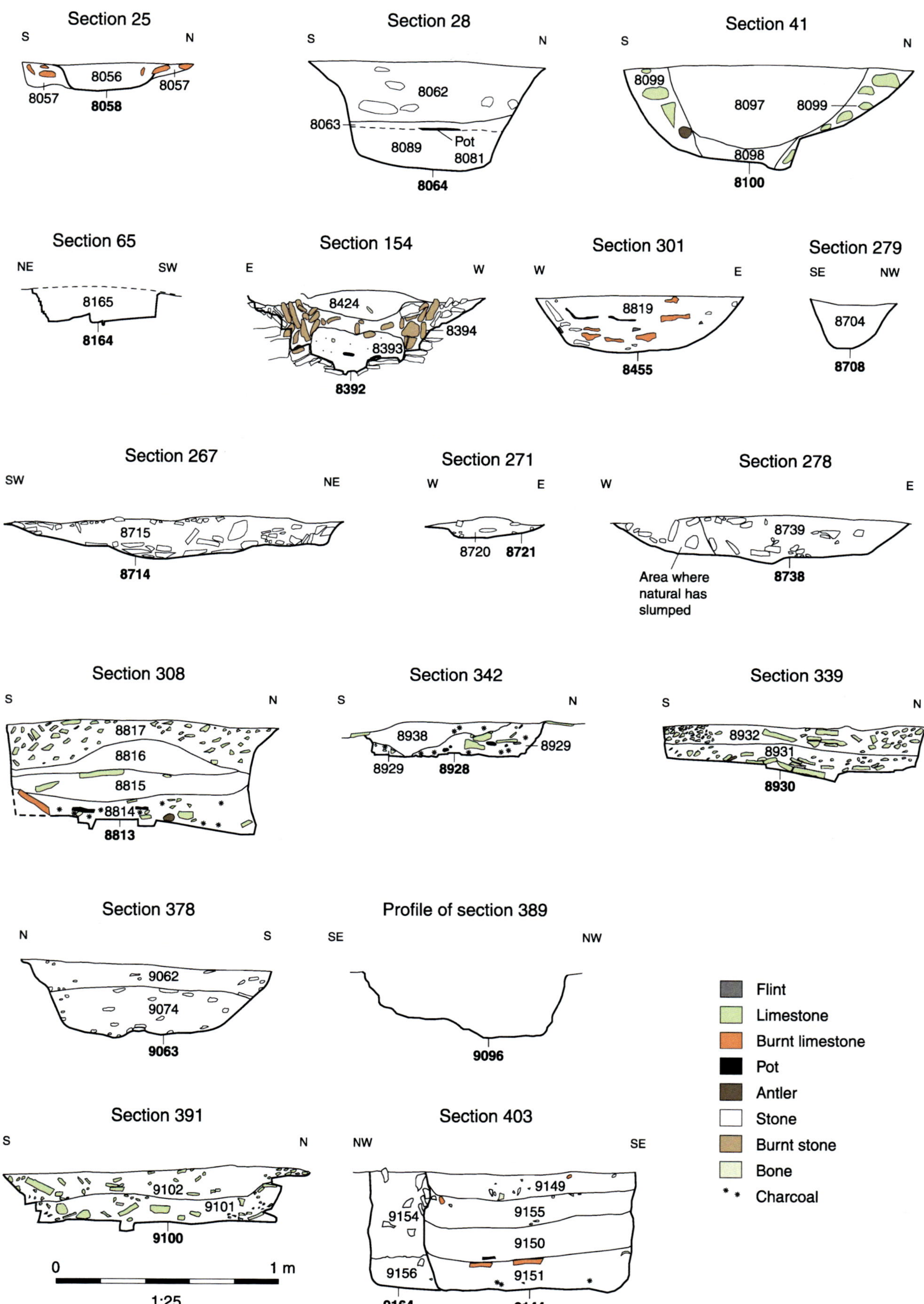

Fig. 7   Phase 1. Sections through Neolithic pits

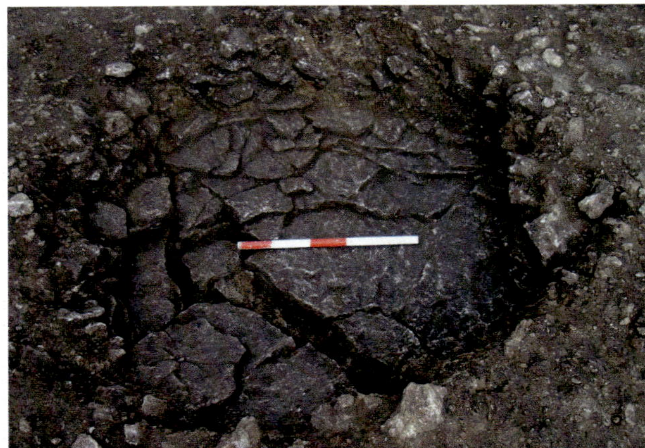

Fig. 8   Neolithic pit 9100

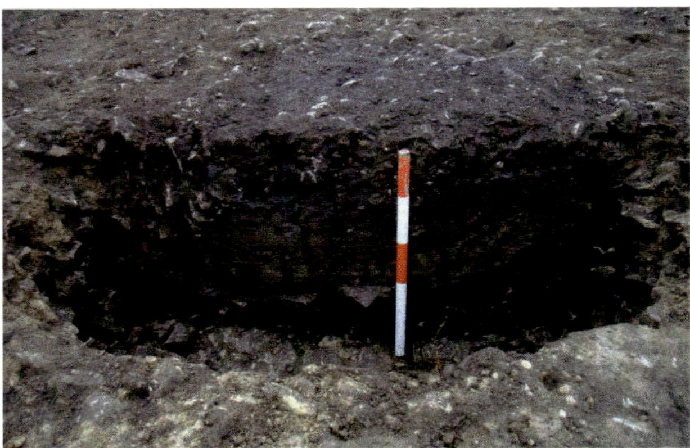

Fig. 9   Neolithic pit 9144

grouped in the centre of the site with pits 8813 and 8930, was dated to 3261-2922 cal BC (95%; NZA-33224). Pit 9096, located near to pits 9063 and 9144 at south-western end of the site, contained a nutshell dated to 2886-2665 cal BC (95%; NZA-33151). At the far eastern end of the site, an antler fragment from pit 8064 and a nutshell from pit 8100 gave closely similar determinations of 2856-2571 cal BC (95%; NZA-33477) and 2863-2673 cal BC (95%; NZA-33140) respectively.

Phase 2 – Beaker to Bronze Age, *c* 2400-1400 BC (Figs 10-14)

The archaeology of the Bronze Age was exclusively funerary in character. Group 8454, uncovered towards the south-eastern part of the site, was a ring-ditch enclosing a central grave that contained an inhumation burial (Figs 10-12). The ditch measured on average 0.65 m wide, 0.22 m deep, and formed a ring 12 m in diameter. Sections dug through the ditch revealed that feature was filled with a silty clay soil, although deposition was uneven; parts of the ditch were filled in single episodes while others – usually the deeper sections – received two, and occasionally three, fills. Small quantities of struck flint, pig and cattle bone, deer antler, and Bronze Age Beaker sherds were recov-

ered from the ditch fill. Two postholes (8993 and 9011) were uncovered on either side of ditch. No dating evidence was recovered, but their arrangement suggests that they were associated with the ditch. The central grave (8588) was rectangular, measuring *c* 2.2 m by 1.3 m, its long axis aligned south-west/north-east. The buried individual (8656) was placed in the empty cut on its right side, with its head at the south end and its legs flexed (Fig. 12). Diagnostic traits on the cranium pointed to male, but the more accurate traits of the pelvis made identification as female more likely. Dental and pelvic elements indicated an age of 30-40 years old (Zochowski and Webb, Chapter 3 below). Strontium isotopes extracted from the teeth suggested a childhood in eastern or southern England (Lamb and Evans, Chapter 3 below). A Beaker was placed on the floor of the grave in between the legs and arms. The grave was backfilled with silty clay in three episodes; the final fill, 8589, contained 270 fragments of animal bone, including substantial portions of the skull and lower legs of a cow. These belonged to a so-called 'head-and-hooves' deposit representing the burial of a hide (see Strid and Nicholson, Chapter 6 below). Dating evidence places the burial in the early Bronze Age. Apart from the Beaker, a radiocarbon date of 2458-2152 cal BC (95%; OxA-20184) was obtained from the skeleton.

Another early Bronze Age grave (1402) (Fig. 13), found during the 2006 evaluation, was located at the north-eastern part of the site. In this case, however, the skeleton (1403) was dated to 2201-2031 cal BC (95%; OxA-20186), indicating that the burial was later than the burial associated with group 8454. The grave was very roughly circular, measuring 1.6 m across its widest extent. The skeleton, which was crouched with its head was at the north end, was fragmentary, but the diagnostic traits suggest that the individual was an adult female over 50 years old (Zochowski and Webb, Chapter 3 below). In contrast to skeleton 8656, strontium isotope results placed the childhood of individual 1403 in more south-westerly areas of Britain (Lamb and Evans, Chapter 3 below). A Beaker, incomplete on excavation, had been placed by the feet. Bone fragments from the redeposited remains of a juvenile burial were also recovered. Two fills were recorded: a layer of sandy clay, which had accumulated before the individual was interred, and a silty clay backfill. The upper deposit contained an area of charcoal that appeared to lie over the legs of the skeleton. Fragments of animal bone were also found within the grave.

A third grave, 1905 (Fig. 14), was later still in date. The skeleton provided a radiocarbon date of 1502-1415 cal BC (95%; OxA-20188), placing the burial at the start of the middle Bronze Age. The grave, aligned east-west, was rectangular and measured *c* 2.2 m long by 0.9 m wide. It appeared to cut an earlier pit (1907). The individual (1903) was laid in the empty grave supine and extended, with

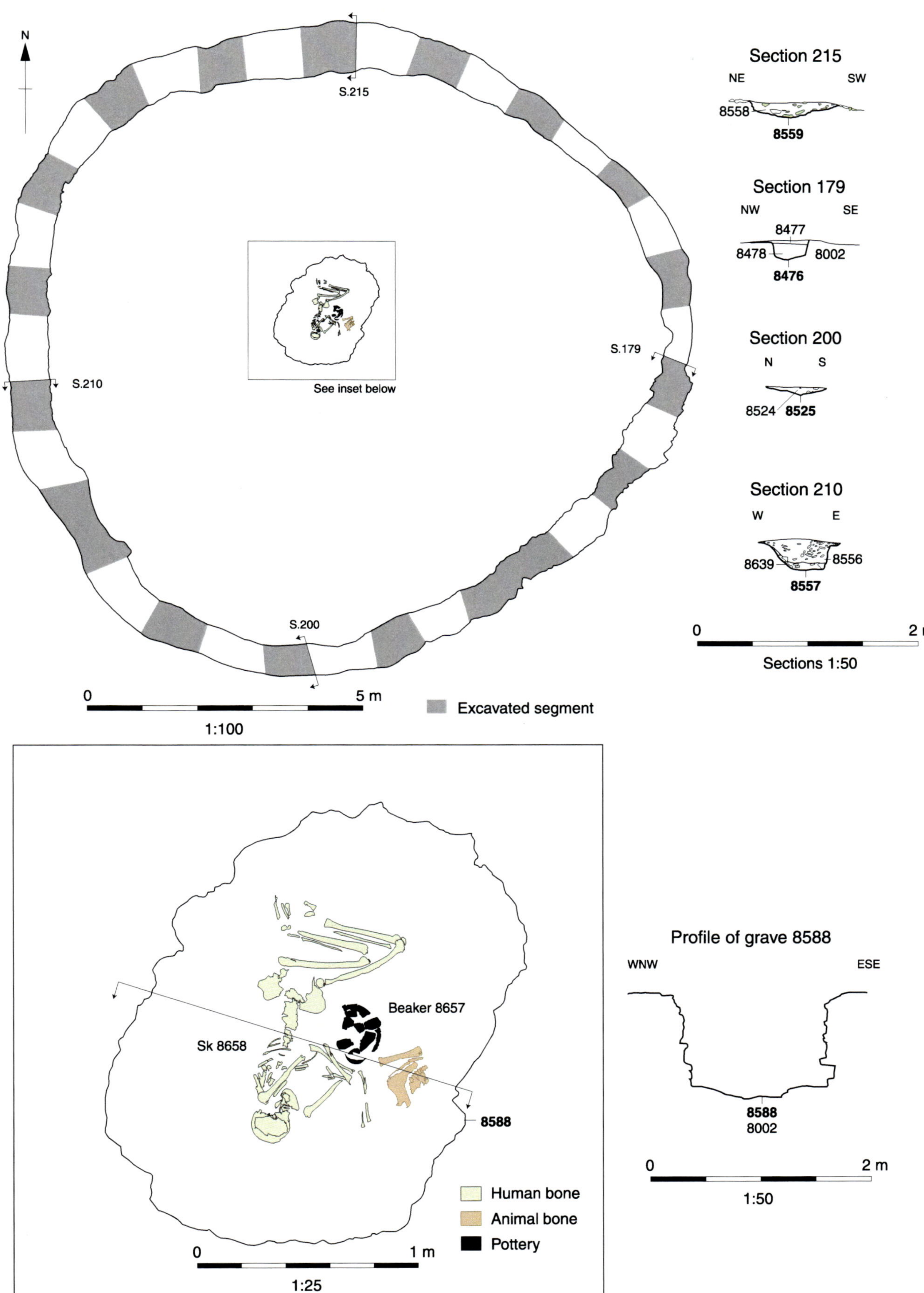

Fig. 10 Phase 2. Early Bronze Age ring-ditch and burial, group 8454

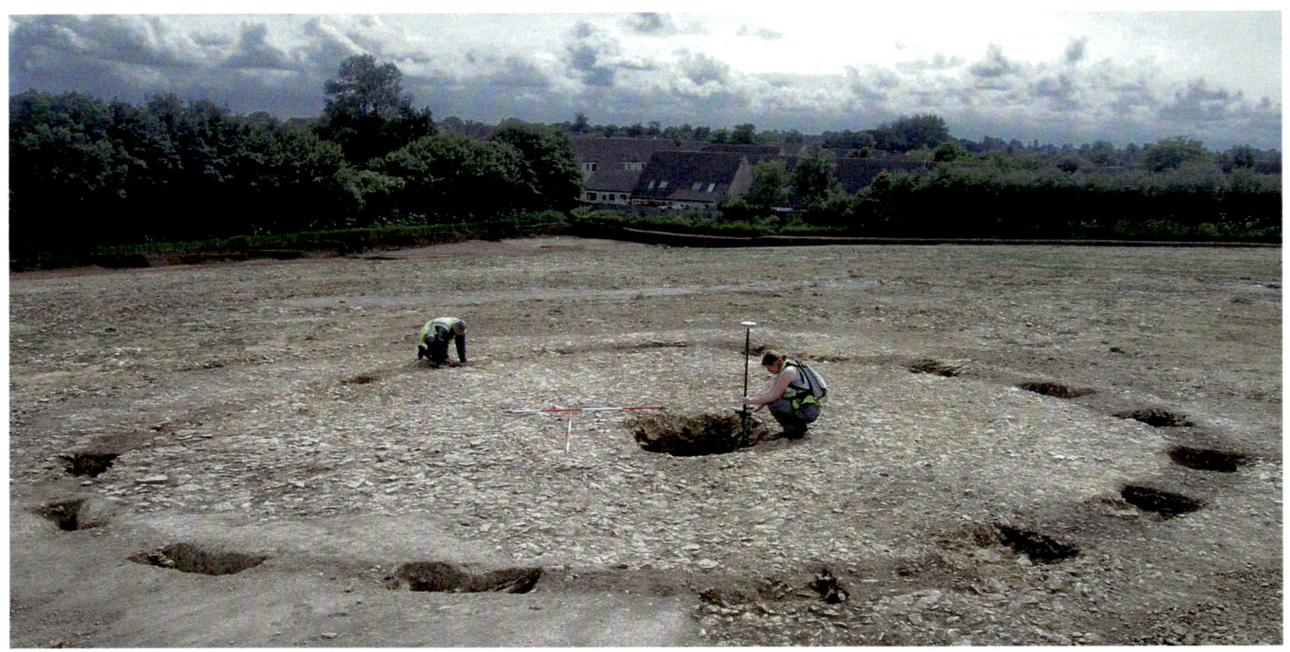

Fig. 11   Round barrow 8454

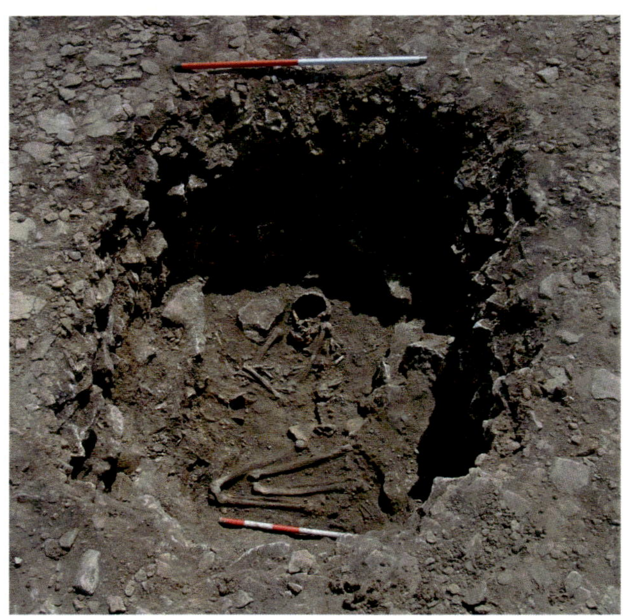

Fig. 12   Central grave 8588

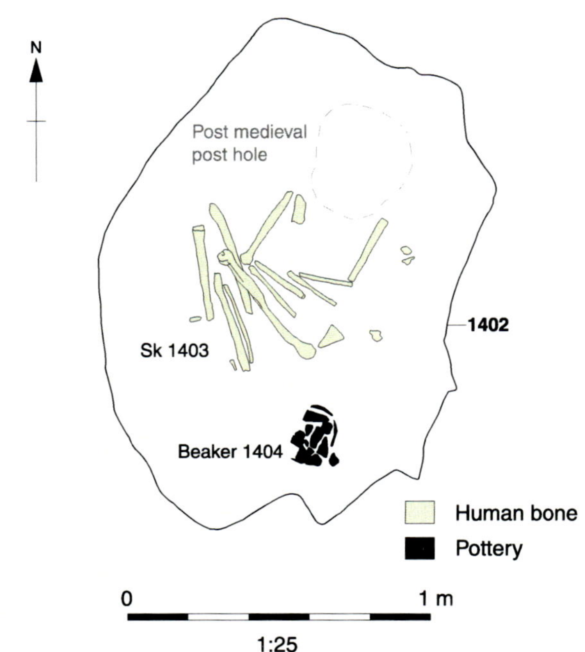

Fig. 13   Phase 2. Early Bronze Age grave 1402

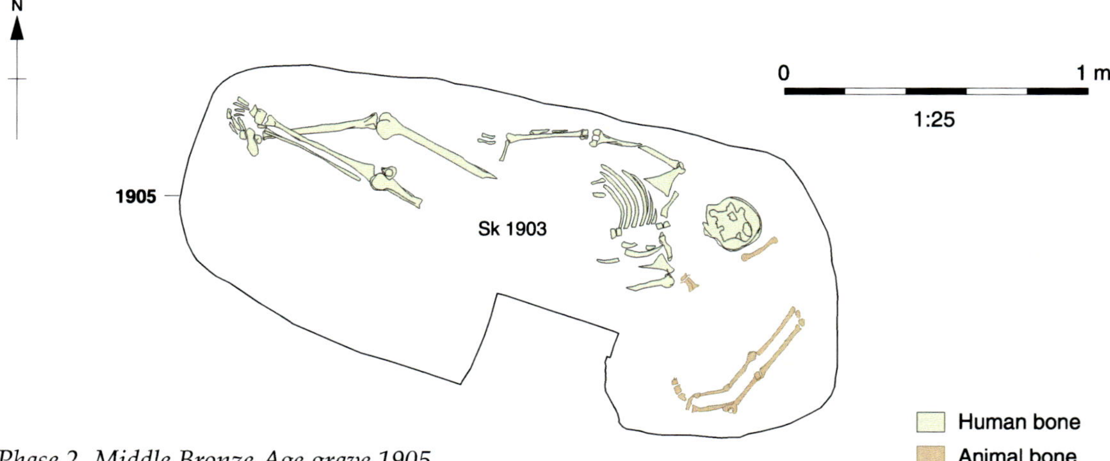

Fig. 14   Phase 2. Middle Bronze Age grave 1905

its head to the east. Evidence from the teeth suggests that the individual was aged 25-35 years at death, while cranial and pelvic traits indicate male. Grave goods were restricted to the hindquarters of a sheep or goat, which were placed next to the head.

Phase 3 – Middle Iron Age, *c* 400-200 BC
(Figs 15-17)

As with the late Neolithic phase, the middle Iron Age was characterised by pit digging, which was similarly widely distributed across the site, though concentrated in the southern half (Fig. 15). Nineteen pits were assigned to this phase on the basis of radiocarbon determinations or the pottery contained in the pits. The features measured on average 0.53 m deep and 1.7 m across. The deepest pit (8311) was 1.15 m deep and 1.5 m wide, while the shallowest (8140) was 0.16 m deep and 1 m wide. Four broad types were discerned. Cylindrical pits, or those with steep sides and flat bases, for example pit 8660 (Fig. 16, section 256), were

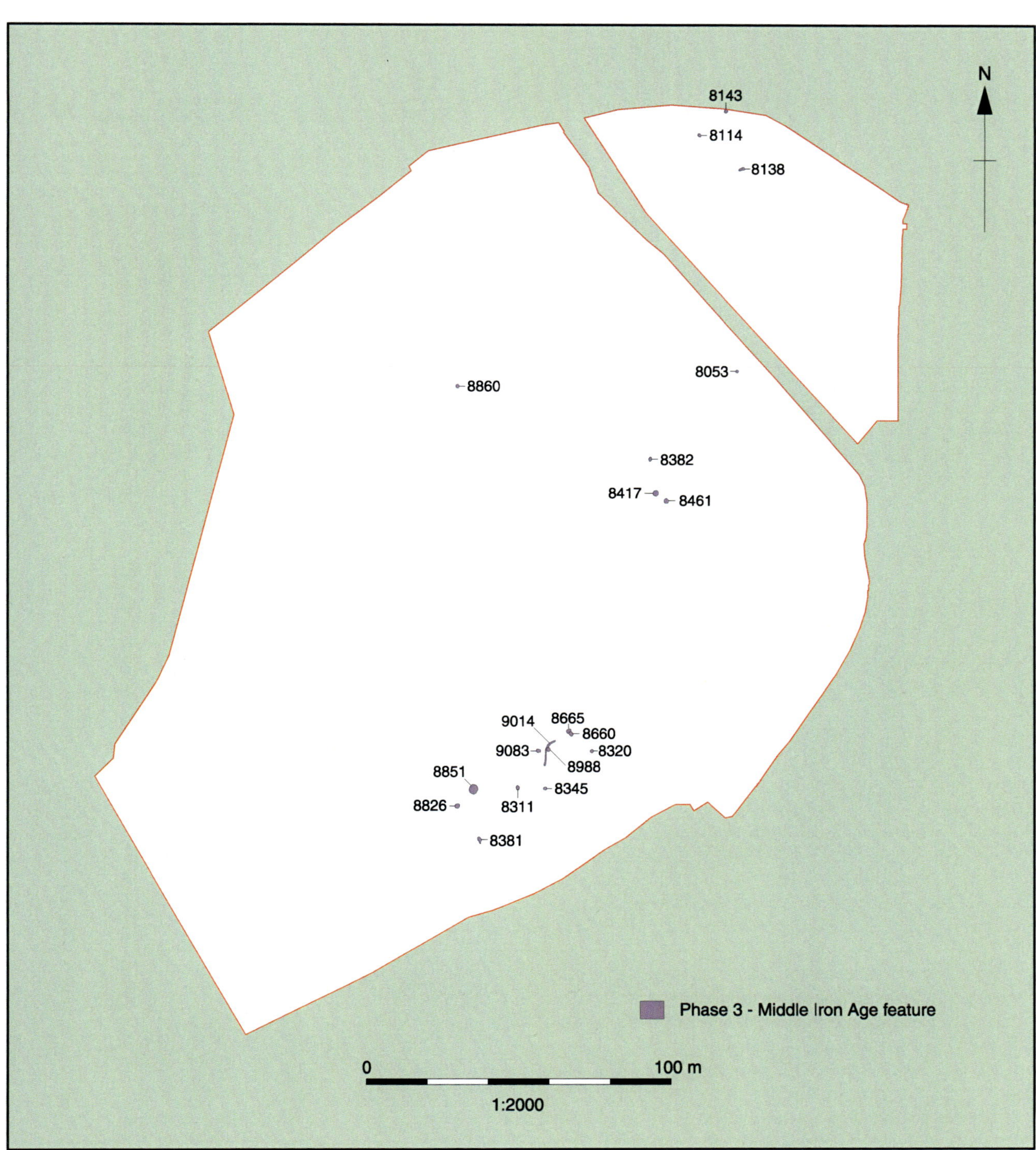

Fig. 15   Phase 3. Middle Iron Age activity

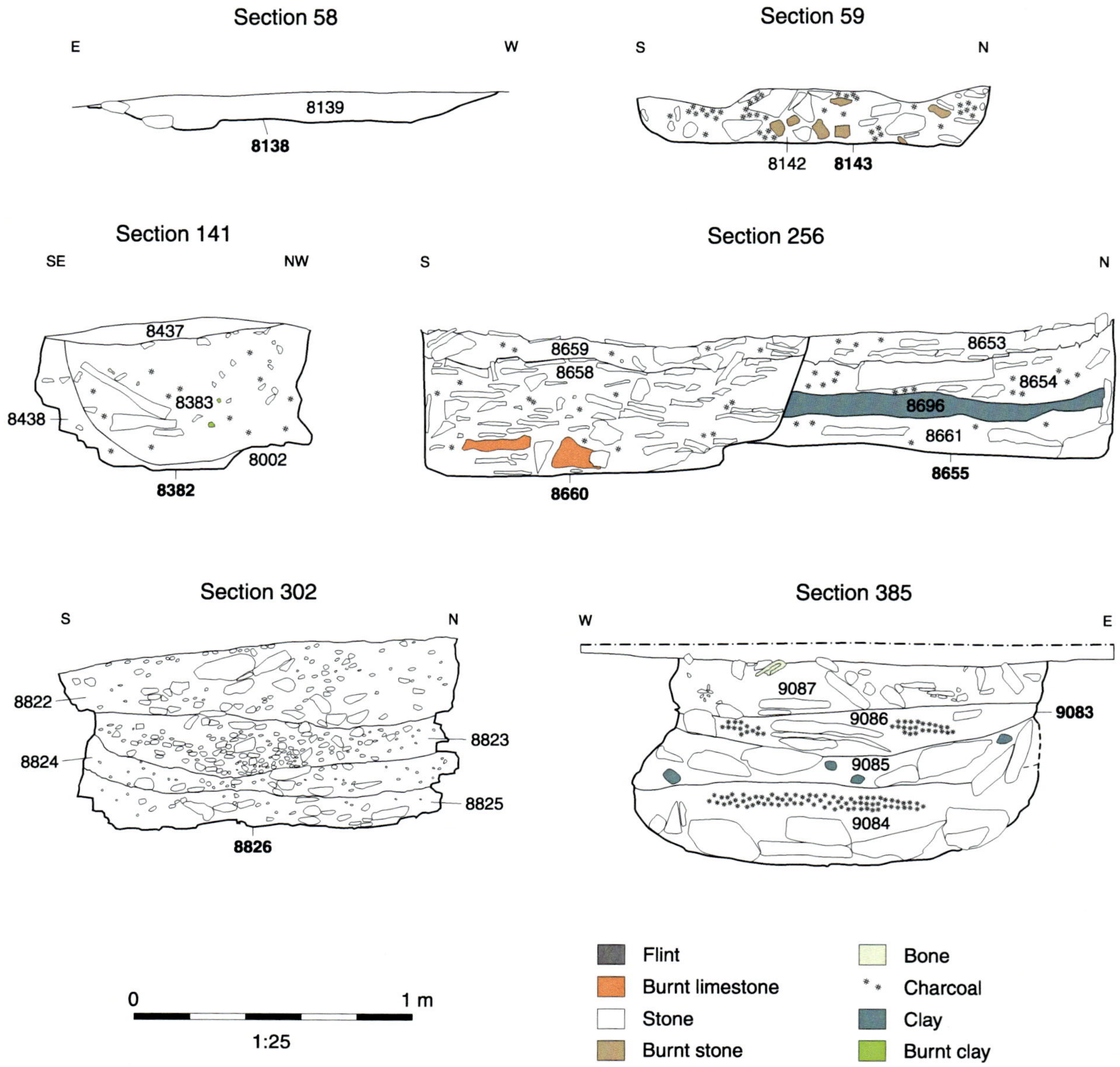

Section 58

Section 59

Section 141

Section 256

Section 302

Section 385

Flint
Burnt limestone
Stone
Burnt stone
Bone
Charcoal
Clay
Burnt clay

0   1 m

1:25

Fig. 16 Phase 3. Sections through Iron Age pits

commonest, followed by those with irregular profiles, which had been cut into solid limestone, among them pit 8826 (Fig. 16, section 302). One pit (9083) (Fig. 16, section 385), had concave sides and base, and was wider at the base than the surface, while a further three survived as little more than shallow scoops, for example 8138 (Fig. 16, section 58).

The pattern of deposits was also similar to that seen among the late Neolithic features. Pits were filled by up to four deposits (pit 8851 with its twelve deposits is exceptional), and overall, the deposits appear to represent deliberate infilling. The silty fills, with varying amounts of limestone, often contained evidence of human activity: charcoal and burnt stones from hearths, pottery and animal bone fragments. Pit 8851 (Fig. 17) contained the articulated skeletons of a dog and a crow or rook.

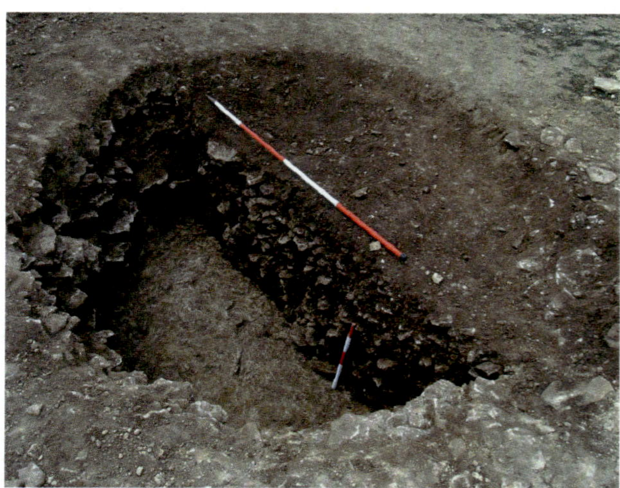

Fig. 17 Middle Iron Age pit 8851

The distribution and shape of the pits and the nature of the deposits naturally invite the conclusion that the features must belong to the Neolithic period. However, dating evidence confirms the later phasing. The crow or rook bone from the fill of pit 8851, on the southern edge of the site, gave a radiocarbon date of 394-209 cal BC (95%; NZA-33476). Another pit, 8143 (Fig. 16, section 59), at the north-eastern part of the site, contained charred grain that provided an almost identical determination of 396-208 cal BC (95%; NZA-33147). Both dates place the episodes of deposition in the middle Iron Age. The pottery present in the remaining pits gives further support for a middle Iron Age phase (Timby, Chapter 4 below; see also Timby 1999, 321-2; fig. 7.7). The fabrics were invariably shell- or limestone-tempered, and the forms included barrel-shaped jars and jars with upright and finger-impressed rims. It is worth noting, too, the paucity of struck flint from the pits. Just five flakes were recovered, compared with over 1,500 pieces from almost the same number of late Neolithic pits. There was a further difference between the Neolithic and Iron Age pits in terms of the animal bone recovered from them. The late Neolithic assemblage was dominated by cattle and pig remains, while the Iron Age assemblage was focused on sheep/goat (see Strid and Nicholson, Chapter 6 below).

No other type of feature was dated to the mid-late Iron Age. Pit 8988 cut curving gully 9014, which, though stratigraphically earlier, was not closely dated. However, it seems more likely that this gully belonged either to Phase 1 (late Neolithic) or to Phase 3 (middle Iron Age), rather than being of Beaker or Bronze Age date (Phase 2).

Phase 4 – Late Iron Age and Roman

Late Iron Age (Phase 4a), c 100 BC-50 AD
(Figs 18 and 19)

The late Iron Age saw the laying out of a ditched enclosure (Figs 18 and 19), located in the centre of the excavated area. The enclosure defined by ditch 8563 was generally oval, measuring some 20 m across its widest extent. It was open along its western side, and there were two short gaps or entrances through the ditch, creating three segments, which essentially defined the northern, eastern and southern sides of the enclosure. A spur was recorded on the east side of the ditch outside the enclosure. The dimensions of the ditch were variable, but the feature measured on average 0.8 m wide and 0.35 m deep (Fig. 18). The ditch was generally filled in two episodes of deposition along its length; terminus 8907 was unusual in having six fills. The deposition was a combination of natural silting and deliberate infilling to judge from the presence of charcoal, pottery and animal bone fragments. Charred grain from a fill of 8907 was radiocarbon dated to 90 cal BC-cal AD 64 (95%; NZA-33149). The dating is supported by some 370

fragments of pottery recovered from the ditch, which were dominated by grog-tempered ware and other late Iron Age fabrics. A small quantity of pottery of Roman date was also recovered, but this was intrusive or collected from upper fills, which had accumulated much later.

The ditch enclosed a number of postholes, which appear to have defined a building. Two groups of three postholes formed roughly-parallel alignments (9159, 9113 and 9135 to the south, 8780, 8767 and 9161 to the north). Another posthole (9157) in between the easternmost postholes may have been associated with the alignments. Another two postholes (9072 and 8614) were assigned to this phase (Fig. 18), but these were north-east of the main groups and appear to be unrelated to the structure. Indeed posthole 8614 lay outside the enclosure. None of the postholes contained pottery or other dating evidence, and so phasing is uncertain, although it is reasonable to suppose that ditch 8563 and the structure were contemporary. Postholes assigned to phase 4b (see below) were cut into a layer of dark silty clay soil (8844), while phase 4a posthole 9072 was sealed by the layer. If the phase 4a postholes were not associated with 8563, then they may well represent a phase of activity separating phase 4a ditch 8563 and phase 4b ditch 8918. The deposit 8844 contained limestone-tempered pottery dated to the late Iron Age and is assigned to Phase 4b.

Other postholes were recorded at irregular intervals within ditch 8563. The postholes were largely confined to the southern part of the enclosure and had been dug into the infilling, rather than the floor of the empty ditch, and therefore were later than the digging and use of the ditch. It is possible that they belong more properly to Phase 4b. The exception was posthole 9066, which had been dug into the edge of ditch cut 9038 and appeared to be filled with the same material that filled the ditch.

A grave (1104) containing an infant burial was cut into enclosure ditch 8563. The burial 1104, covered by a stone, was aligned north/south with the head to the south. The skeleton appeared to be supine, although the bones were displaced and so the exact position was uncertain. A radiocarbon date of 41 cal BC to 75 cal AD (95%; OxA-20187) was obtained from the skeleton. Given its stratigraphic relationship with the ditch, the burial was assigned to Phase 4a, though it may have been deposited at any time up to Phase 4d.

Late Iron Age (Phase 4b), c 100 BC-50 AD
(Figs 19-21)

Overlying the north end of the Phase 4a enclosure ditch 8653 was an irregular oval silty spread (8844). Postholes 8804, 8820, 8842, 9008, 9064, 9080 and 9133 cut 8844. It is tempting to view 8844 as an occupation soil or floor of a roundhouse defined by the postholes, although the stratigraphic relationship between the spread and the postholes would

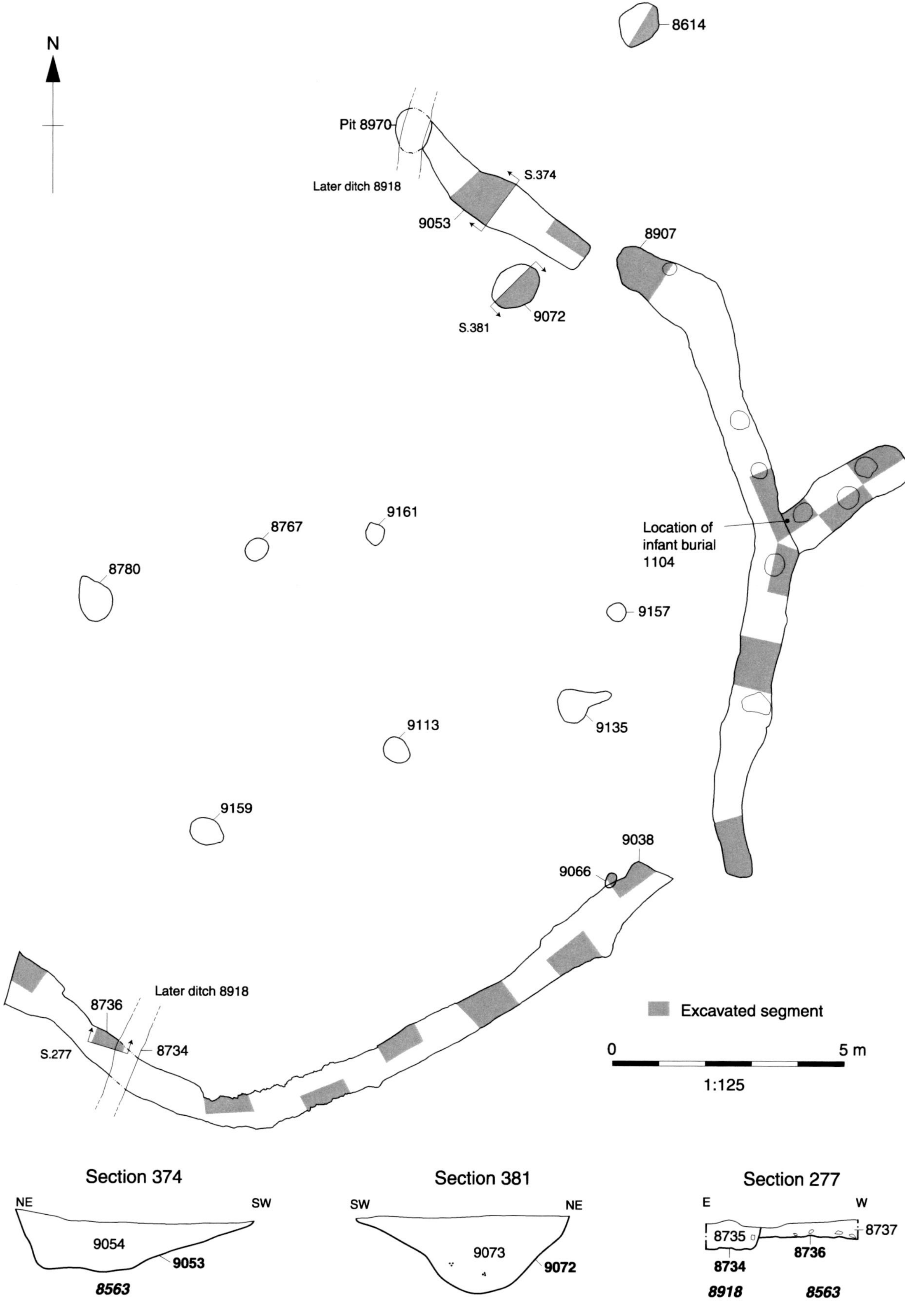

Fig. 18 Phase 4a. Enclosure 8563 and postholes

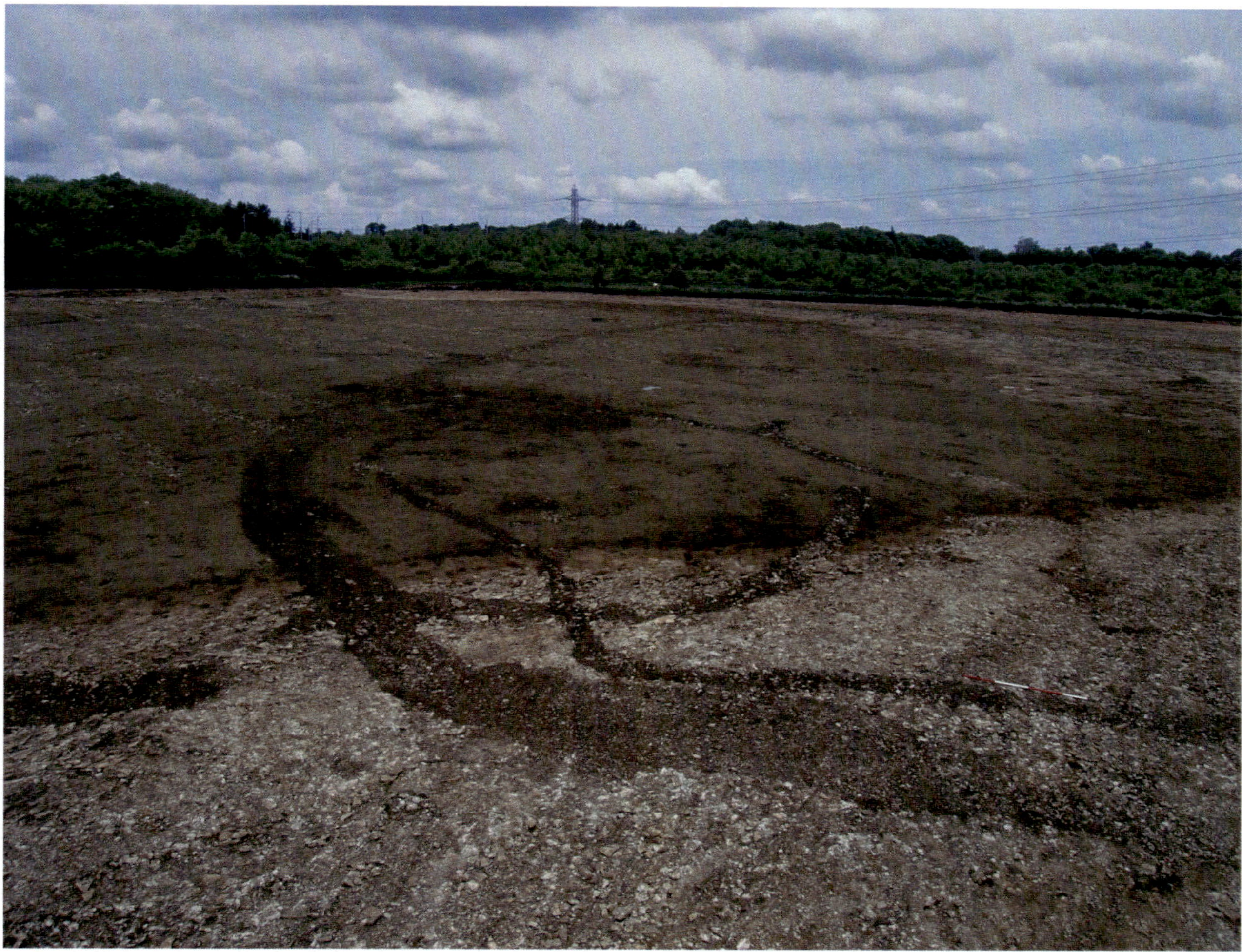

Fig. 19   Phase 4 ditches 8563, 8918 and 8413

seem to rule out this possibility. That said, the positioning of the postholes around the edge of the spread is noteworthy; the excavator suggested that the soil was a levelling deposit that prepared the ground for a structure. Like those assigned to phase 4a, these postholes did not produce strong dating evidence, but for stratigraphic reasons must post-date phase 4a.

Deposit 8844 and the southern end of the Phase 4a enclosure ditch 8563 was cut by gully or ditch 8918 (Figs 19 and 20, section 345; see also Fig. 18, section 277). Ditch 8563 had been largely infilled by this time, although it is possible that parts of it survived as a visible earthwork. Ditch 8918, in plan took the form of broad slightly irregular W, and extended on a roughly north-south alignment for some 50 m. It was examined with ten sections and was generally about 0.66 m wide and 0.17 m deep (Fig. 20). The profile varied from U-shaped to one with concave sides and a flat base, and was more irregular in areas of limestone bedrock (Fig. 20, sections 310, 320 & 345). Deposition was uniform throughout; the ditch was filled in a single episode. The presence of pottery and animal bone fragments suggests that the filling was to a greater extent deliberate. Twenty-seven sherds of pottery were recovered; a range of

late Iron Age fabrics – limestone-tempered, sand-tempered and grog-tempered wares – were recorded. Vessels were confined to jars.

A grave (8723) 1 m long and aligned south-west/north-east was cut into the north end of ditch 8918. It contained a 40-45 year old male inhumation (8724; Figs 20-21). The skeleton was found in a contorted position, which may be due to the relatively small size of the grave, or may be the result of deliberate treatment and positioning of the body. A radiocarbon date of 181 to 41 cal BC (95%; OxA-20185) was obtained from this skeleton. This date is earlier than the date given for the filling of ditch 8918 and does pose a chronological conundrum. The layout of the skeleton offers a possibility that it had been redeposited, but given that the skeleton was more or less in its correct anatomical position, its preservation seems remarkable, even assuming an interval between original burial and relocation of a few years rather than decades. The stratigraphic relationship between ditches 8563 and 8918 (and between 8918 and grave 8723) is secure, though on the basis of the ceramic evidence, the chronological gap separating 8918 and 8563 need not have been particularly long. However, it strains the ceramic evidence to push the filling of ditch

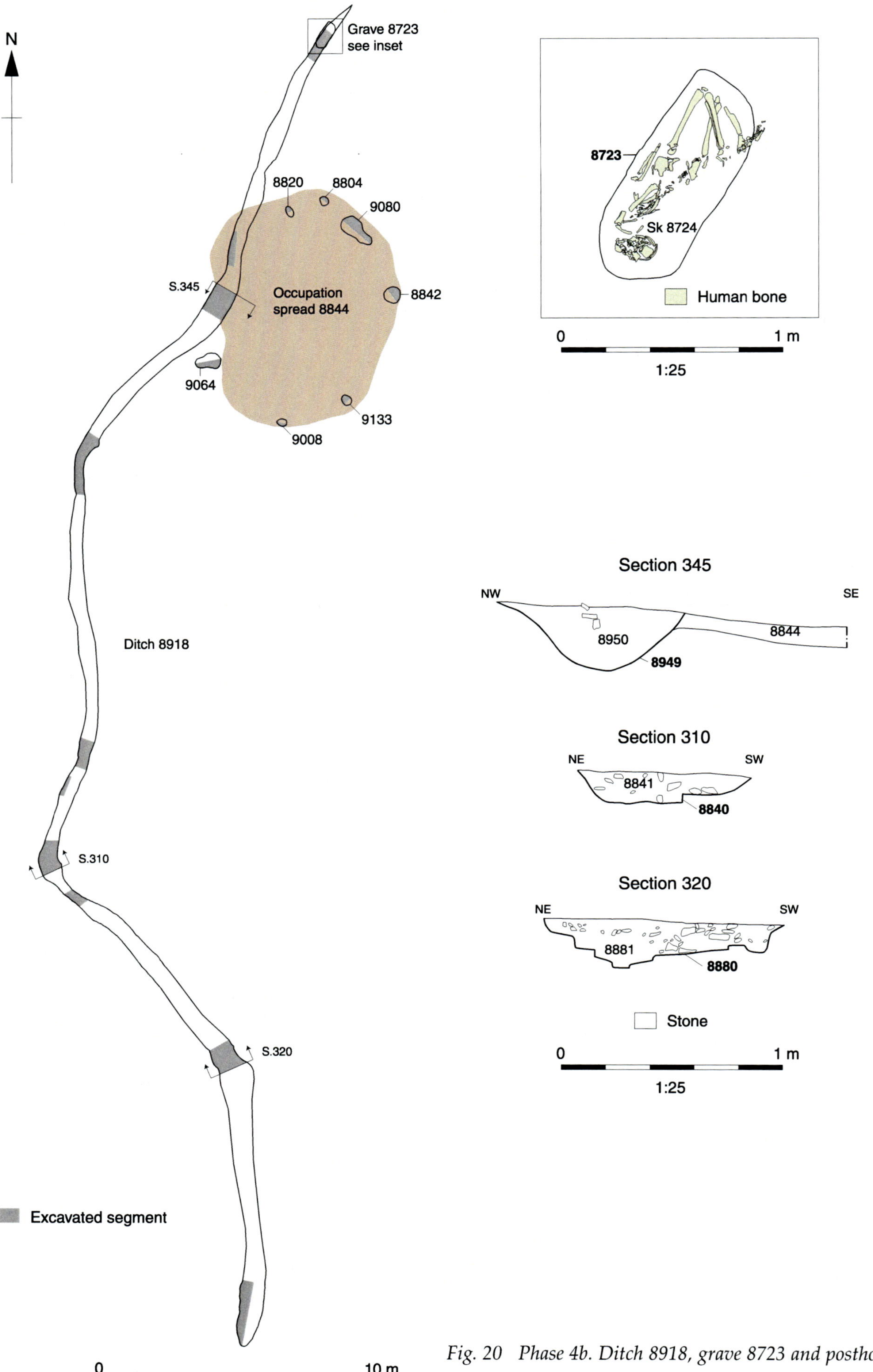

Fig. 20 Phase 4b. Ditch 8918, grave 8723 and postholes

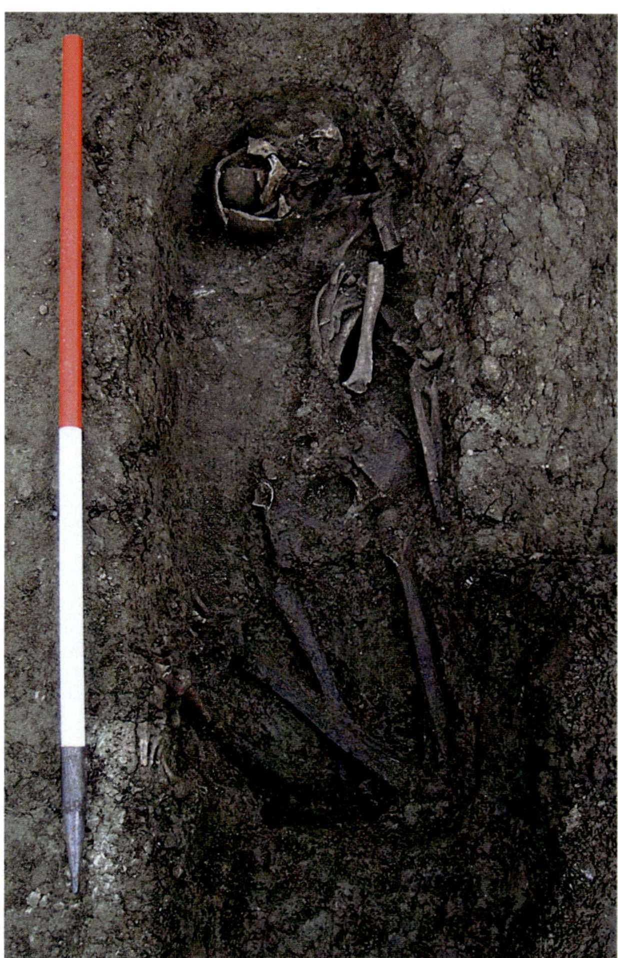

Fig. 21 Burial 8724, Phase 4b

followed the sinuous course of the earlier ditch, suggesting that 8918 was still visible as a ditch or earthwork. In profile, ditch 8413 had concave or steep sides and flat base, though was occasionally U-shaped (Fig. 23, sections 191, 264 & 409). It was filled with up to three deposits, usually silty clay, which contained varying amounts of pottery, animal bone fragments and charcoal, pointing to deliberate dumping. Some natural silting is likely, though; occasionally fills were devoid of finds or had accumulated into hollows created as previous fills settled. Pottery recovered from the feature gave a probable post-conquest, mid-1st century AD, date for the filling of the ditch. Grog-tempered ware, available as bead-rimmed and globular jars, remained the most important fabric, and was accompanied mainly by shelly and limestone-tempered fabrics and Savernake ware. Severn Valley oxidised ware and post-conquest sandy grey ware made a minor appearance. A copper alloy brooch (SF 10097), dated to the 1st century AD, was also recovered from the ditch.

The south arm of the ditch (8665) possibly continued further south (Fig. 22B). Ditch segment 8663 may originally have been part of the ditch, extending the ditch by some 4 m. The south arm (8665) was in any case recut by 8669. The recut measured 0.65 m wide and 0.2 m deep. Its single fill contained 44 fragments of grog-tempered ware. The end of the north arm (8511) of ditch 8413 was also recut by 8514, which had the effect of curling the end of the ditch inwards (Fig. 22A). The recut 8514 was a linear feature 0.6 m wide and 0.18 m deep. It may have continued as either ditch 8535 or 8536, but any relationship between these features was removed when phase 4d ditch 8537 was dug through all three (see Fig. 26).

Ditch 8536, which was 0.65 m wide and 0.06 m deep, cut pit 8448, which measured 0.7 m across its widest extent and 0.06 deep. The excavator suggests that the pit could have been a terminus for 8413, but though the edges of the feature were indistinct, there is nothing to confirm that it belonged to the main ditch. Ditch 8536 was in turn cut by ditch 8535. This was shorter than 8536, but was similar in terms of width (0.75 m) and depth (0.08 m). Feature 8521, which cut 8535, was described by the excavator as a pit, but could have been another ditch terminus. Feature 8516 similarly could have been part of one of the ditches in the sequence, possibly 8535 or 8536. The enclosure curled round further with the digging of ditch 8425. This was somewhat irregular in plan, but was on average 0.84 m wide and 0.13 m deep. Malvernian rock-tempered ware, fine grey ware and shell-tempered ware from 8535 suggest a 1st-century AD date for infilling of this ditch. Sherds of grog-, shell- and limestone-tempered wares in 8536, 8516 and 8425 all suggest a similar date.

8918 (and 8563, for that matter) very far into the second half of the 1st century BC. The assemblage from the ditches was dominated by grog-tempered ware. While the introduction of grog-tempered ware in south-eastern Britain is traditionally dated to the late 1st century BC (cf. Thompson 1982), the Upper Thames Valley saw a later introduction, with grog-tempered ware enjoying its greatest currency during the first half of the 1st century AD (eg Moore 2009, 98). The dating of grave 8723 therefore remains problematic.

Late Iron Age/early Roman (Phase 4c), c AD 1-50 (Figs 19, 22-25)

The early/mid 1st century AD saw an increase in the area of land subject to enclosure with the setting out of a substantial ditch (8413) in the centre of the excavated area (Fig. 22; see also Fig. 19). The ditch, measuring on average 1.46 m wide and 0.41 m deep, curved round to form a semi-circle measuring some 80 m between the tips of its north and south arms. Neither 8511 nor 8665, respectively the north and south ends, was a terminus; the ditch simply petered out at each end. The ditch cut the northern end of Phase 4b ditch 8918 (Fig. 23, section 264), but did not replace it entirely; towards the south, 8413

A group of small round or oval features (8806, 8876, 8910, 8926 and 8936; Fig. 23, section 343), east of the southern arm of ditch 8413 were arranged

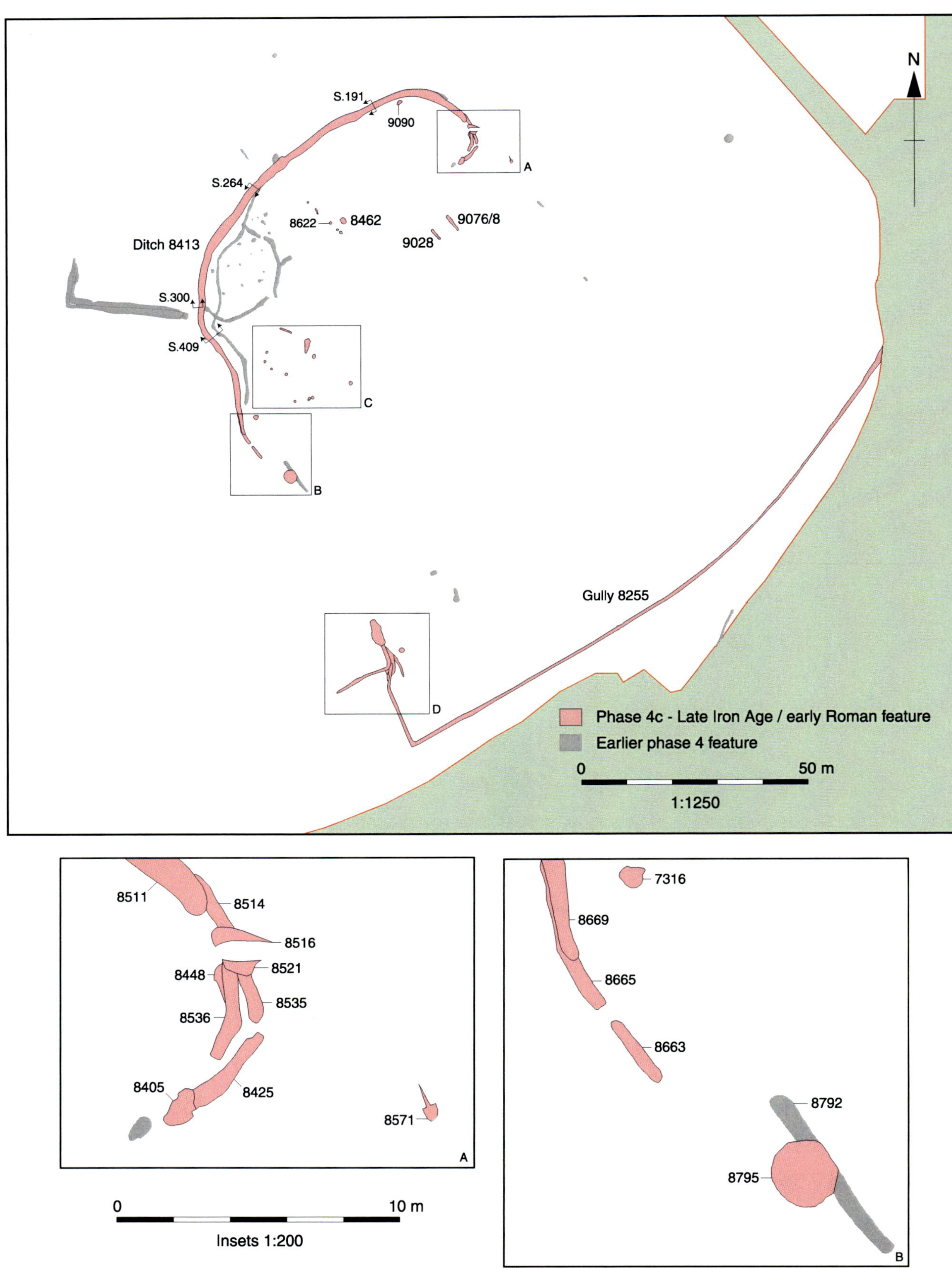

Fig. 22a   *Phase 4c. Ditch 8413, gully 8255 and contemporaneous features*

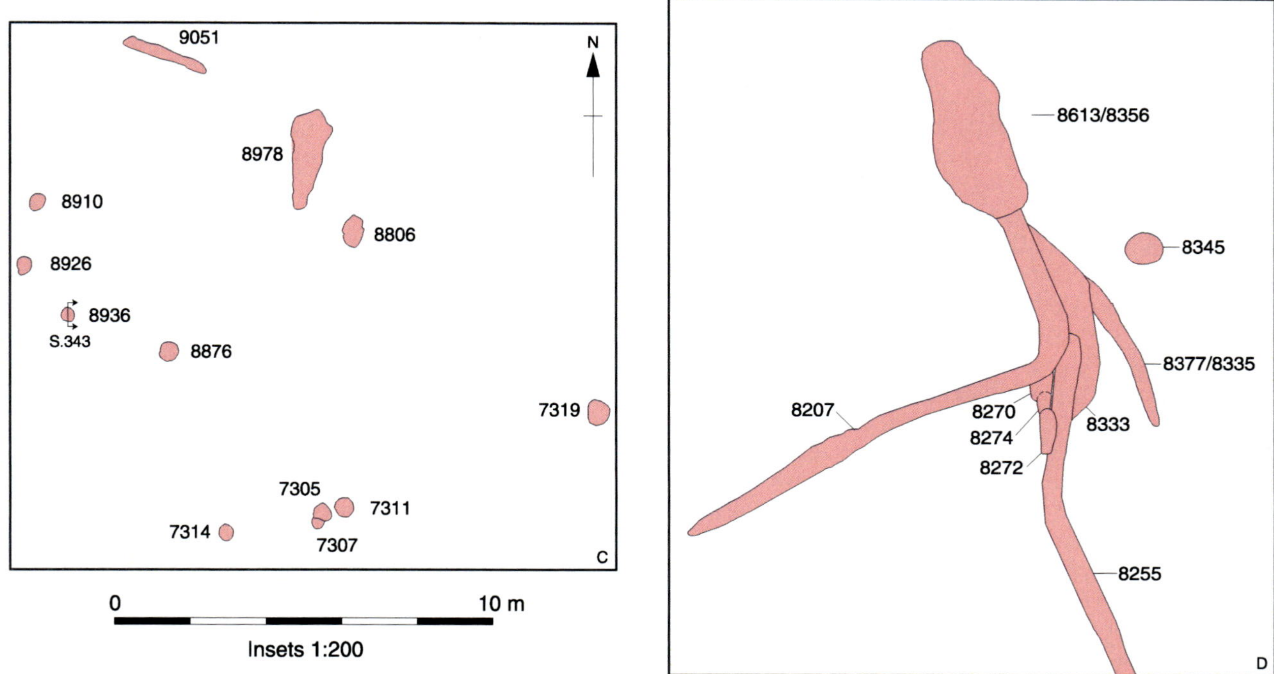

Fig. 22b (above, left and right)   Phase 4c. Ditch 8413, gully 8255 and contemporaneous features

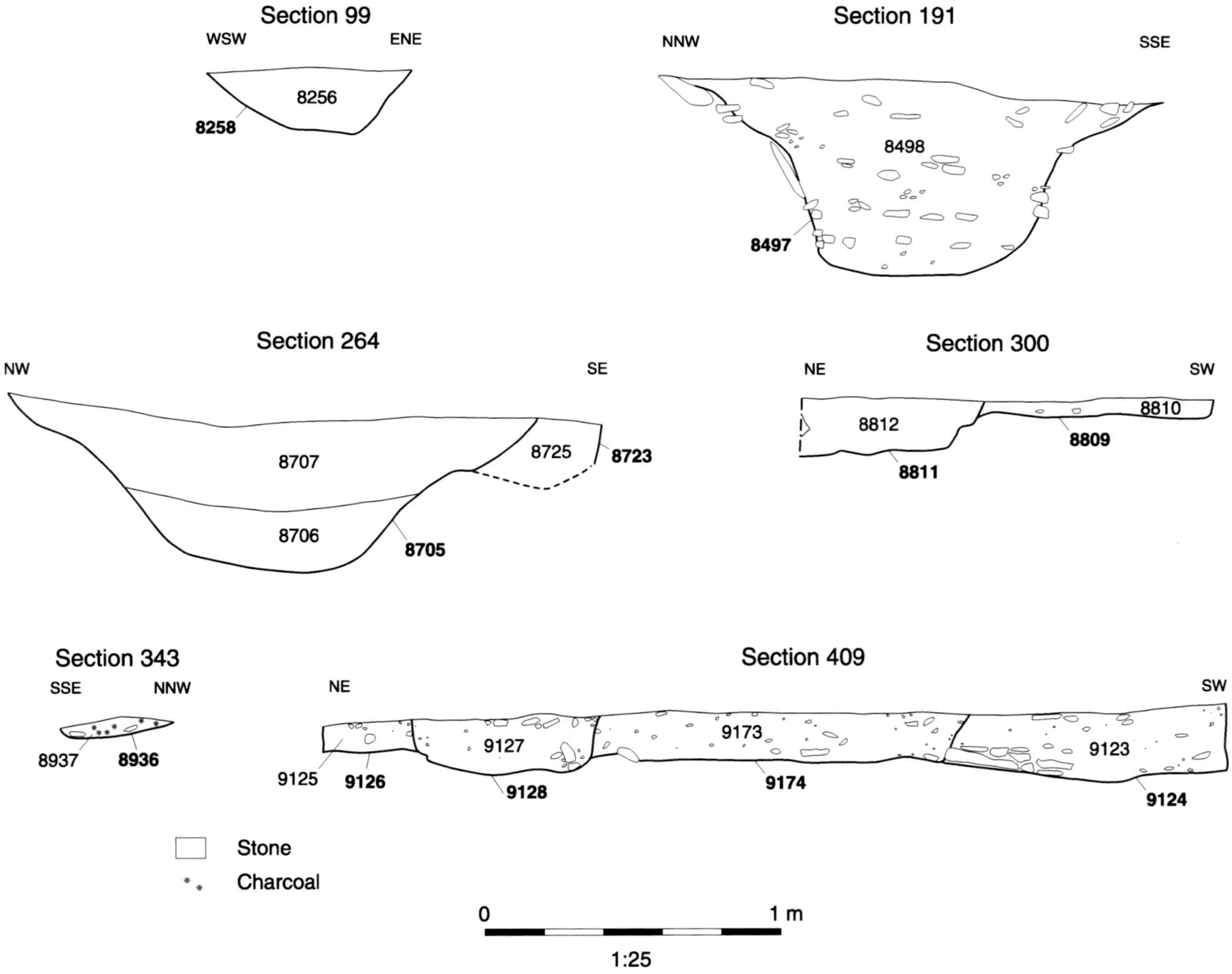

Fig. 23   Phase 4c. Sections through ditch 8413 (showing relationship with 8563 and 8918), posthole 8936, and ditch 8255

roughly in a ring 10 m in diameter (Fig. 22C). They were of similar size, averaging 0.16 m in depth and 0.65 m across their widest extents. The dimensions fall within the range offered by postholes recorded at the site, though the features lack the characteristic V-shaped profile of some of the postholes enclosed, for example, by ditch 8563, nor is there any trace of postpipes or packing. Feature 8876 contained limestone slabs in both of its fills, and it is possible that the slabs functioned as postpads. A near-complete upper stone from a rotary quern (Fig. 24) found in the lower fill of 8806 could have served the same purpose. The alternative view, offered by the excavator, is that the features were severely-truncated pits. The matter cannot be resolved conclusively, though given the arrangement of the features, a structure is tentatively preferred. The irregularly-shaped pit 8978 may have been associated with the features. Presumably it was not incorporated into any structure, but could perhaps have served as a pit for waste or refuse, although just a few pieces of animal bone, pottery and hearth remains were recovered from its fill. A nearby slot (8951) (Fig. 22C), 2.8 m long, 0.3 m wide and 0.09 m deep, was not well dated, but its association with the putative structure is possible, especially if it marked a drain or fence line. The quern provides useful dating evidence for deposition in 8806, as its design is certainly Iron Age. Grog-tempered pottery from feature 8806, as well as from 8876 and 8926, gives a late Iron Age date for the group overall. The dating evidence may place the group in phase 4a or 4b, but a phase 4c date is suggested on the basis of Roman-period sandy oxidised ware from slot 8951.

The southern part of the site was marked by a series of ditches and gullies. Gully 8377/8335 was located some 100 m south-east of ditch 8918 and is tentatively dated to Phase 4c. The gully was 0.4 m wide and survived to a depth of 0.04 m. No dating evidence was recovered from the gully itself, but it was cut by ditch 8333, which measured 0.24 m deep and 1.25 m across its widest extent. Ditch 8333 survived to a length of *c* 6 m, having been cut at its

southern end by gully 8255 and to the north by pit 8613. The ditch was filled with two clay-silt deposits, which included pottery and animal bone fragments. The pottery was identified as Savernake ware, which dates from the mid 1st to early 2nd century. Ditch 8255 was a boundary ditch that ran parallel with the southern boundary of the site for some 135 m, extending beyond the north-western edge of excavation and turning north at its southern end to meet (and cut) 8333 (Figs 22 and 25). The ditch was examined with 21 interventions, which gave average dimensions of 0.71 m wide and 0.3 m deep. A single clay-silt deposit was recorded in most interventions. The deposit appeared to be colluvial in origin, having moved down the slope from the north, and consequently few finds were recovered. A single sherd of late Iron Age or early Roman grog-tempered pottery was collected.

Features 8270, 8272 and 8274 were a series of intercutting pits or heavily truncated ditches which were cut after ditch 8255 had been infilled. Feature 8270 was the earliest of these features, and was cut by 8274, which was cut in turn by feature 8272 which also cut 8255. As no dating evidence was recovered, their placement in phase 4c is uncertain (Fig. 22D). However, 8270 was cut by ditch 8207, which is assigned to this phase. Pit 8613/8356 (Fig. 22D) was roughly oval in plan and had a profile with steep sides and a flat base. The feature, 6 m long, up to 2.4 m wide and 0.94 m deep, contained four limestone-packed fills, which probably represent a number of episodes of deliberate backfilling. Pottery from the feature – a sherd each of grog- and limestone-tempered fabrics – dates these events to the 1st century AD. Function is uncertain, but given its irregular shape and size, the pit may have served as a quarry to extract the underlying natural cornbrash. The sequence of linear features ended with L-shaped ditch, 8207. It cut 8270, but its relationship with pit 8613/8356, which it met at its north end, was uncertain; 8207 does not appear in a section through the pit. The ditch measured on average 0.85 m wide and 0.14 m deep. A clay-silt

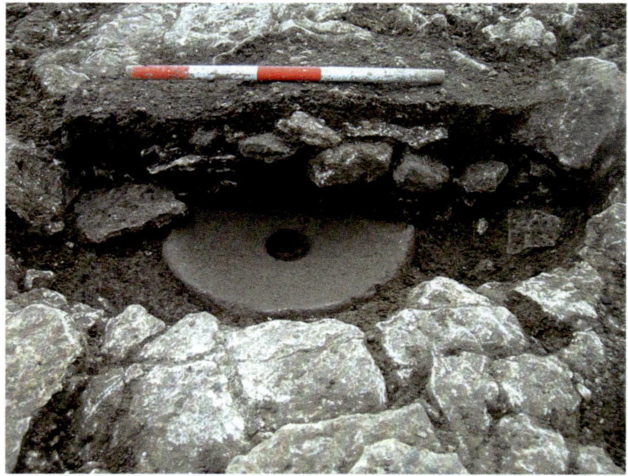

Fig. 24   Pit 8806 with quern, Phase 4c

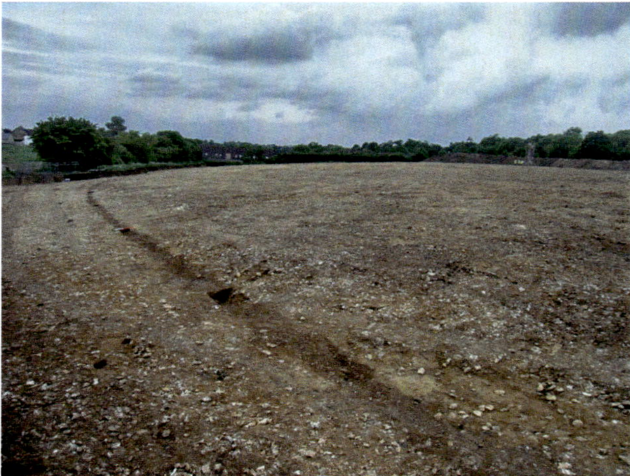

Fig. 25   Ditch 8255, Phase 4c

deposit accumulated, probably though deliberate filling, during the Iron Age or early-Roman period. Animal bone fragments, charcoal and two sherds of shell-tempered pottery were recovered from the feature. There was no indication that the ditch continued northwards beyond the pit, although if ditches 8207 (or 8255) and 8413 were meant to connect in some way, then linear feature 8792, between 8207 and 8413, might provide evidence for this. Its alignment perhaps rules this out, although the ditch potentially fits with the others in terms of chronology; no dating evidence was recovered from 8792, but it was cut by a pit (8795) that contained exclusively late Iron Age pottery, including a high-shouldered jar in grog-tempered ware.

A number of miscellaneous features were assigned to phase 4c. The features were not well dated, but they fit a phase characterised by an expansion of land available for enclosure and occupation. These included two parallel gullies or slots, 9028 and 9076/9078 (Fig. 22). The former was 3 m long, while the latter was 4 m; both were approximately 0.6 m wide and 0.2 m deep, and were 4.5 m apart. Together the slots define the outline of a square or rectangular structure. Slot 9028 contained 300 sherds of pottery dominated by grog-tempered and limestone-tempered wares. Savernake ware was present and was also collected from 9076/9078. The pottery suggests a mid 1st century date for deposition. Pit 9090, (Fig. 22) which measured 1.4 m long, 0.7 m wide and 0.05 m deep, was dug next to ditch 8413. It was filled with a single fill that contained nine sherds of grog-tempered pottery. Another pit, 8642 (Fig. 22), was located further south. This measured 1.6 m long, 1.1 m wide and 0.3 m deep and contained 67 sherds of grog-tempered, limestone-tempered and Malvernian rock-tempered pottery, pointing to a late Iron Age or very early-Roman date. Posthole 8622 (Fig. 8622) was about 2.5 m west of 8642. Two sherds of grog-tempered pottery were recovered from its postpipe. The feature was in alignment with four other postholes, which, though containing no dating evidence, may have been associated, perhaps forming part of a wider episode of land division. Another line of postholes was revealed in an evaluation trench across the south end of 8413. The postholes (7314, 7305, 7307, 7311 and 7319) (Fig. 22C) may have formed part of a fence-line or internal division within the enclosure. Pottery recovered from a number of these features dates up to the mid 1st century AD.

Early Roman (Phase 4d), c AD 50-100 (Fig. 26)

There was further augmentation of enclosure ditch 8413 in the second half of the 1st century AD (Fig. 26). Ditch 9112 extended at right angles from the southern end of the enclosure ditch. It was c 10 m long and averaged 0.92 m wide and 0.34 m deep (excluding the bulbous west terminus). The ditch was filled in one or two episodes; the silty-clay deposits contained 41 sherds of pottery, mainly Savernake ware storage jar sherds, with a smaller proportion (ten sherds) of grog-tempered ware. A mid-1st century date for deposition is likely. It is tempting to link 9112 with ditch 8845, which, after a five-metre gap, forms a right angle with 9112 and potentially a corner of a small enclosure. Ditch 8845 was narrower at 0.6 m, but of comparable depth at 0.38 m. It contained a silty clay fill from which 15 sherds of grog-tempered and limestone-tempered pottery were recovered. On the whole, this assemblage seems typologically earlier than that in 9112, though is not necessarily out of place in the mid-1st century. After it had been infilled, ditch 9112 was cut by two pits, 8800 and 8887, which were filled during the second half of the 1st century. They contained pottery including Savernake and Severn Valley wares. Close by, two recuts (9166/9174 and 8688/8682) were made along the east edge of ditch 8413. Apart from being c 15 m apart, they differed in size – 9166/9174 was the larger, wider and deeper – and it cannot be demonstrated that they were originally part of a single recut. Grey ware from 9166/9174 gave a post-conquest date for deposition.

The northern end of 8413 was effectively extended with a series of ditches (Fig. 26A). Ditch 8537 was a curving feature c 13 m long, 0.91 m wide and 0.46 m deep. Its north end cut phase 4c features 8516 and 8521, and its south end cut the pit or heavily-truncated ditch segment, 8571. It possibly also cut 8578 and 8575, although the relationships are unclear. Ditch 8578, 9 m long, 0.46 m wide and 0.08 m deep, continued the extension, and the sequence was further lengthened with feature 8468, which measured 13 m long, 0.35 m wide and 0.09 m deep. None of the three ditch segments – 8537, 8578 or 8468 – had any direct stratigraphic relationship with one another, and it is possible that they were dug at the same time. The ditches may not have been in use for very long. Pottery recovered from their fills was dominated by limestone-tempered and grog-tempered wares, but included post-conquest material, such as a South Spanish amphora fragment, Savernake ware and fine oxidised ware. These date infilling to the later 1st century or later. Ditch 8606, a short slot up to 1 m wide and 0.2 m deep, has been placed in phase 4d on the basis of its proximity to, and alignment with, ditch 8468, though the pottery recovered from it comprised late Iron Age wares with no certain post-conquest material.

This period of ditch-digging was accompanied by quarry-digging. Group 8895 (Fig. 26B) consisted of nine intercutting pits, located inside the enclosure defined by ditch 8413 where there was an area of natural clay. It was not possible to ascertain dimensions for all the pits, but it is clear that they were variable in size. Pit 8760, for example, measured approximately 4 m long, 2.5 m wide and 0.25 m deep. Pit 9020 was 1.8 m long, 1.4 m wide and 0.3 m deep. That the pits were intercutting meant that there was a sequence – pit 9022 was one of the first pits to be dug, while 8752 (Fig. 26B) was one of the last – but

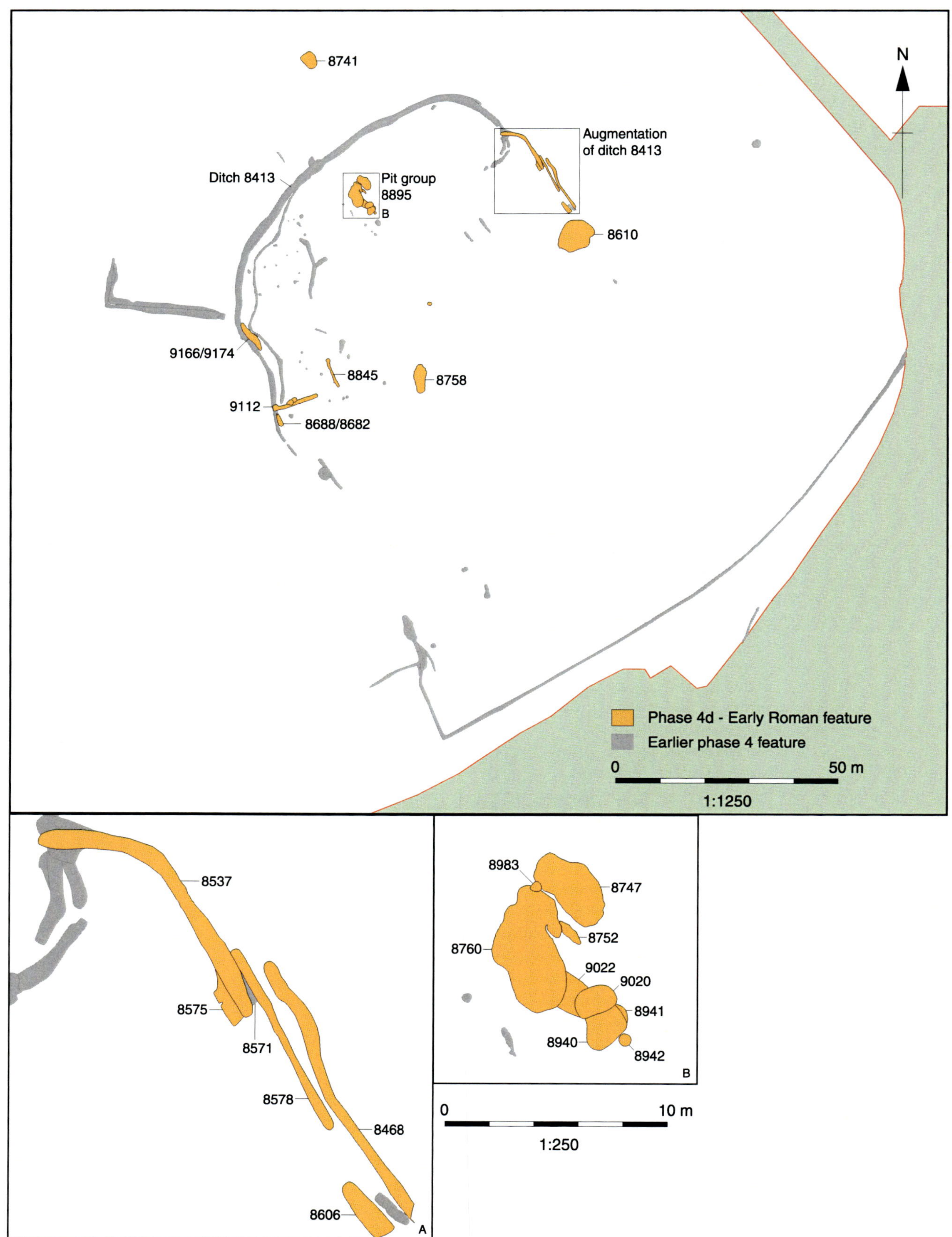

Fig. 26   Phase 4d. Augmentation of ditch 8413 and quarry pit group 8895

they were filled more or less at the same time with a deliberate backfill of redeposited clay mixed with limestone fragments and finds. The large assemblage of 285 pottery sherds recovered from the backfill was dominated by grog-tempered ware, but also contained Severn Valley ware, Savernake ware and sandy grey ware, indicating a date for deposition in the second half of the 1st century.

Another quarry pit (8758) was recorded some 30 m further south. This was sited to exploit the underlying cornbrash and limestone bedrock. Pit 8758 was 6.5 m long by 2.5 m wide and 0.36 m deep. Pottery recovered from the backfill included grog-tempered ware, Savernake ware and a very fine grey ware.

A third area of quarrying is represented by 8610, located *c* 45 m east south-east of group 8895, adjacent to the enclosure ditch extensions, 8537, 8571, etc. This was dug through cornbrash and measured 8.4 m across its widest extent and 0.46 m in depth. Its silty clay backfill included fine oxidised ware, putting deposition into the later 1st century. The pottery assemblage also contained post-Roman material, but this is probably intrusive, having been introduced with the filling of pit 8612, which was dug through the top of the backfilled quarry during the post-medieval period. Pit 8741, north of ditch 8413, was relatively small, though comparable to some of the pits in group 8895, and may also have been a quarry pit. The feature was 3.92 m long, 2.94 m wide and 0.97 m deep. It contained four silty-clay deposits with limestone blocks. Pottery retrieved from the pit included Savernake ware, fine grey ware, sandy grey ware and grog-tempered ware.

Late 1st-4th century AD (Phases 4e and 4f), *c* AD 80-400 (Fig. 27)

The site seems to have been almost totally devoid of activity between the end of the 1st century and the middle of the 3rd century (Phase 4e). Just one feature – cremation grave 8227 – was dated to the phase (Fig. 27) and was dug into the fill of the Phase 4b ditch 8918. The oval grave was 1.3 m across its widest extent and 0.16 m deep and contained charred cereal grain radiocarbon dated to cal AD 86-247 (95%; NZA-33144). A total of 673 g of cremated human bone was recovered. The highly-fragmented character of the bone allowed the individual buried to be identified only as an adult. The bone was found with other material that had been collected from the pyre. Charcoal fragments accompanied the grain, and a bone from a small animal was found among the human remains. Hobnails recovered from the grave indicate that a shoe or pair of shoes had been deposited. Over 1000 iron wood nails were also collected. These were typically small, most measuring up to 25 mm in length, and many were bent. It is likely that the nails belonged to a lightly-built wooden structure, probably a litter that supported the individual on the pyre (see Scott,

Chapter 4 below). The location of the burial within ditch 8918 is potentially significant, as it may represent a continuation of the burial in ditches tradition characteristic of the Iron Age (Whimster 1981, 28), of which graves 8723 and 1104 are examples.

Evidence for activity in the late Roman period (Phase 4f) was similarly limited. Only ditch 8203, a field boundary, was assigned to the phase. The feature stretched across the south-western corner of the site and both ends extended beyond the edges of excavation. The ditch was examined with seven interventions. It was generally about 2.2 m wide and 0.9 m deep. In profile, the ditch generally had convex, almost stepped, sides, and a U-shaped base, which was occasionally more irregular where dug through the limestone bedrock, rather than the cornbrash. The ditch was filled with silty-clay deposits, often with limestone fragments present. Finds recovered from the feature, notably pottery and animal bone, suggests that some deposition was deliberate, although given their fragmentation (each pottery sherd weighed on average 3 g), it is not unlikely that the fills mainly entered the ditch through colluvial action and ploughing. The ditch is not well dated, although a late Roman date is preferred. There was no evidence of recutting. A bronze coin dated to AD 332-3 from the secondary fill suggests that deposits accumulated in the 4th century. Pottery from the feature was residual or broadly dated, but fragments of Dorset black-burnished ware cooking pots present in the assemblage potentially date to the late 4th century. No post-Roman ceramic material was recovered from the feature.

Features broadly dated to Phase 4

A number of features were could not be dated closely within the late Iron Age or Roman period. Typically, these were isolated features which contained at most a few sherds of late Iron or Roman-period pottery. While the evidence was not sufficient to assign features to a sub-phase, it suggests a date broadly within Phase 4.

Phase 4 features included gullies or ditches, pits and postholes. These did not form coherent patterns of activity (although it is possible that associated features had been removed by later ploughing), but suggested that a wider area of land around the central enclosures (see below) was available for occupation. Groups 8206 and 9104 (Fig. 27) were L-shaped ditches and formed more substantial features, but could not be closely dated. The features probably formed the corner of an enclosure (8206) and a subsequent recut (9104). The ditches were practically identical in size; they shared alignment and length and were similar in width (up to 1 m) and depth (up to 0.37 m). Neither contained pottery, but a late Iron Age or early Roman date seems likely given the appearance of the ditches and their proximity to more certain phase 4 enclosures.

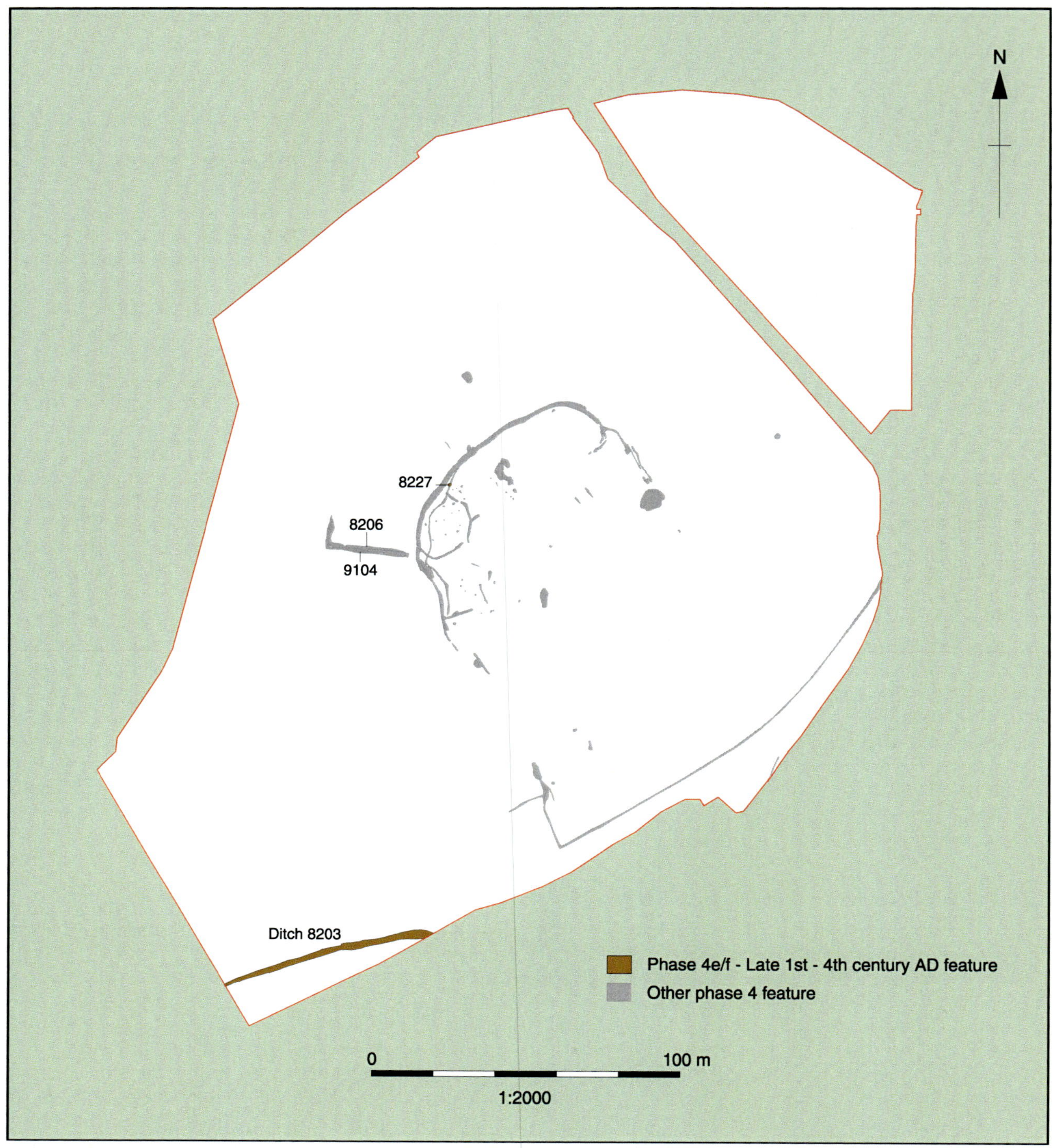

Fig. 27   Features dated to phase 4e and 4f, and broadly dated to Phase 4

Phases 5 and 6 – Medieval and post-medieval, *c* 1100-1800

No features were dated to the medieval period (Phase 5), although two residual sherds of medieval pottery were recovered during the evaluation. These were from a gully associated with a post-medieval hedgerow (Evaluation trench 10). The feature was one of a number assigned to the post-medieval period (Phase 6). Apart from the remains of the hedgerow, a sequence of three field drains, rubbish dumps and landfill along the northern edge of the site, and a modern fence line were identified (Fig. 3). The hedge line corresponded to a kink in the existing field boundaries to the south, which was identified on late 19th-century Ordnance Survey mapping; the hedge line would have been a northern continuation of this field boundary. It is therefore possible to demonstrate that the field system was altered, creating larger fields in recent history. The field drains were stone-lined in the earlier phases and segmented ceramic versions in the later phases; these post-dated the hedge line.

Chapter 3: Earlier Prehistoric Finds

Earlier prehistoric pottery (Figs 28-29)
David Mullin, with a contribution by R A Ixer

A total of 6,600 sherds of earlier prehistoric pottery, weighing 7769 g, were recovered from a number of contexts across the site. Late Neolithic Grooved Ware was recovered from 30 contexts, predominantly from the fills of pits. A near-complete Beaker was recovered from the burial within ring-ditch 8454, and a fragmentary Beaker was also recovered from a burial in what appears to have been an unmarked flat grave (1402).

The pottery was recorded in accordance with the guidance published by the Prehistoric Ceramics Research Group (PCRG 1997), using a x20 hand lens. Four sherds were subject to detailed examination of their fabrics.

Grooved Ware

A total of 1061 sherds of pottery weighing 6432 g were identified as late Neolithic (2900-2100 cal BC) Grooved Ware (Table 2). The pottery was recovered from eleven pits, where it occurred alongside worked flint, animal bone, worked bone, antler and, in three cases, fragments of stone axes.

The fabric of all the vessels was distinctively very shelly, with additional limestone and frequent vesicles. Two sherds were submitted to Rob Ixer (see below) for thin-section analysis and were shown to be of clay from the local Jurassic formations.

It was difficult to distinguish between vessels as the fabrics were so similar, but at least three vessels were identified from rim morphology in pit 8455. Rims and base sherds were infrequent, but nearly

all the wall sherds, and the interior of the majority of the rims, were decorated.

It was possible to reconstruct a complete vessel profile from context 8081 (Fig. 29, no. 1), which conforms to the Woodlands sub-style, as does the decoration on the majority of the other sherds. It was impossible, however, to estimate vessel volumes or indeed have any degree of certainty over the number of vessels represented. The vessel from 8081 has zoned decoration with a fingernail impressed lower section separated by a groove from a plain band. Above this are two grooves separating it from an area of 'lattice lozenge' decoration formed by strips of applied clay which enclose rounded lozenges. The internally bevelled rim is decorated on the inside by an applied strip of clay in a wavy line. This vessel also had at least two post-firing perforations below the rim. Post-firing perforations are recorded from Grooved Ware elsewhere in Britain, and it is generally accepted that they were used to repair broken vessels. Cleal (1988) has indicated that these perforations are more common on Grooved Ware than other traditions of prehistoric pottery and suggests that this implies that Grooved Ware had high symbolic value.

Similarly decorated pottery was recovered from context 9097, but a single sherd from this context is decorated with a chevron design (Fig. 29, no. 3). This has more in common with the Clacton sub-style, as does some of the internal rim decoration from other vessels and in particular the internal wavy line on the vessel from 8081. The latter can be directly paralleled amongst the assemblage from the type-site at Clacton (Hazledine Warren *et al.* 1936, 190 and fig 4).

Kingshill North is one of only a handful of sites within Gloucestershire from which Grooved Ware has been recovered; most Grooved Ware occurs in the area around Lechlade. The majority of this material has been recovered from pits, although possible Grooved Ware appears to have been associated with postholes and other features at Saintbridge, Gloucester (Darvill and Timby 1986, 54) and with tree-throws at Horcott Pit, Fairford (Lamdin-Whymark *et al.* 2009) and Cotswold Community, Ashton Keynes (Brown and Mullin 2010, 6).

At the Loders, Lechlade (Darvill *et al.* 1986, 31 and fig. 3), a single pit contained 83 sherds of Grooved Ware representing at least two vessels. Flint, animal bone and a sandstone rubber were also identified, with cattle, sheep, pig and red deer present within the animal bone assemblage. At a second site in Lechlade, Gassons Road (Boyle *et al.*

Table 2: Quantification of Grooved Ware

Pit	No. sherds	No. contexts	Weight (g)
8058	21	1	39
8064	286	8	2703
8164	17	1	10
8813	59	1	455
8392	69	5	138
8455	305	4	1673
8928	29	2	185
8931	3	1	29
9096	144	3	790
9100	98	3	292
9144	30	1	118
Totals	1061		6432

1998), a series of 15 pits were excavated, one of which (pit 165) contained fragments of at least six Grooved Ware vessels. At Roughground Farm, also close to Lechlade (Allen *et al.* 1993), four pits contained Grooved Ware, a quartzite hammerstone and bone points. Animal bone was also recovered from the pits. The final site from which Grooved Ware was recovered is the recently published assemblage from Cotswold Community (Brown and Mullin 2010, 6), where 13 pits contained small amounts of at least 24 vessels.

The style of the Grooved Ware at Kingshill falls within the Woodlands sub-style, comprising thin walled, tub-shaped vessels decorated with incised lines and converging cordons which is ordered horizontally (Wainwright and Longworth 1971, 238-240). Two vessels, from contexts 8081 and 9097, were decorated with the rare 'lattice lozenge' motif (Cleal 1995), which occurs on this sub-style of Grooved Ware. Other examples which are decorated in a similar way are known from Roughground Farm (Allen *et al.* 1993) and from two sites in Oxfordshire: Tolleys Pit, Cassington (Case 1982a, 124-5) and Barrow Hills, Radley (Barclay and Halpin 1999). The example from Kingshill North is the first confirmed example outside the Thames Valley. While the 'lattice lozenge' motif is uncommon, the Woodlands sub-style occurs widely across Britain from the type site close to Woodhenge, Wiltshire (Stone and Young 1948; Stone 1949) to Dorset (Green 1987), Suffolk (Fell 1952) and Yorkshire (Manby 1974). Cleal (1999) notes that Woodlands sub-style typically occurs in low numbers, usually one to three vessels in pits with other artefacts, and this is indeed the pattern at Kingshill North, where all of the pits containing Grooved Ware also contained worked flint, animal bone and stone axe fragments.

The identification of the vessel from Kingshill North as belonging to the Woodlands sub-style is dependent on the vessel shape and decoration. Some of the decoration overlaps with the Clacton sub-style, however, and it is becoming increasingly apparent that the two sub-styles share many traits, in particular vessel size and form, and that it may be more productive to consider them as aspects of a single tradition, perhaps with a degree of chrono-logical patterning (Garwood 1999). The material from Kingshill North is significant in this respect, as it is somewhat earlier in date than other Woodlands sub-style material, falling within the chronological range of the Clacton sub-style (Garwood 1999, fig 15.6). Also significant in this respect is the chevron decorated sherd from context 9097, a decoration which is typical of the Clacton sub-style, suggesting typological as well as chronological overlap between the sub-styles.

The Clacton sub-style has only been recognised at a single site in Gloucestershire – Cotswold Community (Brown and Mullin 2010, 6) – and although small amounts are known from the Upper Thames Valley (Barclay 1999), the Durrington Walls

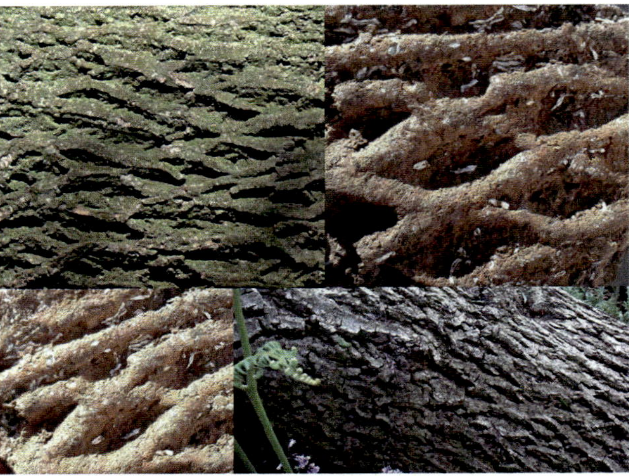

Fig. 28   Ash bark compared with the geometric motif of Grooved Ware

sub-style is more common in the region. The Woodlands sub-style in the Thames Valley (Barclay 1999) is predominantly shell tempered, in contrast to the grog-tempered Durrington Walls sub-style. Barclay (1999) has argued that the use of shell was a deliberate choice and does not reflect local avail-ability of raw materials or a technical choice related to improving firing properties of raw clay. This appears to be the case at Kingshill North as, although the shelly clay used in the fabric occurs locally, it appears to have been selected from a range of materials which would have been equally suitable for potting. This also appears to have been the case at Clifton Quarry, Worcestershire (Edwards 2007) where, although locally occurring, fossilif-erous clay was preferentially selected for use in Clacton/Woodlands Grooved Ware. There is an interesting contrast in the use of fossil shell as a temper within Grooved Ware in the West Midlands (Edwards 2007) and the Thames Valley and the use of marine shell in Wiltshire (Cleal 1994), even on sites far from the coast. Clearly the incorporation of shell within the fabric of Grooved Ware vessels relates to the symbolic meaning of that material, although what that meaning may have been is diffi-cult to detect. A further element worth considera-tion is the 'lattice lozenge' motif. The motif contrasts with the geometric decoration on other sub-styles of Grooved Ware and is unusual within a Clacton/Woodlands context. The decoration has been described by Garwood (1999, 157) as resembling a mesh or net and Cleal (1991, 144) has drawn atten-tion to the presence of a similar design on antler maceheads of the Maesmore tradition. The design also closely resembles the bark of ash and willow trees, both of which can be used for basketry, or may have held wider symbolic meaning (Figure 28).

Beaker

A near-complete Beaker from context 8657, found alongside burial 8656 (group 8454), was represented by 75 sherds weighing 714 g. A single sherd of a different Beaker was recovered from context 2404 in the 2006 evaluation, which is the same context as 8657. A small number of sherds of another Beaker were recovered from 2303, the fill of the ring-ditch surrounding the central grave 8588. A second Beaker burial (1402) was recovered during the evaluation and this was accompanied by 80 Beaker sherds weighing 391 g from a single vessel, which had a profile that could be reconstructed.

The Beaker from 8657 (Fig. 29, no. 5) was tempered with grog and limestone and in fragmentary condition, roughly 85% complete. This vessel can be assigned to Needham's (2005) S-profile class or to Clarke's (1970) 'East Anglian' group. The decoration is horizontally zoned and comprises horizontal lines of tooth-comb impressions with incised zigzags and chevrons. In-filled pendant triangles are present near the base. The form is closest to Clarke corpus no. 406 from Bromley, Kent, which also shares some decorative traits, but the decoration is more closely matched with Wessex/ Middle Rhine Beakers such as Clarke corpus no. 458 from Kinneff, Scotland.

The Beaker from 1402 (Fig. 29, no. 4) had grog and fine flint inclusions. This vessel had many old breaks and was incomplete, but it was possible to reconstruct a complete profile. This Beaker was more difficult to classify, but had a simple, slightly tapered rim, a long neck and very rounded belly and probably fits best within Needham's (2005) "Long Necked" class or Clarke's (1970) southern series. The decoration appears to be all short-comb impressions, but is very irregular and difficult to match with any other examples. The decoration was also very worn suggesting that the vessel was old when deposited and was possibly deposited as sherds.

Clifford (1937) listed a total of eleven Beaker sites from the Gloucestershire Cotswolds, the number having risen to 15 by the time of Clarke's (1970) corpus. At present, a total of 45 sites producing at least 104 Beakers have been identified within the county. The Beakers have been recovered from a number of different kinds of contexts, the most common being pits, where fragmentary Beakers appear to have been deposited alongside burnt material, worked flint and animal bone. The two funerary contexts from Kingshill North are significant, as Beaker burials are rare in Gloucestershire. Grinsell (1961, 14) lists only a single example from a barrow. This is surprising, given the large numbers of round barrows in the county (Grinsell 1961), but it is apparent that Beaker barrows are generally rare in western Britain. The dominance of Beaker finds from pits and other features, rather than burials, in Devon has been pointed out by Quinnell (2003), and this also seems to be the case in Cornwall (Jones 2005) and Somerset (Grinsell 1971; Lewis and Mullin forthcoming).

Beaker burials from Gloucestershire are known, but there is considerable uncertainty if these were recovered from flat graves or from denuded round barrows. At Barnwood, Gloucester, the skeleton of an adult male, accompanied by complete Beaker and flint knife, was recovered in 1927 (Clifford 1930; Clarke corpus no. 277) and a similar burial, again of a adult male, is recorded from Prestbury (Clifford 1938a; Clarke corpus no. 285). A Beaker from a possible flat grave is known from Slaughter Bridge, Bourton on the Water, where it accompanied the body of an adult female (Dunning 1937; Clarke corpus nos 278 and 279), and recent, although unpublished, excavations at Huntsman's Quarry, Naunton (Patrick Foster Associates 2000) uncovered a burial consisting of a crouched inhumation with an associated Beaker vessel and two unretouched flint flakes. It is not certain if this burial was located below a barrow. Fragments of a Beaker were recovered from a burial inserted into the mound of the long barrow at Sales Lot, Withington (O'Neil 1966), and again this burial appears to have been that of an adult male and was accompanied by a fragment of sheet bronze, possibly an ear ring.

In the Upper Thames Valley, a Beaker ring-ditch was located during excavations by Wessex Archaeology at Shorncote Quarry (Barclay *et al.* 1995). This contained a large sub-rectangular grave (grave 121) from which a poorly preserved skeleton and a Beaker, flint dagger, two flint knives and a flint flake were recovered. The skeleton was probably that of a mature male, and had been placed on its left side with the head to the north west. The Beaker was particularly crude and unevenly fired but was decorated with rows of comb impressions. An incomplete Beaker is also recorded from this site. This was recovered from another grave (1007), which contained the skeleton of an adolescent, a flint flake and a penannular bronze bracelet. Elsewhere in the Upper Thames Valley, excavations of an area of the Clemson Memorial Hall, Lechlade was undertaken by the Cotswold Archaeological Trust, and recovered evidence for two Beaker burials (Thomas and Holbrook 1998). The first was in a grave cut aligned approximately north-south and contained the skeleton of an older male and a Beaker, which, though appearing to have been broken in antiquity, held burnt material. The second burial at the site was 7.5 m north of the earlier burial and was in a grave cut aligned east-west. This contained the fragmentary remains of an older infant of 2-4 years buried with a Beaker. An unworked flint flake and a thin copper alloy awl were recovered from among the broken remains of the pot. Excavations by Oxford Archaeology at Cotswold Community School, Somerford Keynes, recovered fragmentary Beaker from a number of pits and from the fill of a ring-ditch, and a total of three inhumation burials were also uncovered at the site. Two of these were accompanied by near-complete Beakers, the other by a fragmentary Beaker, and an incomplete stone wrist guard or bracer was also recovered from one of the burials (Powell *et al.* 2010, 24-5).

A number of Beakers, initially thought to be from a pit associated with a bell barrow at Frampton on

Severn were excavated by Richard Atkinson in 1948, and are now lost, but recent analysis of the archive from this site (Mullin forthcoming; Clarke corpus no. 280) located fragments of another Beaker from below the old turf line of the barrow and suggested that the pit containing the Beaker was earlier than the bell barrow and did not represent a Beaker burial. Similarly, finds from a round barrow at Horsley, otherwise known as the Lechmore barrow, include fragmentary Beaker, but the precise context of this material is not known (Grinsell 1961, 119; Clarke corpus no. 282). An analysis of the finds held by Gloucester Museum (accession numbers A3087-8 and A3085-6) by the author identified a total of five sherds, two of which do not appear to be Beaker. The remaining three sherds are heavily abraded; one sherd is comb impressed, the others appear to be decorated with incised lines or comb impressions. Beaker was found in the round barrow at Ivy Lodge, Woodchester (Gardiner 1930; Clarke corpus no. 300), but again its precise context is uncertain and subsequent excavation by Clifford (1950) did not locate any further Beaker. Clifford (1937, 162) also records three sherds from a round barrow at Taynton excavated by Rolleston and housed in the Ashmolean Museum, but again the context of these finds are not clear.

Beaker is most frequently found within pits in Gloucestershire and is often associated with burnt material, worked flint and human or animal bone. Beakers found in these pits are often fragmented and the number of vessels represented can vary from two to over thirty. A cluster of such pits was excavated at Roughground Farm, Lechlade (Allen *et al.* 1993), where five pits contained a total of 200 sherds, representing at least 36 individual vessels. Over 150 worked flints were recovered from these pits, as well as two fragments of sandstone 'cushion stones' and four quartzite hammerstones and animal bone, including cattle and pig.

An excavation at Trinity Farm, Bagendon, undertaken by Oxford Archaeology (then the Oxford Archaeological Unit) during the A417 road improvement scheme in 1996 and 1997 also recovered a series of pits containing Beaker (Mudd *et al.* 1999b). Here three pits contained 164 sherds of Beaker pottery from at least 14 vessels. Pit 8 contained hazelnut shells, flint scrapers, cores and flakes, and some fragments of burnt limestone and hazelnut shells were also recovered from Pit 10. Large numbers of Beakers were also recorded at Cirencester Polo Club, Daglingworth (Nichols 2004), where a single pit contained 90 sherds of Beaker, representing a minimum of eight vessels. Animal bone, including cattle and possible wild boar was also collected from the feature.

A number of sites across the county have produced pits with smaller assemblages of Beaker. Three pits containing small amounts of Beaker, worked flint and burnt stone were excavated by Oxford Archaeology at Horcott Pit in the Upper Thames Valley (Lamdin-Whymark *et al.* 2009), and

at Station Road, Kemble, work in 2001 by the Gloucestershire County Council Archaeology Service uncovered two pits containing eight fragments of decorated Beaker from two separate vessels and charcoal (Nichols 2001; Evans and McSloy 2006). Two pits containing quantities of Beaker pottery, flint and animal bone were excavated at Warren Farm, Toddington, one of these pits also containing charred hazelnut shells. Similar pits were excavated at Oxpens Farm, Yanworth. The sites at Toddington and Yanworth were excavated as part of the work on the Esso Midline Pipeline (Smith and Cox 1986). An archaeological watching brief undertaken by Cotswold Archaeology at Home Farm, Ebrington, revealed a rectangular, clay-lined pit containing a single sherd of Beaker (Cotswold Archaeology 2003), and single pits are also recorded at Totterdown Lane, Horcott (Pine and Preston 2004), Cirencester Rugby Club (Hicks 1999), Bredon Road, Mitton, Tewkesbury (Barrett 2004), and Netherhills, Frampton-on-Severn (Mullin forthcoming). Very fragmented Beaker is also recorded from Saintbridge, Gloucester (Garrod and Heighway 1984), where it was recovered from three postholes that also contained worked flint. A posthole containing fingernail impressed Beaker and worked flint was recovered during excavations along the Wormington to Tirley pipeline at Bank Farm Site B (Coleman *et al.* 2006, 21) and work at the GPO, Berkeley Street, Gloucester, also recovered some Beaker, although the context for this is unclear (Hurst 1972).

Curiously, Beaker has been recorded at Iron Age hillforts on the Cotswolds. A single Beaker sherd was found in the 1925 excavations at Leckhampton Camp (Burrow *et al.* 1925; Clarke corpus no. 283), although Darvill (1987, 84) suggests that this may, in fact be Iron Age in date. A Beaker sherd was recovered from the old turf line below the rampart at Shenbarrow Camp (Fell 1961; Clarke corpus no. 287). At Crickley Hill, Beaker was recorded from the old ground surface below the ramparts, where it was interpreted as potentially representing the remains of an occupation layer (Dixon 1994, 220).

Beaker was recorded from the interior of a number of Cotswold long barrows and this probably represents the deliberate backfilling of the passage, as recorded at West Kennet (Piggott 1962). At Eyeford (Clark 1925, 94), possible Beaker sherds were recovered from the mound above a cist near the centre of the barrow, and Beaker is also recorded from Swell VI and Swell VII (Clifford 1937, 161). Clifford (1937, 162) also notes Beaker from an unpublished excavation at the Westcote Heath long barrow, Great Rissington. Rather more securely recorded are the Beaker fragments from the antechamber at Notgrove (Clifford 1938b; Clarke corpus no. 284), where it was interpreted as forming part of material brought to the site to deliberately block the passage and entrance.

Two or three sherds of Beaker were recovered from the area of a burnt mound at Sandy Lane,

Charlton Kings, Cheltenham, although their identification is not certain (Leah and Young 2001). Possible Beaker sherds were also recorded from excavations at the henge at Condicote (Saville 1983). This pottery was recovered from the internal ditch and was mostly undecorated, but was identified as being associated with the Beaker series and potentially either domestic or coarse ware Beaker. Such Beaker is rare from Gloucestershire, but known from Horcott Pit (Lamdin-Whymark *et al.* 2009), Roughground Farm (Allen *et al.* 1993), Bank Farm, Dumbleton (Coleman *et al.* 2006) and Cirencester Polo Club (Nichols 2004).

Three sites have produced Beaker from ditches. At Rudgeway Lane, Tewkesbury (Walker *et al.* 2004) and Holme Hill, Tewkesbury (Hannan 1976), the Beaker was residual, and this is also probably true of Beaker from the Beeches, Cirencester (Young 2001). At Leaze Farm, Lechlade, Beaker and possible Peterborough Ware were found in a later feature (John Moore Heritage Services 2001), and a single sherd of Beaker was found in a Roman layers at Gloucester Business Park Link Road, Hucclecote (Thomas *et al.* 2003). Beaker has also been found in unstratified contexts on a number of sites, such as Shorncote Quarry (Hearne and Adam 2000, 35) and The Buckles, Frocester (Darvill 2000).

Clifford reported a find of a Beaker during the course of gravel digging at Shurdington Gravel Pit in 1935-36 (Clifford 1937; Clarke corpus no. 288), and O'Neil and Bunt (1966) recorded another found during the excavation of a water-main trench in Hall Road, Leckhampton. Further Beaker, probably excavated from near Homme House, Dymock, was also recorded from the catalogue of the sale of a miscellaneous collection of antiquities from a country house in 1964 (Clifford 1964).

Very few Beaker fabrics have been recorded in detail within Gloucestershire in contrast to those from northern Somerset (Russell and Williams 1998) and Wiltshire (Cleal 1995). The only material from the county to receive detailed petrographic analysis is that from Roughground Farm, Lechlade (Allen *et al.* 1993), where a total of three main fabric groups were identified. These consisted of grog-tempered (Fabric 3), grog-and-shell-tempered (Fabric 4) and flint-tempered (Fabric 5) wares with-and-shell tempered ware (Fabric 4) being the most common. This appears to have been used for all types of vessels at the site, with flint tempered fabric tending to be found in the larger and thicker-walled vessels and grog temper fabric used for the finer vessels.

Macroscopic work on the Beaker from burial 1 at Memorial Hall, Lechlade (Thomas and Holbrook 1998) identified grog, quartz and limestone in the temper, although the Beaker from burial 2 at the same site was entirely grog-tempered. A similar grog temper is also recorded from Gloucester Business Park Link Road, Hucclecote (Thomas *et al.* 2003) and the Beakers from both grave 121 and from grave 1007 at Shorncote were also grog-tempered (Barclay *et al.* 1995). A substantial sherd of fingernail

impressed Beaker from Bank Farm Site B (Coleman *et al.* 2006, 38) was similarly grog-tempered while the Beaker from Bredon Road, Mitton (Barrett 2004) was grog-and-quartz-tempered, and the Beakers from Cirencester Polo Club were grog-tempered, grog-and-limestone-tempered, and grog-and-flint-tempered. At Trinity Farm, Bagendon, calcite temper was identified, alongside grog temper, grog-and-sand temper, and grog-and-limestone temper. The calcite temper identified at Trinity Farm appears to be the only recognised occurrence of this inclusion in Beaker in the county, although it is known from northern Somerset, where limestone was also exploited as temper (Russell and Williams 1998).

It can be seen that the Beakers from Gloucestershire are typically grog-tempered but can also have shell, flint, quartz and limestone added as tempering agents. Only a single example of calcite temper is known from the county and grog-and-limestone temper appears to be the most commonly occurring fabric type. It is uncertain if these inclusions relate to local potting 'recipes', handed down through generations of potters (Cleal 1995), or if they relate to the form and function of the vessels, with finer vessels tending to have a pure grog fabric (Allen *et al.* 1993). It is, however, noticeable that the inclusions in Beaker pottery from Gloucestershire contrast with those found in Wiltshire (Cleal 1995) where limestone is rarely used, and have more in common with Beakers from northern Somerset, where limestone was more commonly exploited, although Russell and Williams (1998) point out that Beakers from Mendip tend to be purely grog-tempered. The presence of flint in the fabric of the Beakers from Kingshill North, Roughground Farm, Cotswold Community and the nearby Cirencester Polo Club is suggestive of imported Beakers, as flint does not occur naturally on the Cotswolds.

Catalogue of illustrated pottery (Fig. 29)

1. **Lozenge lattice decorated Grooved Ware vessel** of the Woodlands sub-style from context 8081. Fossil shell fabric.
2. **Decorated Grooved Ware rim** of the Woodlands sub-style from context 8819. Fossil shell fabric.
3. **Chevron decorated Grooved Ware sherd** from context 9097. Fossil shell fabric.
4. **Long-necked Beaker** from context 1404. Grog and flint fabric.
5. **S-profile Beaker** from context 8657. Grog, fossil shell and limestone fabric.

Fabric descriptions R A Ixer

Introduction

Grooved Ware from pit 8064 (context 8081) and pit 9096 (context 9097) and Beakers from graves 8588 (context 8657) and 1402 (context 1404) were subject to examination. Initially the exposed surfaces, cut surface and thin-section of the four sherds (as

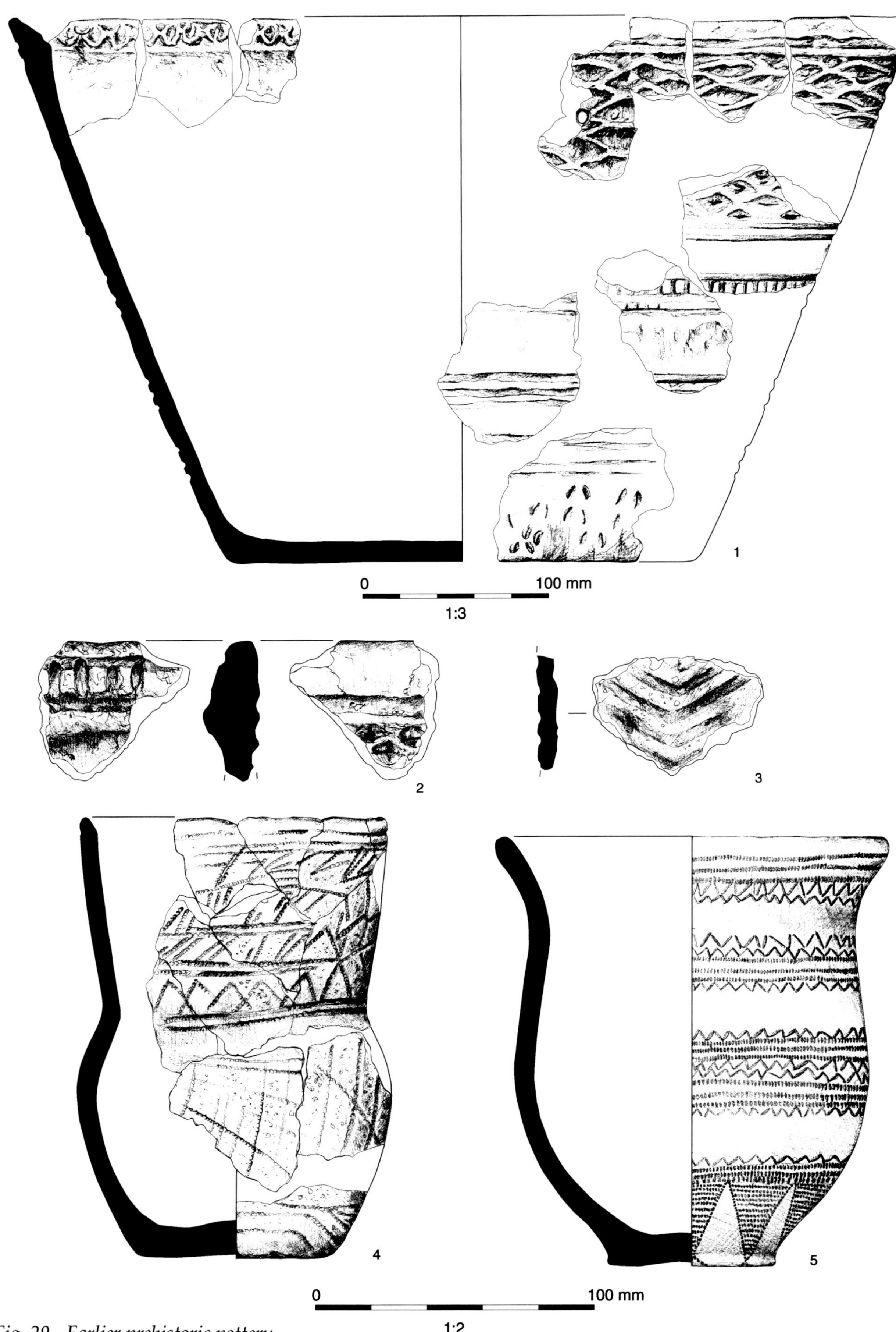

Fig. 29   Earlier prehistoric pottery

provided) were investigated using a x20 hand lens and the Geological Society of America rock-colour chart. A standard thin section was prepared from each of the pottery sherds (after impregnation with resin) and the sherds were investigated using transmitted light petrography. The emphasis of the report is on providing detailed petrographical characterisation of the sherds with an emphasis on their manufacture and the geographical provenance of the raw materials.

Local geology of Cirencester

Cirencester overlies the Middle Jurassic Great Oolite limestones, but immediately to the south lie the Cornbrash limestones and Oxford Clay and Kellaway Beds. As elsewhere, the Jurassic clays have little surface expression other than making for heavy soils. Drift deposits are present in the area and these include boulder clays with chalk flints.

Grooved Ware

The clay in both Grooved Ware pots is almost devoid of fine-grained, monocrystalline quartz and muscovite but carries abundant, small micrite and sparry calcite clasts, less than 0.2mm in diameter. The clay is therefore unusual and is perhaps a marl (a calcareous clay); it is unlikely to be a glacial clay but probably is from the local Jurassic formations.

The pots are ungrogged and it is quite possible that the pots are untempered and that a shelly clay has been fired, or the pots have been tempered with a range of different limestones and Jurassic fossil debris. Although the fossil debris is broadly similar in the two pots, the range of limestone is different. Fossiliferous limestones and shelly clays crop out/are present close to Cirencester, the latter especially to the south. All the components of the pots could be local.

Beakers

The clay in both Beakers has abundant, fine-grained, monocrystalline quartz and muscovite laths; muscovite is more abundant in the vessel from context 8657. The clay may be an unworked, naturally, silty clay or it may have been cleaned. It is probably not a deepwater Jurassic clay.

Both Beakers are heavily grogged and therefore clearly tempered. The grog has a cleaner clay (carries fewer, fine-grained non-plastics) than the main paste; this is especially true of the very clean clay within the grog of the vessel from context 1404. In both pots the grog and main paste carry the same non-plastic tempering material, namely flint/chert in the vessel from context 1404 and shell/limestone in that from context 8657. Very local inhomogeneities in the grog suggests that it is itself grogged (grog-in-grog).

The Beakers have temper in addition to the grog. The vessel from context 1404 has fine-grained angular flint and that from 8657 fossiliferous limestone; the fossil assemblage is Mesozoic in age. Both sherds share the same paste/main clay with

quartz and muscovite and there is little that is diagnostic about this clay. However, it is unlikely to be a deep water Mesozoic clay. The flint in both the grog and main paste of the vessel from context 1404 may be from local drift material (boulder clay) so making the pot local, but as the main chalk outcrops (with their flint bands) are more than 20 kms to the south of Cirencester, the pot could be non-local. The shelly limestone in grog and main clay of the vessel from context 8657 is Jurassic in age and local Jurassic limestone crops out close to Cirencester.

Lithics *David Mullin*

Introduction

A total of 1764 worked flints were recovered from 102 contexts. The material was dominated by waste flakes, but scrapers and cores were recovered from pits containing pottery and other material (Table 3). The flint assemblage is the largest associated with Grooved Ware in Gloucestershire and has few parallels.

The flint was catalogued according to a broad debitage, core or tool type. Information about burning and breaks was recorded. Due to the high level of patination of the assemblage, it was not possible to identify raw material type, although some good quality black flint was noticed on fresh breaks. Cores were classified according to the number and position of their platforms, following Clark (1960). Core maintenance pieces were classified to the following criteria. Core rejuvenation flakes are pieces representing the removal of the top or bottom of a core in order to improve the flaking angle of the platform. Core trimming flakes are

Table 3: Lithics: identification and quantification (fragment count)

Description	Total
Primary waste	42
Secondary waste	85
Tertiary waste	816
Chips	361
Cores	10
Core rejuvenation tablets	16
Core trimming flakes	222
Narrow blades	14
Blade-like flakes and blade shatter	98
Microlith	4
Microdenticulate	2
Scrapers	50
Knife	1
Point	1
Misc. retouched flakes	5
Utilised flakes	32
Burnt flint	76
TOTAL	1764

flakes which remove a substantial part of a core in order to aid working by removing an imperfection in the core, a miss-hit or other impediment to flaking. The nature of any remnant flake scars on the dorsal surface of core trimming flakes was noted.

Flakes were classified following Saville (1990, 155), which allows an identification of the stage in the core reduction process to which the flake belongs. Terminations such as hinge fractures were noted. Chips are defined as pieces measuring less than 10 mm by 10 mm. Flakes were classified as blade-like or a s blades according to ratio length to breadth, with a greater length to breadth ratio being classified as blades. Mid-sections of blades with no bulb of percussion were classified as blade shatter (Andrefsky 1998, 81-3). Retouched pieces were classified according to standard morphological descriptions (Bamford 1985; Healy 1988; Bradley 1999; Butler 2005).

Worked flint recovered from the environmental sample residues was also recorded, while the presence of burnt unworked flint was noted but the material was not retained.

Results

Condition

The flint was generally in a good condition, and generally the assemblage was fresh and unrolled.

Raw materials

The high level of patination noted on all of the flint made identification of raw materials very difficult. However, a variety of materials could be noted from fresh breaks, indicating diverse origins such as good quality chalk flint and poorer quality gravel flint.

Technology and dating

The majority of the flint was recovered from pits which contained Grooved Ware pottery of late Neolithic date. Although the assemblage is dominated by waste – chips form 20% of the total assemblage (and 28% of the waste) – this probably reflects the retrieval of smaller pieces from the sieved fills of pits. Nevertheless, waste comprises over half of the assemblage in every pit, with the proportion of waste being over 70% in the majority of cases.

Cores and core-related pieces – in particular core trimming flakes and rejuvenation tablets – form the next highest proportion of the assemblage. This reflects the active maintenance of cores and the preparation of good flaking surfaces, although the high number of hinge and step terminations appears to reflect relatively low knapping skill. The cores tend towards blade, rather than flake-based technology and many have prepared and abraded platforms. There is also evidence for the use of both hard and soft hammers. The Levallois core from context 8393 (pit 8392) is noteworthy, as this technology is associated with the production of petit tranchet derivative arrowheads, dating to the late Neolithic; one such arrowhead was found in the topsoil at Kingshill North.

Scrapers were the commonest form of tool; every pit (with the exception of 8929 and 8164) contained at least one, while pit 8813 contained 21, a selection

Table 4: Lithics: quantification by type and context (fragment count)

Description	8455	8813	8928	8930	9096	9100	9144	8058	8100	8064	8738	8164	8392
Primary waste	40	17	4	3	-	2	-	1	2	-	-	1	-
Secondary waste	10	27	7	13	1	13	2	-	2	1	-	3	3
Tertiary waste	60	313	62	59	7	55	1	10	31	42	4	67	54
Chips	5	9	84	43	52	96	-	-	8	8	-	-	40
TOTAL WASTE (%)	85	72	92	81	71	82	27	58	60	64	50	88	83
Cores	1	3	3	2	2	-	-	-	-	-	-	-	1
Core rejuvenation tablets	-	2	2	3	1	1	1	-	-	-	-	-	-
Core trimming flakes	7	81	5	7	11	25	4	2	11	16	3	5	9
TOTAL CORE-RELATED (%)	6	17	6	8	17	13	45	11	15	20	37	6	8
Narrow blades	-	-	-	-	3	-	-	-	4	1	-	-	1
Blade-like flakes and blade shatter	10	29	3	9	4	7	1	3	5	3	-	5	8
Microlith	-	-	-	-	-	1	-	-	-	-	-	-	-
Microdenticulate	-	1	-	-	-	-	-	-	-	-	-	-	-
Scrapers	3	21	-	4	1	1	1	2	6	8	1	-	1
Misc. retouched flakes	-	1	-	-	-	-	1	1	2	-	-	-	-
Flint axe fragment	1	1	-	-	-	-	-	-	-	-	-	-	-
TOTAL	136	505	170	145	84	202	11	19	72	80	8	81	117

of which are illustrated in Figure 30. Very few other kinds of tools are present and miscellaneous retouched pieces are also rare. The end scrapers form over half the scraper assemblage, but side-and-end scrapers are also present. The angle of retouch varies, as does the size of each scraper, probably reflecting a toolkit used for a variety of purposes. Only one thumbnail scraper contemporary with the Beaker phase of the site was recovered, but this came from the topsoil and cannot be directly assigned to this phase.

Flakes of flint axes were recovered from ring-ditch 8597 (group 8454), pit 8747, and pits 8813 and 8455; that from 8597 comprised the butt-end of the axe.

A low proportion of the flint recovered from the site was burnt – less than 4% of the assemblage – and burnt material occurred in low numbers (less than 20) in all of the pits from which it was recovered.

Contexts

Nearly all of the flint was recovered from pits containing Grooved Ware pottery of late Neolithic date. Few earlier pieces were present (four microliths) and no certain later material could be identified (Table 4).

Discussion

The majority of the flint from Kingshill North was recovered from pits containing rich finds assemblages including Grooved Ware pottery, animal bone and burnt material. Lamdin-Whymark (2008, 121) describes the distinctive characteristics of Grooved Ware associated flint assemblages as a high proportion of retouched tools, high levels of burning and breakage and the presence of knapping debris, especially refitting pieces. Wainwright and Longworth (1971, 254-61) consider the most common type of flint tool from Grooved Ware context to be the scraper, followed by transverse arrowheads, serrated flakes and knives. Flakes and cores are also common among these assemblages. The lack of evidence for deliberate breakage of implements, especially scrapers, and the lack of formal tools or other retouched items and the few burnt items from the pits at Kingshill North is therefore unusual.

Although scrapers are the most abundant artefact type from the pits at the site, they form only a small proportion of the assemblage, the 21 scrapers from pit 8813 forming only 4% of the total content of the pit, which is dominated by waste flakes (72%) and cores (17%). The presence of a high proportion of

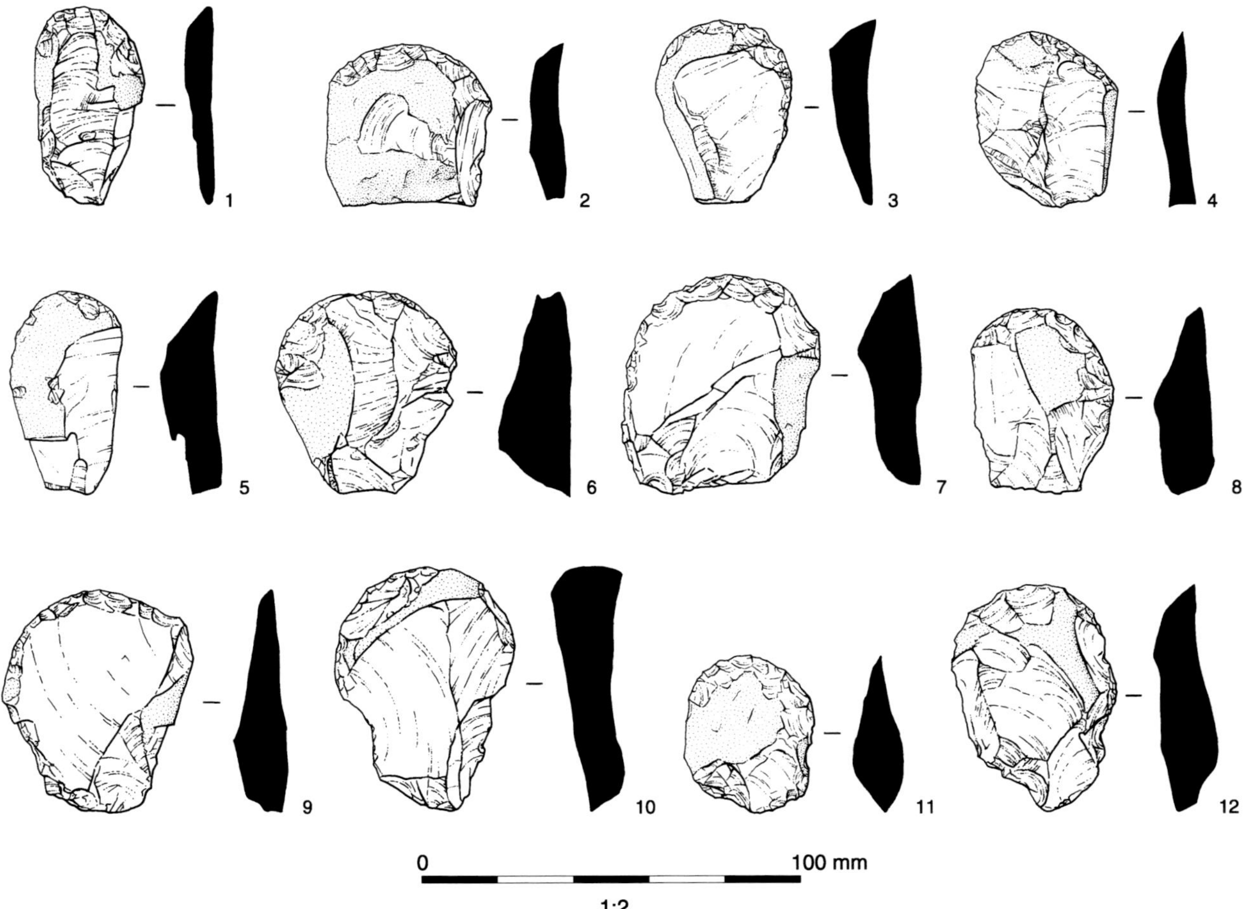

Fig. 30 Earlier prehistoric lithics

knapping waste is suggestive of deliberate working-down of cores for incorporation, along with their waste material, into the pit fills. There are, however, very few refits between flakes and cores within the pit fills, again an unusual aspect for a Grooved Ware associated assemblage. Few refits could likewise be found between assemblages from different pits, suggesting that each was filled in a discrete episode with no mixing of material between pit fills.

There are very few Grooved Ware assemblages from Gloucestershire with which to compare the pits at Kingshill North. A total of 675 flints were recovered from two fills of a pit at Frampton on Severn, Gloucestershire (Mullin forthcoming), but this contained no pottery. The pit was, however, radiocarbon dated to the late Neolithic. Many small chips were present in the assemblage, as well as six cores, 13 scrapers and two chisel arrowheads. At Clifton Quarry, Worcestershire, also in the Severn valley, two late Neolithic pits contained over 200 flints and over 800 chips (Mann and Jackson 2007). The flint here, however, was very fragmented and burnt. The assemblage contained a variety of tools including a fabricator, knife, retouched flakes and a scraper.

In the Upper Thames valley, to the south east of Cirencester, a total of 135 pieces of flint were recovered from pits containing Grooved Ware at Roughground Farm (Allen *et al.* 1993); most were in very fresh condition and of good quality chalk flint. The assemblage was dominated by scrapers and utilised flakes, but the pits also contained a high proportion of unmodified waste. At Horcott Pit (Lamdin-Whymark *et al.* 2009), two pits containing Grooved Ware were excavated. These contained waste flakes, an oblique arrowhead of late Neolithic date, and a side scraper, but the flint assemblages were much poorer than those at Kingshill North.

Catalogue of illustrated flint (Fig. 30)

1. **End scraper** from pit 8813
2. **End scraper** from pit 8813
3. **End scraper** from pit 8813
4. **End scraper** from pit 8813
5. **End scraper** from pit 8813
6. **End scraper** from pit 8813
7. **End scraper** from pit 8813
8. **End and side scraper** from pit 8813
9. **End and side scraper** from pit 8813
10. **End scraper** from pit 8813
11. **End scraper** from pit 8813
12. **End scraper** from pit 8813

Stone axe heads *Fiona Roe, with a contribution by Roger Taylor*

Introduction

Three pits (8100, 8455 & 8928) produced fragments of stone axe heads, and one pit (8813) produced a complete small stone axe. Pits 8813, 8455 and 8928 also contained Woodlands style Grooved Ware (see

Mullins above). Pit 8100 produced no pottery but a radiocarbon date of 2863–2673 cal BC (95%; NZA-33140), obtained from a nutshell suggests that it should be of similar late Neolithic date. Three of the axes were made from Cornish greenstone and one flake was of Group VI Langdale stone from the Lake District.

Description

The axe heads from three of the pits were made from Cornish greenstones, a term used for altered igneous rocks. The details have been confirmed in two cases by thin sectioning, with petrological identifications by Dr Roger Taylor on behalf of the South Western Implement Petrology Committee (see Taylor, below). In the case of the thin-sectioned incomplete axe head from pit 8455 (context 8819, SF 10079), the description of the minerals suggests that although the rock could not be attributed to the Group I variety of Cornish greenstone, it nevertheless bears quite a close resemblance to it. This axe head consists of the butt end only and there are traces of battering where the break occurred, so that it seems as if the damage may have been deliberate. The second thin section, taken from one of two small axe fragments from pit 8928 (context 8929), indicates another Cornish greenstone with some similarities to SF 10079, but it probably did not come from the same implement. A complete small axe from pit 8813 is made from a slightly different material but Roger Taylor agrees as a result of macroscopic examination that it is likely to be another Cornish greenstone. It is clear that this late Neolithic community had some links with the South West, as discussed below. The fourth axe head, which came from pit 8100 (8098), is only represented by a thin flake without any surviving polished surface, but appears to be of the Group VI Langdale stone from the Lake District, a distinctive green-grey tuff that was widely used for axe heads.

All four pits with axe heads in them contained other finds, which help to demonstrate the wider picture, especially since there seems to be some correspondence between the occurrence of axe heads and especially large assemblages of pottery or flints. Pit 8455, in which the broken butt end of an axe head was found (8819, SF 10079) also contained 305 sherds of Grooved Ware, the largest collection of pottery from any of the Grooved Ware pits on the site (see Table 1). The highest number of flints, 505 (including 21 scrapers), came from pit 8813, which also contained the complete axe head (8814; SF 10077). In view of this, it is perhaps no coincidence that pit 8928, which had two small greenstone axe head fragments in it (8929), also contained a high proportion of flints amounting to 170 items. Artefacts of bone also seem to have had some significance in the deposits made in the Grooved Ware pits on the site. One key pit, 8813, with its complete axe head and large quantity of flints, also contained five bone pins together with a bone awl, a worked rib and a spatula. The pins are not the more elaborate variety of skewer pin known mainly from burial contexts (Montague 1995) but simpler worked bone points. Another three such bone pins came from pit 9100, along with 202 flints, the second highest amount from the Grooved Ware pits. The deposition of animal bones is also of interest, with the occurrence of an articulated neonatal pig in pit 8455 along with an axe head fragment, while there is a predominance of bones of young pigs generally, including 51 bones found in pit 8928, which also contained two axe head fragments. Pit 8064, which had the second largest quantity of Grooved Ware sherds, also produced a bird bone, although unfortunately it has not been possible to identify it more closely.

By contrast, the pit in which the small flake of Langdale stone was found (8100) contained no pottery and only 72 flints, although a sandstone pendant was retrieved, along with an antler and a quartzite hammerstone which could have been used together for digging out the pit. There appears to have been less of consequence here, as if these items were considered to be more mundane. The flake of stone axe head material is so insubstantial that its presence in the pit could simply be fortuitous. It also seems less likely that the occurrence of flakes from polished flint axes in Grooved Ware pits could be of particular significance. These were found in addition to stone ones in pits 8813 and 8455, but were also recorded from two altogether different contexts, from 8596, the fill of ditch 8597, which is part of the Beaker ring ditch and barrow, and again from 8748, which is the fill of pit 8747 in an early Roman group of pits, 8895. Such finds, which are not uncommon, may merely represent the re-use of broken flint axe heads.

Catalogue of stone axe heads

1   **Axe head**, 2 fragments (Fig. 31, no. 1). Cornish greenstone. Pit 8928, context 8929

2   **Axe head**, complete (Fig. 31, no. 2). Cornish greenstone. Pit 8813, context 8814, sf 10077

3   **Butt end of axe head** (not illustrated). Cornish greenstone. Pit 8455, context 8819, sf 10079

4   **Flake from axe head** (not illustrated). Group VI Langdale rock. Pit 8100, context 8098

Discussion

The clearest indication of a meaningful deposit in a Grooved Ware pit comes from Clifton Quarry, Worcestershire, where excavations in 2006 revealed a group of six or more axe heads, which were mostly burnt and were associated with large sherds of Durrington Walls style pottery and numerous flints (Mann and Jackson 2009). The axe heads were made from varied materials, including the Group I Cornish greenstone, which was used for a burnt blade end broken into four pieces. This provides a useful indication that an incomplete Cornish axe might have been deliberately included in a particular deposit. Similar circumstances were met with at Boscombe Down, Wiltshire, where two Cornish greenstone fragments, possibly from the same axe head, were found in a pit along with Woodlands style pottery and a very large assemblage of flintwork that includes over eighty scrapers (Wessex Archaeology, in prep). Fragmentary axe heads founds in Grooved Ware pits frequently show traces of damage from burning, though others, including an example from Kingshill North (8819), seem to have been deliberately destroyed in a way that is replicated at Rotheley Lodge Farm, Leicestershire, where two axe heads made from Group XX (Charnwood) axe heads were broken up (Hunt 2006, 238).

Bone artefacts did not survive at Clifton Quarry but seem to have been a particular characteristic of the Grooved Ware pits at Kingshill North (see Mullin below, 'Worked bone and antler'). The assemblage of eight bone artefacts in pit 8813 contributes towards the apparent special nature of

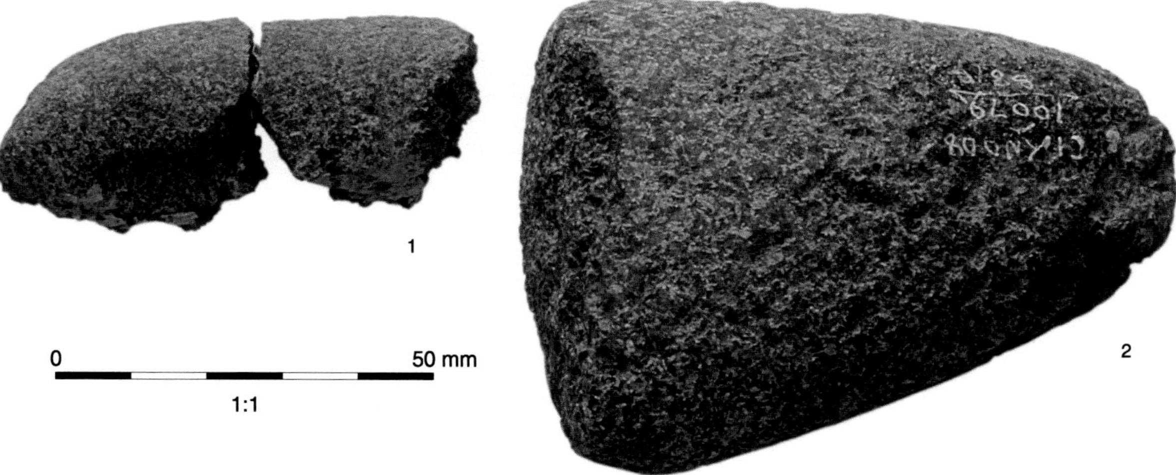

Fig. 31 Stone axes

the deposits in this particular pit. Bone pins have been found in some numbers at sites such as Durrington Walls (Wainwright and Longworth 1971, 181; Parker Pearson *et al.* 2009, 36), although they are not in fact of common occurrence in Grooved Ware pits. A notable exception is the pair of pits at Woodlands, near Woodhenge (Stone and Young 1948), which yielded three bone pins or awls. One of these came from Pit 1, which also contained a complete and high quality flaked flint axe and the damaged blade end of another, a Group VII example from North Wales. The assortment of finds from these pits also included abundant flints and fragments from sea shells, all of which are once again suggestive of a deliberate placement of some kind. A tentative conclusion can be made that other finds of fragmentary or damaged stone axes in Grooved Ware pits, but maybe not small flakes, may also have been of some contemporary significance, even though they may have had fewer special items associated with them

By no means all pits with Grooved Ware pottery in them also contain axe heads, whether complete or otherwise, but some 40 instances have been recorded to date (Roe 1999; Roe in prep a). Analysis of axe heads both from these pits and from other Grooved Ware associations shows that the largest proportion, some 49% of the non flint axe heads, were made from Cornish materials, whether Groups I and III greenstone, other unattributed greenstones or rocks on the borderline between the two (Roe in prep a and b). In this respect the finds from Kingshill North are entirely typical. Such axe heads may not have been obtained by direct contact with the south west, but rather by passing along the line from person to person in exchange systems that would have bestowed prestige upon the recipients (Bradley and Edmonds 1993, 12). The connections with Cornwall, even if tenuous, must have had some importance during the late Neolithic, as is also shown by the use of Cornish materials to make mace-heads (Roe 2001, 141). Axe head fragments of the same varieties of stone have also been recorded from major henge monuments such as Durrington Walls (Wainwright and Longworth 1971, 183), Woodhenge (Cunnington 1929, 77) and Stonehenge, where six pieces are known although here they are not from well recorded contexts (Clough and Cummins 1988, 157-8). In Gloucestershire Cornish materials (Groups I and III and greenstone) account for approximately 23% of the axe heads recorded from the county, being found in greater numbers even than the popular Langdale axe heads. Most of these finds are however undated and the axe heads from Kingshill North are the only ones known at present from Grooved Ware contexts in the county. Other examples though have been recorded in Oxfordshire, since a Group I axe head fragment is known from pit 917 at Barrow Hills, Radley, where bones of young pigs were also recorded (Barclay

and Halpin 1999, 77; Roe 1999, 228) and a greenstone axe head came from pit P at Sutton Courtenay, along with finds that included five flint scrapers and a bone point (Roe 2003, 134).

Some recurrent themes can be detected amongst the finds from all these late Neolithic sites, including axe heads that were burnt or otherwise damaged, a preference for Cornish rocks, the deposition of large assemblages of pottery and of flints, especially collections of flints with numerous scrapers, while bone artefacts seem also to have had some significance. The preponderance of young pigs among the animal bone at Kingshill North (see Strid and Nicholson, Chapter 6 below) is another key point. The presence of these piglets calls to mind the suggested midwinter culling of young pigs at Durrington Walls (Pitts 2008, 16), and it could be that the winter solstice was being celebrated in a similar manner in Gloucestershire. The majority of the pits at Kingshill North did not contain axe heads or indeed very much at all in the way of finds, but six pits, five of which had very limited finds assemblages, did contain fragments of fired clay, which could have been utilized as oven linings, quite possibly within the pits. Burnt limestone that could have been used for heating ovens and for other methods of cooking was recorded at Kingshill North along with charcoal fragments; evidence for burning or ashy layers has frequently been noted in many Grooved Ware pits generally and could again be traces of cooking. It is possible that ceremonies were taking place which could have involved both the cooking and eating of young pigs and which may have included the subsequent deposition of stone axe heads along with the kitchen debris. There is much that remains mysterious at all these sites, but it is clear that the community at Cirencester was following traditions that were shared with other late Neolithic groups around the country.

Axe head petrology Roger Taylor

Stone axe from pit 8455, context 8819, SF 10079

Greenstone (Epidiorite). Amphibole, fibrous aggregates weakly pleochroic bluish green to nearly colourless. Pyroxene as occasional colourless cores within amphibole. Feldspar as diffuse altered areas between amphibole. Some indication of grain length up to 1 mm. Ilmenite, opaque granular aggregates tending to form skeletal crystals up to 0.6 mm. Leucoxene, pale brown mineral non-pleochroic non-birefringent areas and interstitial to some ilmenite aggregates. It has not proved possible to match this example to the published descriptions of Cornish axe groups with any degree of certainty. South Western Implement Petrology Committee Serial Number 1974/ G138.

Stone axe (two fragments) from pit 8928, context 8929

Greenstone with traces of relict ophitic texture

derived from a doleritic parent rock. Feldspar, extensively replaced by sericitic mica, plagioclase lathes with an original crystal length up to 0.8 mm. Amphibole, pleochroic, light bluish green to greenish buff, as aggregates completely replacing pyroxene. Some aggregates indicate the outlines of pyroxene crystals mainly less than 1 mm occasionally up to 1.5 mm long. Some amphibole also appears to invade and partially replace feldspar. Ilmenite, interstitial skeletal grains substantially replaced by leucoxene.

Other earlier prehistoric worked stone
Ruth Shaffrey

Late Neolithic

A small pebble found in pit 8100 (fill 8097) was deliberately pierced and suspended on a cord or string (SF 10054). This was apparently used as a pendant as there is evidence for suspension, but it was also modified along the lower edge, which is bevelled, although it is not clear whether this was deliberate or that it occurred through use. Neolithic contexts also produced a single hammerstone, broken at one end and with some percussion wear (SF 10095). This made use of a quartzite pebble of a type easily collected from local deposits of northern drift (Sumbler *et al.* 2000, 73).

Catalogue of Neolithic worked stone

SF 10054 **Pendant** (Fig. 32). Very fine-grained sandstone. Naturally flat pebble of slightly irregular shape. Pierced with small amount of wear in the top of the hole suggesting it was suspended on a slim cord or string. The lower end of the stone is bevelled possibly as a result of use wear. Measures 53 x 44 x 7 mm. Fill of pit 8100 (8097). Late Neolithic.

SF 10095 **Hammerstone** (not illustrated). Quartzite pebble, broken at one end and with some percussion wear Measures 57 x 59 x 49 mm. Fill of pit 9096 (9097). Late Neolithic (Grooved Ware).

Beaker to Bronze Age

Two chunks of limestone demonstrate no signs of having been shaped or used, but may have been collected with use in mind (SF 10058, 10059); they are naturally perforated, so could have been intended for use as weights (see discussion in 'Later prehistoric and Roman worked stone' below). No other worked stone was recovered from these phases.

Catalogue of Beaker to Bronze Age worked stone

SF 10058 **Pierced stone** (not illustrated). Shelly limestone. Unshaped and naturally perforated. Measures 57 x 53 x 22 mm. Fill of ditch 8559 (8558). Phase 2: Beaker – Bronze Age.

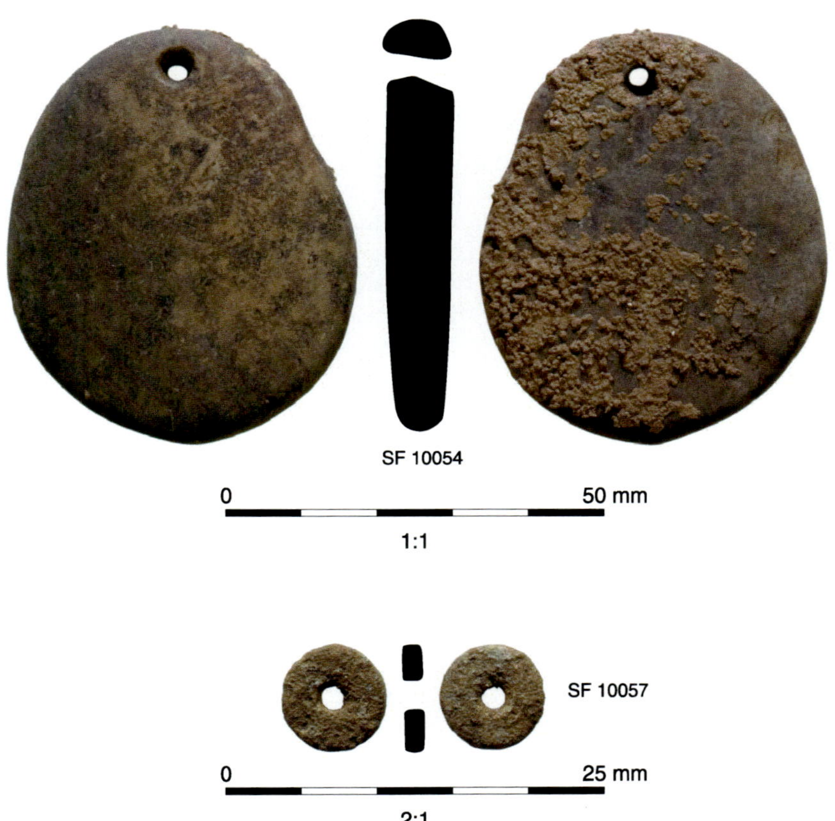

Fig. 32   Worked stone objects, phases 1 and 2

SF 10057 **Bead** (Fig. 32). Measures 6mm diameter. Fill of ditch 8528 (8529). Phase 2: Beaker – Bronze Age.

Earlier prehistoric worked bone *David Mullin*

A total of 16 worked bone objects were recovered from six contexts. The majority were recovered from late Neolithic pits, and a single object was recovered from the fill of the Beaker grave 8588. Objects include bone awls, pins and spatulae. Awls are defined as points made from longitudinal bone splinters where the articular end is retained as a handle. The ends are subsequently ground or polished to from a point. Pins are distinct from awls as they have their articular end removed and the shaft, as well as the tip, are polished or ground (Wainwright and Longworth 1971, 181). Spatulae are usually made from antler, although bone examples are also known (Smith and Simpson 1966, 134) and tend to be worked at both ends, either being finished in a rounded or chisel-like and pointed manner.

Late Neolithic pits

All the worked bone was recovered from pits which also contained Grooved Ware pottery, worked flint and other objects. Context 8057, the fill of pit 8058, contained the broken tip of a bone pin measuring 12 mm long. A broken tip, probably of a pin, was also recovered from context 8089, the fill of pit 8064. This also contained a bone awl with a broken tip and the chisel-end of a bone spatula made from a large mammal rib. Context 8814, the fill of pit 8813, contained the greatest number of worked bone implements, comprising a bone awl, fragments of five bone pins (although as these are fragments it is uncertain if some of these are also awls), a worked rib fragment and the rounded-end of a spatula. The spatula fragment is identical to the antler spatula recovered from Barrow Hills, Radley (Barclay *et al.* 1999, fig. 4.23), and appears to have been burnt and is not a part of the spatula from context 8057. The awl is made on a cattle metatarsal, while two of the pin fragments are from roe deer metatarsals. The worked rib (SF 10078) is highly polished along both surfaces and appears to have been shaped into a handle at one end. The two fills of pit 9100 (9101 and 9102) contained three bone pins. One of these (SF 10085) is of roe deer bone. Another (SF 10089/10090), though complete, was not identifiable to species.

Horn cores were recovered from pit 8058, which contained worked bone, but the horncores were from sheep, which were not usually exploited in the Neolithic period. Antler was recovered from 13 contexts, a total of four from late Neolithic pit 9096, three from pit 8930, two each from pits 8058 and 8100, with single examples recovered from pits 8064, 8738, 8813, 9100 and 9144.

Beaker burial

Context 8641, the fill of burial 8588 enclosed by the Beaker ring ditch (8454), contained a fragment of the tibia of cattle or deer with a smoothed and rounded tip. A fragment of deer antler was recovered from the ditch itself (context 8452); see Strid and Nicholson, Chapter 6 below.

Discussion

The assemblage of pins, awls and spatulae from Kingshill North is one of the largest from south-west Britain. The association of bone pins and awls with Grooved Ware is well-known and has been noted at sites such as Durrington Walls, Wiltshire (Wainwright and Longworth 1971, 181-185), Mount Pleasant, Dorset (Wainwright 1979) and Seven Barrows Gallop, Oxfordshire (Howell and Durden 1996). Grooved Ware pits are rare from Gloucestershire, but Grooved Ware and bone pins were found at Roughground Farm, Lechlade (Allen *et al.* 1993), where two broken pins were found in a pit. Further down the Thames Valley, three awls, a bone pin and two spatulae were found at Barrow Hills, Radley (Barclay *et al.* 1999). Two of the awls and the pin were associated with Grooved Ware, whereas the spatulae and remaining awl were recovered from Beaker burials. Awls are also known from the Thames Valley at Barton Court Farm, Abingdon (Wilson and Miles 1986) and Cassington (Case 1982a), and a pin has also been recovered from Vicarage Field, Stanton Harcourt (Case 1982b).

Antler and bone spatulae have been discussed by Smith and Simpson (1966, 134-9), who consider them to be male-associated grave goods with Beaker burials, possibly associated with leather working. They are rare in Grooved Ware contexts, all the local examples coming from Beaker graves (Barclay *et al.* 1999, 235), and none is recorded in the most up-to-date gazetteer of Grooved Ware finds in Britain (Longworth and Cleal 1999).

The worked bone from burial 8588 is unusual in this context, as although pins, awls and spatulae are well-known Beaker grave goods, worked bone is infrequently found with burials of this date and more usually takes the form of buttons and belt-rings (Clarke 1970, 260-265). The form of the worked bone object is unusual and may be some form of burnisher.

Catalogue of illustrated pins, awls and spatulae (Fig. 33)

1. **Bone awl**, 125 mm long x 24 mm wide; context 8089, fill of pit 8064, Phase 1
2. **Bone awl**, 110 mm long by 27 mm wide; context 8814, fill of pit 8813, Phase 1
3. **Bone pin fragment**, 70 mm long x 10 mm wide; context 8814, fill of pit 8813, Phase 1
4. **Bone pin fragment**, 38 mm long x 11 mm wide; context 8814, fill of pit 8813, Phase 1
5. **Bone pin fragment**, 32 mm long x 12 mm wide; context 8814, fill of pit 8813, Phase 1
6. **Bone pin fragment**, 80 mm long x 15 mm wide; context 9101, fill of pit 9100, Phase 1

7. **Bone pin fragment**, 82 mm long x 11 mm wide; context 9101, fill of pit 9100, Phase 1
8. **Bone pin**, 157 mm long x 12 mm wide; context 9102, fill of pit 9100, Phase 1
9. **Bone pin tip**, 48 mm long x 6 mm diam; context 8089, fill of pit 8064, Phase 1
10. **Bone spatula fragment**, 53 mm long x 17 mm wide; context 8814, fill of pit 8813, Phase 1
11. **Worked rib**, 77 mm long x 14 mm wide; context 8814, fill of pit 8813, Phase 1
12. **Bone spatula tip**, 73 mm long x 37 mm wide; context 8089, fill of pit 8064, Phase 1
13. **Worked tibia fragment**, 87 mm long x 31 mm wide, context 8641, fill of burial 8588, group 8454, Phase 2
14. **Bone pin tip** (not illustrated), 12 mm long x 2 mm diam; context 8057, fill of pit 8058, Phase 1
15. **Worked roe deer metatarsal** (not illustrated), 30mm long x 10mm wide, context 8814, fill of pit 8813, Phase 1
16. **Worked roe deer metatarsal** (not illustrated), 39mm long x 10mm wide, context 8814, fill of pit 8813, Phase 1

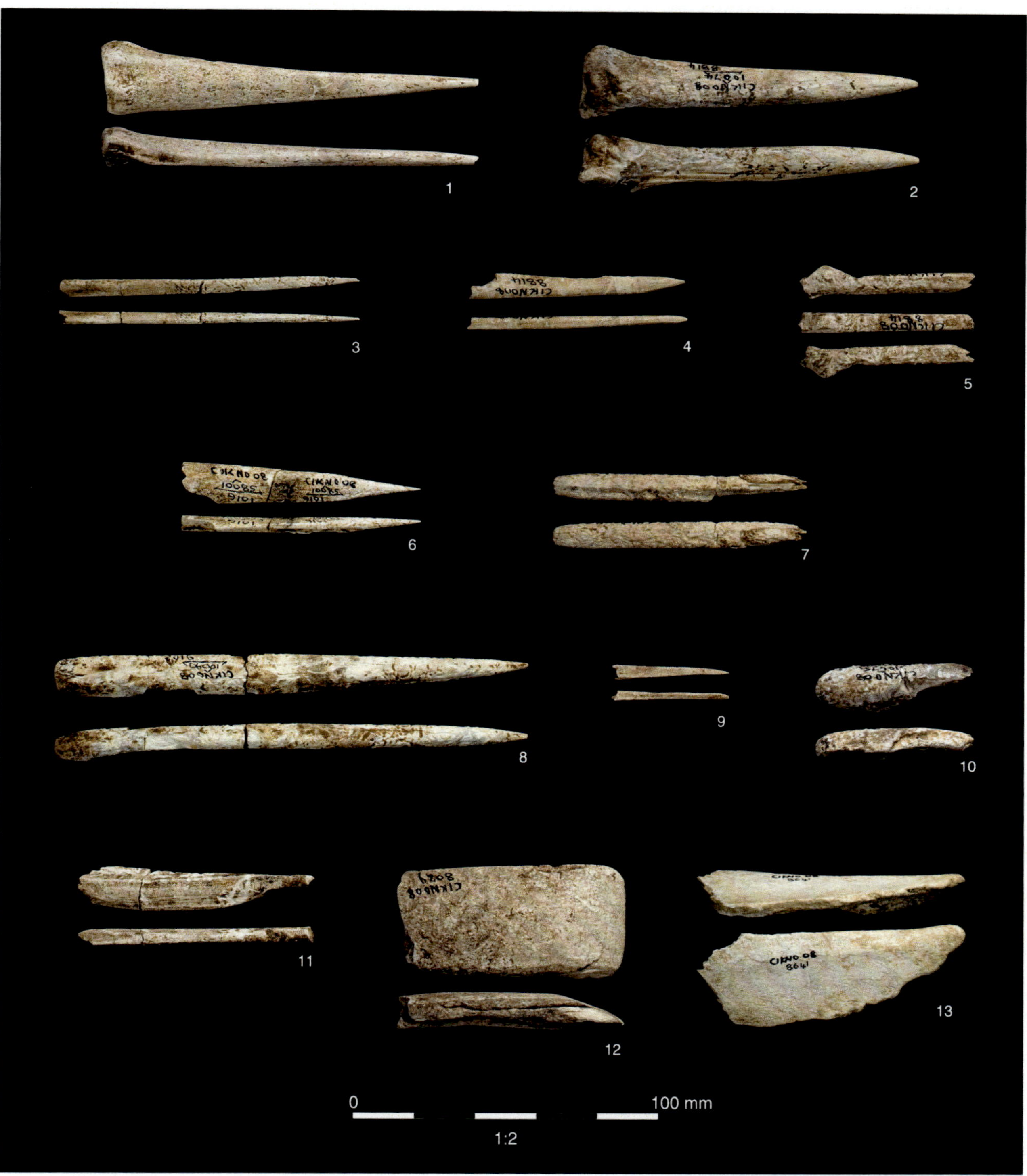

Fig. 33 Worked bone objects, phases 1 and 2

Human remains from earlier prehistoric burials
Alistair Zochowski and Helen Webb, with a contribution by Angela Lamb and Jane Evans

Introduction

Standard anthropological and palaeopathological examinations were undertaken in accordance with published guidelines (Brickley and McKinley 2004). Condition and completeness were assessed and an inventory was complied listing all the elements that survived. Condition was scored with reference to published criteria (McKinley 2004,16). Estimation of sex was based on observations of pelvic and cranial morphology (Buikstra and Ubelaker 1994). Adult ages were estimated based on a combination of methods including those that refer to late fusing epiphyses (Scheuer and Black 2000), dental attrition (Brothwell 1981; Miles 1962) and the metamorphosis of the pubic symphyses and auricular surfaces of the pelvis.

Phase 2 – Beaker to Bronze Age

Skeleton 1403, grave 1402

This skeleton was in a poor condition, consistent with grade four of McKinley's criteria. This means that all bone surfaces were eroded, but the general profile of bones had been maintained (McKinley 2004, 16). The skeleton was very fragmentary and only between 25% and 50% of it had survived. Skull, long bones and pelvis were all present to some degree. There was also a juvenile right femoral head from another burial. The vertebrae, hands, feet and ribs were predominately absent.

The skeleton was estimated to have been an older adult at death (approximately over 50 years of age), based on the auricular surface. No other age indicators could be examined.

An unpronounced protuberance on the occipital bone of the skull suggested that the individual was possibly female. This feature was the only indicator of sex that had survived. Sex estimation using the skull is not as accurate as it is using the pelvis. Accuracy is further reduced if estimations are based on one skull feature alone (Buikstra and Ubelaker 1994). This estimate is therefore very tentative.

The skeleton completely lacked any maxilla or mandible, but 13 teeth were present. These were poorly preserved, exhibited heavy attrition and were difficult to identify. Among them was evidence for calculus and caries. Calculus was observed on the mandibular molars as a grey/white deposit on the enamel surfaces. Known colloquially as 'tartar', calculus is formed by the mineralisation of organic material and bacteria and, as such, reflects the lack of importance (or perhaps inability owing to illness) given to maintaining healthy teeth. It accumulates on the teeth faster when there is a high protein and/or carbohydrate diet, the bacteria favouring an alkaline oral environment. Calculus is

a significant cause of periodontal disease and subsequent tooth loss. It is not possible to say whether the present skeleton had periodontal disease and tooth loss because of the missing jaw bones. Caries was present on the left and right second molars and first left molar of the mandible. Dental caries involves the destruction of the enamel surface, the dentine (internal part of the tooth) and cement (outer layer of the roots). This is caused by the acid produced by the bacteria present within dental plaque (Hillson 1996, 269). The cavities were large and affected the occlusal and lingual surfaces of the teeth.

Stature could not be estimated for this skeleton because the bones were too fragmentary to measure. No pathology or non metric traits were observed.

Skeleton 8656, grave 8588 (group 8454)

This skeleton was 75% complete and, with the exception of the vertebral column, was relatively intact. Bone condition was good, or grade two after McKinley (2004,16). Thus, there was moderate erosion on some bone surfaces. The sternal epiphysis of the clavicle had fused, indicating an age of at least 25 years (Scheuer and Black 2000). The degree of attrition on the molar teeth suggested an age of between 25 and 35 years. However, not all molar teeth were available to appreciate the full pattern of wear, thus this estimate is less reliable. Degenerative changes on the auricular surface of the pelvis indicated an age of approximately 30-40 years. Overall, it was concluded that this individual was a mature adult of between 30 and 40 years of age at death.

Sexually dimorphic features of the cranium had survived, including the right supra-orbital ridge and the occipital protuberance. These suggested a male. This was not corroborated by other characteristics; the anterior mandible was rounded suggesting a female, and the pelvis also had female characteristics. Given the greater accuracy of the pelvis over the skull in sex estimation, it was concluded that the individual was probably female.

The individual's dentition was almost complete and included a total of 19 teeth. All these teeth exhibited calculus. Using Ogden's (2005) system, mild periodontal disease was identified on the jaw bones. A single carious cavity was located on the mesial aspect of the 3rd left mandibular molar. There was also a small periapical cavity on the alveolar bone of the left mandible in the area of the first molar. The circumscribed margins of the cavity, coupled with its small diameter (less than 3 mm) are consistent with a periapical granuloma. Periapical granulomas, or foci of chronic inflammation around the apex of the tooth, arise when the pulp of the tooth is inflamed, secondary to caries or trauma. On the present individual an associated carious cavity was not observed. Cribra orbitalia was present on the right orbit and was graded as slight (type 1) after Stuart-Macadam (1991). Cribra orbitalia is believed to be caused by iron deficiency anaemia

(Stuart Macadam 1991), with dietary deficiency, malabsorption (due to gastro-intestinal infection or parasites), blood loss and chronic disease being among the main causes. Anaemia tends not to leave traces on adult bone (Stuart Macadam 1991) and, therefore, the example described here probably relates back to a time during the individual's childhood, the only time when skeletal lesions relating to this disease are manifest.

Other pathology includes osteophytosis, or new bone formation on or around joint margins. This was present on the vertebral column and on the right femoral head. It is extremely common, and is seen in association with several different conditions (for example, osteoarthritis and trauma), as well as on its own as a normal accompaniment to ageing. No other associated pathological changes were observed on the present skeleton. Limited areas of the skeleton were available for examining the presence and absence of non-metric traits. Of note was the presence of Allen's fossa on the left femur. This is a depression near the superior margin of the femoral neck, close to the border of the femoral head. In the past this trait was regarded as a marker of activity and was linked to rapidly descending steep slopes and / or walking on rough terrain. However, the extent to which its manifestation in bone is genetically controlled is far from clear.

The central Beaker burial was assigned context number 2405 in the 2006 evaluation, and a 5th metacarpal from a right hand and a pisiform bone from the left hand, both from an adult individual, were assigned to this context. The metacarpal was 100% complete and was graded as a 2 on the IFA scale (McKinley 2004). The pisiform was graded 1 on the IFA scale (McKinley 2004).

Funerary practice

Skeletons 1403 and 8656 date to the early Bronze Age or Beaker period. Both had been buried in individual graves, in a crouched position, in keeping with the burial tradition of this period. The older adult female, 1403, was buried within a large, N-S aligned sub-oval pit, cut into the natural limestone. The head, at the south end of the grave, had been heavily disturbed by a modern posthole. The individual had been buried in a crouched position, with the torso laid on its back, the arms crossed over the abdomen and the legs tightly flexed at the knees, both tilted over onto their right side. A complete, but fragmentary Beaker had been placed at the north end of the grave, just to the west of the feet. Mature adult female 8656 was buried on her right side with her legs flexed at the knees and her arms flexed at the elbows, her hands towards her right shoulder. Her head was to the south west of the grave, with her feet at the north east. The skeleton was buried within a sub-rectangular grave (8588) inside ring ditch 8454 and was accompanied by a Beaker. Both burials were buried in large graves. It is likely that this additional space would have created a greater opportunity for the visual display of the deceased and their grave goods to mourners at the grave-side, and probably represents an important stage in the funerary ritual preceding interment (Thomas 1991).

Skeleton 1903, grave 1905

This skeleton was moderately fragmented. The condition of the bones was poor with erosion covering large areas of bone surface as reflected by a grade four after McKinley (2004,16). Between 50%-75% of the skeleton had survived, all elements being present to some degree with the exception of the hands which were missing most of their bones.

Dental attrition indicated an age of between 25 and 35 years, but ante-mortem loss of some molars, combined with the loss if teeth post mortem, means that this is not a reliable estimate. Degenerative changes on the auricular surface suggested an age of over 50 years and is the age estimate assigned to this individual. Sex estimation was based upon observations of cranial features and one pelvic indicator. The sciatic notch on the pelvis was narrow and 'V' shaped, indicating a male (Buikstra and Ubelaker 1994, 18). This was corroborated by features of the skull including a pronounced occipital protuberance, square mandible and mastoid processes that were vertical and large, all traits that are seen in males (Schwartz 1995, 280). Overall the individual was robust with pronounced muscle markings.

Twenty-one teeth and both the maxilla and mandible were available to explore the dental status of the individual. All teeth were heavily worn and three (upper left molars) had been lost ante-mortem. Calculus was present on all of the mandibular teeth and the left maxillary central incisor. Four carious cavities were observed and involved mandibular and maxillary teeth. There was also a granuloma on the alveolar bone below the right first molar. This measured 3-5 mm in diameter and was probably associated with the caries that involved the first molar. Periodontal disease was present and was mild or severe. Overcrowding was noted for the mandibular incisors and canines.

Based on the maximum length of the left tibia, the individual was estimated to have been approximately 1.83 m tall. Non-metric traits included a septal aperture on right and left humeri. This is identified as hole in the olecranon fossa of the distal humerus. It is usually more common among females than males. Pathological conditions included cribra orbitalia on the left orbit (grade 1 after Stuart-Macadam 1991, 109). Osteophytosis was observed on the joint margins of the right knee (distal femur) and left shoulder. There was also evidence of degenerative disc disease in the cervical spine and osteoarthritis in the thoracic spine. Degenerative disc disease is identified in dry bone as increased porosity on the surfaces of the vertebral bodies. The condition is mainly caused by degeneration of the intervertebral discs and is associated with increasing age.

The individual was lying in a supine (on the back) position with his arms by his side and his left leg crossed over his right at the ankle. Inhumation burials of middle Bronze Age date are exceptionally rare within Britain, the most common practice being cremation, usually associated with Deverel Rimbury pottery. At the eastern end of the grave, just to the left side of the head, an articulated animal foot/leg was found, probably the remains of a joint of meat that had been deliberately placed within the grave. This is also exceptionally uncommon.

A complete, third proximal phalanx was found within a fill of grave 1905. Its condition was grade three using McKinley's (2004) system. The bone was from an adult and showed no evidence of pathology. It is possible that it belonged with skeleton 1903.

Strontium and oxygen isotope analysis
Angela Lamb and Jane Evans

Introduction

Two teeth each from two Beaker-period individuals (skeletons 8656 and 1403) were received by NIGL for isotope analysis.

Analytical method – Sr (strontium) isotopes

The available enamel surface of the teeth was abraded from the surface to a depth of >100 microns using a tungsten carbide dental bur and the removed material discarded. Thin enamel slices were then cut from the tooth using a flexible diamond edged rotary dental saw. All surfaces were mechanically cleaned with a tungsten carbide bur to remove adhering dentine. The resulting samples were transferred to a clean (class 100, laminar flow) working area for further preparation. In a clean laboratory, the samples were first cleaned ultrasonically in high purity water to remove dust, rinsed twice, dried down in high purity acetone and then weighed into pre-cleaned Teflon beakers. The samples were mixed with ^{84}Sr tracer solution and dissolved in Teflon distilled 16M HNO_3. Strontium was collected using Dowex resin columns. Strontium was loaded onto a single Re Filament with TaF following the method of Birck (1986) and the isotope composition and concentrations were determined by Thermal Ionisation Mass spectroscopy (TIMS) using a Thermo Triton multi-collector

mass spectrometer. The international standard for ^{87}Sr/^{86}Sr, NBS987, gave a value of 0.710250 ± 0.000006 (n=8, 2σ) during the analysis of these samples. Blank values were in the region of 100pg. Data are presented in Table 5.

Analytical method – Oxygen isotopes

Small fragments of clean enamel (15-20 mg) were treated to extract PO4 radicals and precipitated as silver phosphate, using the method of O'Neil *et al.* (1994). The fragments of enamel were cleaned in concentrated hydrogen peroxide for 24 hours to remove organic material and subsequently evaporated to dryness. The samples were then dissolved in 2 M Nitric acid and transferred to clean polypropylene test tubes. Each sample was then treated with 2 M potassium hydroxide and 2 M hydrogen fluoride to remove calcium from the solution by precipitation. The samples were then centrifuged and the supernatant added to beakers containing ammoniacal silver nitrate solution and heated gently to precipitate silver phosphate. The silver phosphate was, rinsed, dried and weighed into silver capsules for analysis. Oxygen isotope measurements on each sample were analysed in triplicate by thermal conversion continuous flow isotope ratio mass spectrometry (TC/EA-CFIRMS). The reference material NBS120C, calibrated against certified reference material NBS127 (assuming δ^{18}O of NBS127 = +20.3‰ versus SMOW; IAEA, 2004), has an accepted value of 21.70‰ (Chenery 2005). The reproducibility of NBS120C during this set of analyses was 21.70‰ ± 0.38 (1σ, n=8). Drinking water values are calculated using Levinson's equation (Levinson *et al.* 1987), after correction of +1.4‰ for the difference between the average published values for NBS120C used at NIGL and the value for NBS120B used by Levinson *et al.* (1987) (Chenery *et al.* in press). Data are presented in Table 5.

Discussion

The premolar and second molar teeth initially calcify between 1.5 and 2.5 years of age (van Beek 1983) and hence they record early childhood environment. The first molar starts calcifying at birth (van Beek 1983) and hence will record a pre-weaning signature for both Sr and oxygen. Individual 8656 has a PM2 Sr value of 0.70857 and an M2 value of 0.70872. The values are consistent with a childhood spent on chalklands typical of

Table 5. The strontium and oxygen isotope composition of Kingshill North tooth enamel.
DW = drinking water δ^{18}O values calculated using Levinson et al. (1987) according to Chenery et al. (2010).

Sample	tooth	ppm	87Sr/86Sr	δ^{18}O	1sd	drinking water	1sd	n
CIKNO-08-SK8656	URPM2	36.81	0.708566	17.09	0.20	-8.06	0.44	3
CIKNO-08-SK8656	LLM2	35.96	0.708720	17.64	0.09	-6.87	0.20	2
CIKNO-08-SK1403	ULPM2	43.94	0.708939	18.10	0.16	-5.86	0.34	3
CIKNO-08-SK1403	LLM1	57.63	0.709620	18.70	0.06	-4.57	0.14	2

southern and eastern England. For individual 1403, the PM2 value of 0.70894 is also typical of chalklands, but the more elevated isotope composition of the first molar, 0.70962, is likely to be inherited at least in part from the mother and hence does not reflect the individual's childhood origin.

The drinking water $\delta^{18}O$ range in human tooth enamel of United Kingdom locals is estimated to be between -8.7 and -4.7. Individual 8656 records values of -8.06 (PM2) and -6.87(M2) consistent with a childhood in southern England. Individual 1403 records a value of -5.86 (PM2) suggesting the childhood origin in the more south-western region of England. The first molar from this individual gives -4.57. This 'warm' signature is probably due to a component of additional fractionation caused by a pre-weaning diet and corroborates the suggestion that the Sr signal is not recording the direct biosphere input.

Conclusions

The strontium isotope results for both individuals support a childhood founded on chalklands. The oxygen isotope composition suggests that 8656 could be from eastern or southern England, while 1403 is probably from more south-westerly areas. Such combinations of values do not exclude certain continental options, but the most likely origin of these two individuals is from the chalklands of England.

Chapter 4: Later Prehistoric and Roman Finds (Phases 3 and 4)

Middle to late Iron Age pottery *Jane Timby*

Introduction and methodology

The archaeological work at Kingshill resulted in the recovery of approximately 675 sherds of later prehistoric pottery, weighing 27.1 kg. The assemblage was extremely poorly preserved with an overall average sherd size of just 4 g. Pottery was recorded from some 109 individual contexts, many of which produced fewer than five sherds.

The assemblage was sorted into fabric groups based on the principal inclusions present and further sub-divided on the basis of the size and frequency of the inclusions, following the recommended guidelines for the analysis of later prehistoric pottery (PCRG 1997). Very small crumbs were counted and weighed only. The sorted sherds were quantified by count and weight for each recorded context. Details such as surface finish, was noted along with evidence for use in the form of sooting, residues or leaching.

Description of fabrics and forms

Five basic ware groups were identified: calcareous, sandy with limestone/shell, flint, Malvernian rock, and grog-tempered. Three of the groups are further sub-divided giving a total 14 defined fabrics (Table 6). The commonest group is the calcareous wares including fossil shelly wares and Jurassic oolitic limestone-tempered wares, with varying quantities of fossiliferous matter, both fabrics occurring in various grades and mixtures. In addition the calcareous group contained Palaeozoic-limestone and calcite-tempered wares.

Overall calcareous wares (Jurassic source limestone and shelly wares) account for 66% by count, 76.8% by weight of the total later prehistoric assemblage. Most or all of these wares could have been locally made. The Palaeozoic limestone-tempered wares are imports to the site probably originating from the area of May Hill, the Woolhope Hills or Glass house Hill, south of Newent on the other side of the Severn. These sherds account for 14.1% by count (8.8% by weight). More imports to the site are the flint-tempered wares which account for 1.5% by count (6.7% by weight), the Malvernian sandstone-tempered group, representing 11.3% by count (5.4% by weight), and the Malvernian rock-tempered represented by a single sherd. The local mixed sandy with calcareous wares account for just 0.7% by count (0.5% by weight), while the grog-tempered wares contribute less than 1%.

Calcareous/shelly

SH1: a moderate to common frequency of coarse fossil shell and very sparse fossiliferous matter. Shell fragments up to 5 mm.

Table 6: Middle-late Iron Age pottery (sherd count & weight)

	Fabric	Description	No	No %	Wt	Wt %
Calcareous	SH1	coarser fossil shell	5	0.7	58	2.1
	SH2	finer sparser shell	5	0.7	57	2.1
	SH3	very dense fine shell/limestone	5	0.7	38	1.4
	CA	mainly calcite	5	0.7	10	0.4
	L1	dense limestone and fossil shell	250	37.0	1046.5	38.6
	L2	mainly oolitic limestone, some fossil	88	13.0	461	17.0
	L3	mixed shell/fossil and oolitic limestone	100	14.8	408.5	15.1
	L00	miscellaneous limestone	2	0.3	3	0.1
	MALREB	Palaeozoic limestone-tempered	95	14.1	239	8.8
Sandy/calcareous	SALI	sandy with limestone/shell	5	0.7	13	0.5
Flint	FL	calcined flint-tempered	10	1.5	181	6.7
Malvernian	MAL RE A	Malvernian rock-tempered	1	0.1	17	0.6
	MAL RE C	Malvernian sandstone-tempered	76	11.3	147	5.4
Grog (LIA)	GR	grog-tempered	6	0.9	21	0.8
CRUMBS	OO	undiagnostic small crumbs	22	3.3	12	0.4
TOTAL			675	100.0	2712	100.0

SH2: a sparse to common frequency of predominantly fossil shell fragments finer than 5 mm.

SH3: sparse fine fossil shell fragments in a very calcareous clay matrix which at x20 magnification contains a fine admixture of very fine shell and limestone.

L1: common to moderate frequency of ill-sorted limestone and fossiliferous matter including fragments of bryozoa, shell and other detritus.

L2: Common to abundant frequency of oolitic limestone, mainly as discrete ooliths and rarely as a conglomerate. Very occasional fossiliferous matter is also present. Mainly fine (less than 2 mm).

L3: Common inclusions of oolitic limestone with a mixture of shell and other fossiliferous detritus 2 mm in a fine calcareous matrix.

CA: calcite-tempered ware. A sparse to moderate frequency of calcite in crystalline form. The source of this ware is not known, possible contenders being the Malvernian area or the Mendips (cf. Allen 1998).

MAL RE B: Palaeozoic limestone-tempered ware (Peacock 1968, fabric B). The likely source of the clays used for this ware are within the Woolhope limestone series (Morris 2005), which outcrops south of the Malverns in the May Hill area, Glasshouse Hill and the Woolhope Hills (Worssam *et al.* 1989).

SALI: sandy, slightly micaceous ware with rounded quartz (\$ 0.5 mm) and sparse limestone, some as ooliths or voids (up to 2mm) and/or fossil shell fragments.

Non-calcareous

FLINT: a generally black compact, hard fabric with a red-brown or grey interior tempered with a sparse to moderate frequency of crushed, calcined, angular flint.

MAL RE A (Peacock 1968, fabric A; Tomber and Dore 1998, 147). Metamorphic/ igneous rock-tempered ware originating from the Malvern Hills.

MAL RE C (Peacock 1968, fabric C) Malvernian/ Forest of Dean sandstone-tempered ware. A black ware with a brownish exterior and quite a compact, gritty textured fabric. The paste contains a rare scatter of fine quartz sandstone inclusions 1–2 mm in size and sparse sub-angular quartz and rare limestone.

GROG: a usually brown, occasionally black, ware with a soapy feel containing a sparse to moderate frequency of sub-angular to rounded grog /clay pellets. Equivalent of Cirencester fabric C (Williams 1982, 201).

Vessel forms

Most of the assemblage was very fragmentary, making it difficult to confidently ascribe rims to forms. All the pots were handmade with unfinished, smoothed, or more rarely burnished, finishes. Only 17 rim fragments were recorded and most of these were too small to measure or identify to overall form shape. The only decoration present is some slight finger-tipping on one vessel rim (Fig. 34.4). Most of the rims come from vessels in the calcareous group with two in fabric MAL RE B, single examples in fabric MAL RE A and the grog-tempered ware.

Amongst the featured sherds are some barrel-shaped vessels with in-turned rims (Fig. 34.6), smooth globular-profiled jars or bowls with simple rims (Fig. 34.1-3) and vessels with flaring rims (Fig. 34.5, 7). These vessels are all typical of middle Iron Age forms and can be paralleled, for example, amongst middle Iron Age assemblages from sites to the east within the Cotswold Water Park, and the Upper Thames Valley and to the west (see below for discussion of contemporary sites). Two joining sherds from pit 8747 possibly base sherds come from an uncertain form with a central opening.

Evidence of use

Evidence for use was observed on a number of vessels in terms of external sooting or burnt internal residues and interior surface pitting where calcareous inclusions have been leached out. No limescale deposits were observed. All the deposits were on calcareous wares with five examples with internal sooted residues and six with external sooting. Five of these eleven sherds came from pit 8851.

Dating

Dating the assemblage is slightly problematic due to the very small sizes of the individual feature assemblages and of the degraded state of the sherds themselves. As noted by Morris (2005, 136), any ceramic phasing has to be based on an established minimum quantity of material generally accepted to be around 25 sherds. On this basis just eight of the Kingshill features qualify: seven pits (8311, 8320, 8382, 8655, 8851, 8901 and 8988) and one ditch (8419, group 8425). It is clear that there are a small number of redeposited sherds present dating to the earlier prehistoric period. The absence of any decorated wares, carinated or angular forms or obvious early Iron Age rim forms along with the coarser shell-tempered wares more typical of this period suggests that there was no earlier Iron Age activity at the site. The featured sherds are indicative of a middle-late Iron Age phase of occupation. Both the Malvernian rock-tempered (MAL RE A) and Palaeozoic limestone-tempered wares (MAL RE B) were in circulation from the middle Iron Age period, continuing with little evident technological change into the early Roman period. There is surprisingly very little sandy ware with limestone and no sandy wares proper which feature on most other middle Iron Age sites in the region. Conversely there is a much higher proportion of Palaeozoic limestone-tempered ware and flint-tempered ware compared with most middle Iron Age and middle-late Iron Age sites in the Cotswold Water Park. At many sites in Gloucestershire where there is a late Iron Age-early Roman transition, there is clear evidence of an increasing presence of grog-tempered wares from the early 1st century AD alongside with Palaeozoic limestone-tempered wares.

Phase 3

Just over 50% of the later prehistoric assemblage came from contexts allocated to Phase 3. Within this group Jurassic source calcareous wares very much dominate, accounting for 88.8% by count. There were 17 sherds of sandstone-tempered ware, all from pit 8771 and thus likely to be from one vessel. Single sherds of MAL RE B and flint-tempered ware are present.

Phase 4

Only four sherds of MAL RE B were recovered from posthole 8731 (group 8563) in Phase 4a. A single flint-tempered sherd was recovered from Phase 4b. Slightly more significant amounts of pottery were recovered from Phases 4c and 4d (125 and 115 sherds respectively) and were either residual or demonstrate continued currency of the pottery in the 1st century AD. MAL RE B wares account for 40% of the assemblage from 4c and 14% of the assemblage from 4d, the latter being slightly skewed by a 59 small sherds of MAL RE C. Small quantities of both flint and grog-tempered ware are also present in both. At least one feature in Phase 4c, pit 8830, is likely to be early Roman. Of the contexts allocated to Phase 4c – ditches 8268 (group 8255), 8421 and 8419 (both in group 8425), along with pit 8829 – all contain small quantities of grog-tempered ware and are thus likely to date to the 1st century AD. Similarly in Phase 4d the later prehistoric wares appear in a number of early Roman pits (8747, 8741, 8752, 8887 and 8900) when the ware may well have still been in circulation.

Affinities

The composition of the assemblage differs slightly from other known middle Iron Age sites nearby. Immediately to the south-east along the A419 is the site of a middle Iron Age enclosure at Preston, and slightly beyond is a second enclosure at Ermin Farm (Mudd *et al.* 1999b). The early-middle Iron Age assemblage from Preston is dominated by Jurassic limestone-tempered wares with a very small number of sandy wares but no clear regional imports (Timby 1999, table 7.7). The dominant fabric at Preston (L2) equates with L1 here. A similar range of wares was documented from Ermin Farm (Timby 1999, table 7.8) where again, apart possibly from a few sandy wares, there are no regional imports. By contrast the middle-late Iron Age site at Highgate House near Birdlip to the north-west of Cirencester had an assemblage dominated by sherds of MAL REB (57.8% by count) accompanied by a range of

Jurassic limestone wares and a few sherds of MAL RE A. This might suggest an influx of MAL RE B to this area in the later part of the Iron Age.

Pottery from a number of other middle Iron Age sites within the Cotswold Water Park has been studied over recent years, notably Shorncote Quarry (Brossler *et al.* 2002); Eysey Farm (Timby 2008), Dryleaze Farm (Timby 2010) and Horcott (Harrison and Timby 2004). These appear to show a typical progression from a dominance of local calcareous wares in the early Iron Age accompanied by increasing numbers of sandier wares moving into the middle Iron Age. Generally speaking, most of the assemblages are plain with a small number of exceptions. Moving through the middle Iron Age into the late Iron Age, the assemblages start to diversify with a number of regional imports reaching the sites; glauconitic sandy wares, flint-tempered wares and the various Malvernian area wares demonstrating an expansion of trading networks at this time. The apparent absence of the transition into the sandier wares at Kingshill could conceivably indicate either a slight hiatus or shift in occupation during the latter part of the middle Iron Age but the quality of the assemblage is poor and such subtle changes are difficult to identify.

Catalogue of illustrated sherds (Fig. 18)

1. **Globular-shaped vessel**, probably a bowl with a simple, slightly out-turned rim. Fabric: L2. Pit 8311 (8309), Phase 3.
2. **Barrel-shaped** or **ovoid vessel with an in-turned rim**. Fabric: SH2. Pit 8320 (8323), Phase 3.
3. **Ovoid-bodied vessel with a short, vertical rim**. Orange-brown surfaces with a dark grey core. Fabric: L3. Pit 8851 (8947), Phase 3.
4. **Wide-mouthed vessel with a vertical, squared rim** and hint of a slight carination at the break. Lightly finger-tipped upper rim surface. Fabric: SH3. Sooted exterior. Pit 8951 (8946), Phase 3.

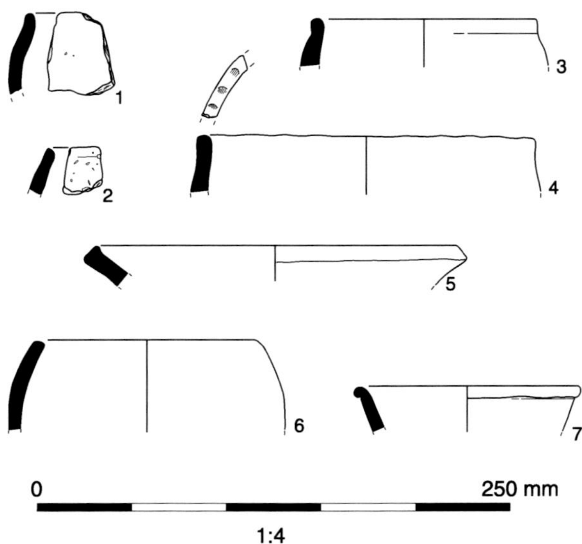

Fig. 34 Middle to late Iron Age pottery

Table 7: Late Iron Age and Roman pottery, quantification by fabrics

Fabric	Sherds	%	Weight (g)	%	MV	%	EVE	%
Amphora fabrics								
A10 Buff ware amphora	1	0	224	2				
A11 South Spanish amphora	1	0	94	1				
Black-burnished wares								
B10 Black-burnished ware category 1	119	6	241	2	1	1	0.64	6
Calcareous wares								
C10 Shelly ware	1	0	3	0				
C20 Limestone-tempered ware	1	0	5	0				
Late Iron Age/early Roman wares								
E20 Fine sand-tempered ware	35	2	149	1	2	3	0.13	1
E30 Coarse sand-tempered ware	14	1	175	1				
E40 Shelly ware	49	2	206	15	3	4	0.09	1
E50 Limestone-tempered ware	331	15	941	7	8	10	0.58	5
E60 Flint-tempered ware	31	1	260	2				
E80 Grog-tempered ware	675	31	4771	35	30	39	4.47	42
E80(RS) Red-surfaced grog-tempered ware	224	10	1191	9	7	9	1.28	12
G21 Malvernian rock-tempered ware	151	7	768		7	9	0.86	8
Oxidised wares								
O10 Fine oxidised ware	5	0	6	0	2	3	0.06	1
O20 Sandy oxidised ware	4	0	7	0				
O30 Wiltshire sandy oxidised ware	5	0	11	0				
O40 Severn Valley ware	29	1	112	1	1	1	0.08	1
O60 Calcareous oxidised ware	1	0	22	0				
O80 Oxidised storage jar fabric	16	1	186	1				
White-slipped ware								
Q10 Fine white-slipped oxidised ware	7	0	15	0				
Reduced wares								
R10 Fine grey ware	9	0	23	0				
R101 Very fine grey ware	10	0	20	0				
R20 Coarse sandy grey ware	9	0	39	0				
R30 Medium sandy grey ware	64	3	323	1	2	3	0.27	2
R35 Wiltshire grey ware	18	1	122	1				
R39 Alice Holt sandy grey ware	1	0	21	0				
R50 Black-surfaced ware	94	1	183	1	5	6	1.05	10
R90 Reduced storage jar fabric	68	3	1253	9	1	1	0.45	4
R95 Savernake grey ware	160	7	2339	17	8	10	0.84	8
Samian wares								
S20 South Gaulish samian ware	3	0	4	0				
S30 Central Gaulish samian ware	1	0	1	0				
White wares								
W20 Sandy white ware	2	0	22	0				
W30 Fine (imported) white wares	8	0	8	0				
Unidentified								
Z Unidentified pottery	3	0	4	0				
TOTALS	2150	-	13749	-	77	-	10.8	-

5. **Sharply everted, squared rim.** Black throughout. Fabric: L3. Sooted on the top of the exterior rim. Pit 8795 (8967), Phase 4.
6. **Barrel-shaped** or **ovoid vessel** with a simple, undifferentiated in-turned rim. Fabric: MAL RE A. Ditch 8571 (8569), Phase 4c.
7. **Rolled rim, everted necked vessel.** Fabric: L3. Pit 8582 (8583). Unphased.

Late Iron Age and Roman pottery *Edward Biddulph*

Introduction

Some 2150 sherds, weighing 13.7 kg, were recovered from the excavation (Table 7). A fraction over half of the assemblage (52% by weight) was recovered from deposits dated to the late Iron Age and up to the mid 1st century AD (phases 4a, 4b and 4c). A further 37% belonged to the early Roman period, while 5% of pottery was collected from late Roman deposits. The remainder of the assemblage could not be closely dated within Phase 4. This is a substantial addition to the 231 sherds recovered from the evaluation stage of fieldwork (Timby 2006). Overall, the condition of the pottery was moderate to poor. The average sherd weight of 6 g is indicative of relatively small fragments, and on average, just 15% of the circumference of each rim survived. This made form identification difficult (many vessels could only be assigned to broad vessel class), although recording was possible at a sufficiently detailed level to address key themes of supply, chronology and function.

The assemblage was sorted within context-groups into 'sherd-families' – for example the fragments of a single vessel or the mass of undiagnostic sherds in the same fabric – and quantified by sherd count, weight in grammes, vessel count based on rims, and rim-EVEs, which records the surviving percentage of a rim (a complete rim is recorded as 1 EVE, half a rim as 0.5 EVEs). The data were entered on to a database (one record per sherd-family). Each record was given a date range, and a context-group date was entered on the basis of the group's constituent record dates. Fabrics and forms were identified using standard Oxford Archaeology guidelines (Booth nd), though reference was occasionally made to regional typologies, for example the *Camulodumum* series (Hawkes and Hull 1947) and Webster's Severn Valley ware corpus (Webster 1976).

Assemblage composition and pottery

Phases 4a and 4b describe a stratigraphic sequence, but are otherwise contemporaneous in terms of ceramic dating; their assemblages have therefore been combined here (Table 8). In total, this group accounted for 25% of the entire assemblage by EVE. The pottery was dominated by grog-tempered wares, which represented 72% of the phase group. Most of this comprised reduced fabrics (E80). Forms identifiable to type (as opposed to broad class) were

confined to necked jars, though other types of jars may have been available. There is a hint that one of the necked jars was a pedestal jar; the base was broken in such a way to suggest that the footring extended into a deeper pedestal. As red-surfaced grog-tempered fabrics tend to be finer than the reduced fabric, a beaker in this ware is expected. A beaker, possibly a butt-beaker, was also recorded in the reduced fabric. Malvernian rock-tempered (limestone) ware (G21) was another important category, taking a 21% share of the phase assemblage by EVE. The ware emerged in the middle Iron Age – and indeed was present in the middle Iron Age settlement, identified as fabric MAL RE A (see Timby, this volume) – and continued in use in the region into the 2nd century AD (Timby 1999, 322). Vessels recorded in this group were restricted to one of the fabric's commonest forms, a barrel-shaped jar with everted rim. Fabric R50 was another limestone-tempered ware; its source is unknown, but a reasonably local origin is likely. Sand-tempered (E20 and E30), shell-tempered (E40) and flint-tempered (E60) fabrics were present during the late Iron Age, but were very minor components of the assemblage. Grog-tempered fabric – Savernake ware (R95) – was recorded in small quantities. The prevailing view places the ware's origin in the mid 1st century (Swan 1975; Timby 1999, 324). This is not the assemblage with which to challenge the conventional dating, and given that a range of post-conquest wares (R20, R30, R50, O10, Q10) were also collected from Phase 4a deposits, the Savernake ware could well be intrusive. It is not unreasonable to suppose that parts of enclosure 8563, from which

*Table 8: Pottery from late Iron Age deposits (phases 4a and 4b). Quantification by EVE. Forms: C jars (general), CB barrel-shaped jars, CE high-shouldered necked jars, CP pedestalled jar; E beaker. * = present, but no with no rim surviving.*

Ware	C	CB	CE	CP	E	Total EVE	%
E20						*	
E30						*	
E40						*	
E50	0.05					0.05	2%
E60						*	
E80	0.28		0.27	1	0.14	1.69	62%
E80(RS)					0.05	0.05	2%
G21		0.58				0.58	21%
O10	0.01					0.01	1%
O80						*	
Q10						*	
R20						*	
R30						*	
R50	0.12					0.12	4%
R90						*	
R95			0.23			0.23	8%
Total	0.46	0.58	0.5	1	0.19	2.73	-
%	17%	21%	18%	37%	7%	-	-

*Table 9: Pottery from late Iron Age/early Roman deposits (Phase 4c). Quantification by EVE. Forms: C jars (general), CB barrel-shaped jars, CC narrow-necked jars, CE high-shouldered necked jars, CG globular jars, CH bead-rimmed jars, CN storage jars; E beaker; H bowls (general), HA carinated bowls. * = present, but no with no rim surviving.*

Ware	C	C/H	CB	CC	CE	CG	CH	CN	E	HA	Total EVE	%
E20	0.09										0.09	3
E30											*	
E40	0.03										0.03	1
E50	0.18		0.14			0.05					0.37	10
E60											*	
E80	0.2	0.29	0.06		0.25		0.21			0.1	1.11	30
E80(RS)	0.13			0.88							1.01	28
G21	0.06		0.19								0.25	7
O40				0.08							0.08	2
O60											*	
O80											*	
R10											*	
R20											*	
R30											*	
R50									0.6		0.6	17
R90											*	
R95								0.06			0.06	2
W20											*	
Total	0.69	0.29	0.39	0.96	0.25	0.05	0.21	0.06	0.6	0.1	3.6	-
%	19	8	11	26	7	1	6	2	17	3	-	-

*Table 10: Pottery from early Roman deposits (Phase 4d). Quantification by EVE. Forms: C jars (general), CB barrel-shaped jars, CC narrow-necked jars, CD medium-mouthed necked jars, CE high-shouldered necked jars, CG globular jars, CN storage jars; E beaker; H bowls (general), HA carinated bowls. * = present, but no with no rim surviving.*

Ware	C	CB	CC	CD	CE	CG	CN	E	H	HA	Total EVE	%
A11											*	
E20		0.04									0.04	1
E40	0.03										0.03	1
E50	0.08							0.08			0.16	5
E60											*	
E80	0.38		0.86					0.04	0.14	0.12	1.54	48
E80(RS)											*	
G21		0.03									0.03	1
O10								0.05			0.05	2
O40											*	
O80											*	
R10											*	
R101											*	
R20											*	
R30					0.08						0.08	2
R35											*	
R39											*	
R50				0.25		0.08					0.33	10
R90							0.45				0.45	14
R95				0.07		0.1	0.35				0.52	16
W30											*	
Z											*	
Total	0.49	0.07	0.86	0.32	0.08	0.18	0.8	0.17	0.14	0.12	3.23	-
%	15	2	27	10	2	6	24	5	4	5	-	-

Savernake ware was recovered, remained open for deposition after AD 43. There is also the possibility, though, that a form of Savernake ware existed in the years approaching the conquest period as potters were introduced to different styles (chiefly 'Belgic') and influences.

Compared with phases 4a and 4b, a larger amount of pottery was deposited during the latter part of the late Iron Age and beginning of the Roman period (Phase 4c; Table 9). Some 33% of pottery by EVE was recorded in deposits assigned to this phase. In broad terms, there was little difference between phases 4a and 4b on the one hand and Phase 4c on the other. Grog-tempered wares continued to dominate the assemblage, although the fabrics collectively took a smaller share of 60%. The reduced fabric (E80) was available, again largely as jars. There was greater variety, though; high-shouldered necked jars were joined by bead-rimmed and barrel-shaped types. Carinated bowls were also recorded. Red-surfaced grog-tempered ware was almost as well represented as the reduced fabric, though this was due to the anomalous survival of a near-complete jar rim. A storage jar was present in Savernake ware (R95). Barrel-shaped jars in Malvernian rock-tempered ware (G21) continued to arrive at the site though they were less important in this phase. Part of the market for this ware appeared to have been taken up by more local limestone-tempered fabrics (E50), in which barrel-shaped jars were also available. Other wares of late Iron Age tradition remained a minor part of the assemblage; jars were identified in shelly ware (E40) and sand-tempered fabrics (E20). The range of essentially post-conquest wheel-thrown, sand-tempered wares was more diverse, although few forms were identified by rim. A beaker was recorded in black-surfaced ware (R50), while a narrow-necked jar was seen in Severn Valley oxidised ware (O40).

Pottery recovered from deposits dated to the second half of the 1st century AD (Phase 4d) took a 30% share of the entire assemblage by EVE (Table 10). Pottery of late Iron Age tradition made a smaller contribution to the group compared with Phase 4c, although grog-tempered ware remained the best-represented fabric within it. This is partly due to the good survival of a narrow-necked jar, although the fabric remained reasonably diverse in terms of vessel types. It is noticeable, however, that some of the standard jar forms – high-shouldered jars and bead-rimmed or globular jars – were no longer available in the fabric, but were instead taken up by producers of wheel-thrown sandy reduced wares. This appeared to restrict grog-tempered ware to forms approaching a specialist use – the narrow-necked jar (possibly for liquids), a beaker, and fine carinated bowls (including an example reminiscent *Cam* 212). Other wares of late Iron Age tradition were present, but like grog-tempered ware, made a smaller contribution than in Phase 4c. As noted, the main jar forms were supplied in

sandy reduced wares. Black-surfaced ware (R50) was dominant among these fabrics. The ware – identical to grey wares (for example R30) except for its darker surfaces – may have represented a continuation of the late Iron Age tradition, whose fabrics (for example E80 and G21) usually had dark grey or black surfaces, though was based on post-conquest technology. That said, the presence of a typical late Iron Age form – a high-shouldered necked jar – in fabric R30 indicates that aspects of earlier traditions could be expressed in different ways.

Most of the reduced wares had been made reasonably locally, but pottery was arriving from further afield. Savernake ware (R95) was more important in this phase compared with the earlier phases. This is reflected in the increased range of forms available: a medium-mouthed jar, a globular jar, and a storage jar. Possibly in imitation of fabric R95, local potters increased the output of their storage jar products (fabric R90). North Wiltshire potters were also responsible for sandy grey ware (R35); unsurprisingly, the fabric was present in small quantities; production would not increase until the mid 2nd century (Biddulph 2010, 35). Fabric R101 was a fine grey ware a dark core, and micaceous fabric with occasional calcareous fragments. It was present in small quantities here, though a reasonably local source is suspected; the fabric was present at Cotswold Community where a beaker and Gallo-Belgic-style cup, both dating to the early Roman period, were found (Biddulph 2010, 31). Another fragment of grey ware was identified as coming from Alice Holt (R39), though this is a late Roman fabric and certainly intrusive. Severn Valley oxidised ware (O40) was present, though no rims survived. Fragments of a butt-beaker were recorded in fabric W30, a fine white ware possibly imported from northern Gaul. A definite import was a fragment of a South Spanish amphora (A11).

No context-groups were dated exclusively to the mid-Roman period (*c* AD 120-250), and Phase 4e, which encompasses this period was represented by an unfurnished burial only. A single small sherd of Central Gaulish samian ware was dated to the 2nd century, but it was found in late Roman ditch 8203 and so was residual. In fact, the ditch was the only feature to be assigned to the late Roman period (Phase 4f). Pottery collected from the ditch was consistent with a late Roman date, but carried a broad date range that did not necessarily confine the group to that period (Table 11). The date for the ditch derived from a coin dated to AD 332-3, which suggested that the pottery was deposited in the 4th century. Though it is possible that 81% of the pottery by sherd count could have been used in the 4th century, it is also possible – likely, even, given the amount of known residual pottery present – that the group was somewhat older than the date of deposition and had been redeposited. If that were the case, the group implies 2nd-century activity in the area. The presence of Central Gaulish samian

Table 11: Pottery from late Roman deposits (Phase 4f)

Ware	Sherds	Weight (g)	EVE
B10	119	241	0.64
C10	1	3	
E40	2	15	
O20	3	1	
O30	5	11	
O80	2	39	
Q10	6	14	
R10	3	5	
R30	35	192	0.19
R35	17	117	
R95	3	45	
S20	3	4	
S30	1	1	
W30	7	5	
Total	207	693	0.83

has already been noted, but in addition, the black-burnished ware (B10) did not arrive in any quantity before the AD 120. Just two vessels were identified by rim. Both, one in black-burnished ware, the other in a sandy grey ware (R30), were cooking jars with everted rims.

Pattern of pottery deposition

The pottery was collected from a restricted range of features. The bulk of the assemblage was recovered from ditches, naturally reflecting the dominance of the feature type at the site (Table 12). Pottery was deposited into pits only when there were pits (or quarries) available to receive material in the second half of the 1st century AD (Phase 4d). Even then, more pottery was deposited into ditches than pits. In terms of pottery condition, the pottery entering ditches was in marginally better condition than the pottery in pits (Table 13). The mean sherd weight (calculated by dividing weight by sherd count, with values expressed in grams) of pottery in ditches was higher than that of pottery from pits, indicating that sherds were larger, on average, and may have undergone fewer episodes of disturbance and

Table 12: Pattern of pottery deposition – quantification by EVE

	Phase 4a/4b	Phase 4c	Phase 4d	Total EVE	%
Ditch	2.1	2.74	1.83	6.67	69%
Gully			0.09	0.09	1%
Pit		0.86	1.36	2.22	23%
Structural	0.63		0.63		7%
Total EVE	2.73	3.6	3.28	9.61	

redeposition. However, the difference of 4 g hardly seems significant, and it is reasonable to suggest that ditches and pits both received material that was very fragmented. Their assemblages are likely to represent pottery subject to redeposition long after initial breakage. This is consistent with the view given by the general paucity of structures across the site that the excavated area was located away from the core of settlement.

Aspects of pottery use

There was little evidence of pottery use (beyond, that is, standard assumptions deriving from vessel shape, for example jars being used for cooking and beakers for drinking). Three pieces had been drilled after firing. Three or more holes had been drilled through the body sherd of a Savernake ware storage jar. The holes were possibly made to effect a repair, though this is not certain. Another storage jar, in fabric E80 (or possibly Savernake ware), was transformed into a strainer-type vessel as at least one hole was knocked through its base. A grog-tempered pedestal jar had its pedestal removed and its base perforated with at least three holes to form a strainer. Evidence of burning was recorded on a number of pottery fragments, but these were associated with very few identifiable forms. The narrow-necked jar mentioned above (Phase 4d) was burnt externally and so may have been used to heat liquids.

The pottery in its regional context

Comparison of broadly contemporaneous pottery assemblages from the region reveals ceramic zones or areas of cultural difference. The pottery from Kingshill North, dominated as it is by locally-produced coarse wares, closely resembled that from Cotswold Community. The site, some 5 km south of Kingshill North, was similarly characterised by grog-tempered wares and other wares of Iron Age tradition (E wares), as well as black-surfaced and Savernake ware and other wheel-thrown reduced (R) wares (Table 14). The sites were matched, too, by

Table 13: Pattern of pottery deposition: mean sherd weights (MSW) by phase and feature type

	Phase 4a/4b (g)	Phase 4c (g)	Phase 4d (g)	Overall MSW (g)
Burial	13			13
Ditch	8	6	13	9
Gully	14		3	9
Natural		13		13
Pit		4	6	5
Spread	4		6	5
Structural	6	2		4
Overall MSW	7	6	8	8

their relatively small proportions of Gloucestershire/Severn basin wares, including Malvernian rock-tempered ware and Severn Valley ware, and paucity of fine and specialist wares, such as samian and mortaria. The assemblages from both sites, then, generally exhibited profiles weighted towards local producers. There was far less concordance between the post-conquest assemblage of Kingshill North (phases 4c and 4d) and pottery attributed to the earliest activity in Cirencester itself. The defensive ditch of Leaholme fort, which pre-dated the town, produced an assemblage dated *c* AD 45-75 (ceramic phase 1 – Cooper 1998, 325). The striking aspect about this group is its large quantity of imported wares, notably South Gaulish samian and Lyons ware, which collectively took a 68% share of the assemblage by vessel count. Oxidised wares were well represented, too, for which Kingsholm flagons were chiefly responsible. Clearly the military supply pattern was very different from supply to a native settlement, even one so close to the fort. The military market did not eschew locally suppliers completely, but it had to fit the cultural traditions brought by the soldiers, for example the preference for flagons, and that excluded potters with restricted, essentially pre-conquest, repertoires. A similar dichotomy between civilian and military markets was noted at Kingsholm, Gloucester (Cooper 1998, 327). On first impression, the assemblage belonging to the first civilian phase of Cirencester (ceramic phase 2 – AD 75-100/120) continued the military traditions, given its relatively high proportion of samian and oxidised wares, for example (Cooper 1998, 328). That said, while we do not have a contemporaneous assemblage from Kingshill North for comparison, there are signs that pottery supply to the town returned largely to local suppliers as trade links with Gloucester and elsewhere disappeared with the army (Cooper 1998, 329). This is evident from the increased proportion of grey wares, mainly Wiltshire (Table 14). This also helps to explain the peculiar distribution of wares in an assemblage associated with the town defences at Trinity Road and dated to AD 70-100 (McSloy 2008, 99). Two assemblages can be offered by Ditches, the site of a late Iron Age enclosure and early Roman villa (Trow *et al.* 2009). Group A, from the enclosure ditch, dated to AD 45-55, while group B2, a quarry deposit, may have dated up to *c* AD 70 (Moore 2009, 107, 114). Both, though, have a largely identical composition. Wares of Iron Age tradition made an important contribution to the groups, and it is this factor that sets them apart from Cirencester. But it does not necessarily move them closer to the Kingshill North profile. Though the levels of wheel-thrown reduced wares was similar, the Ditches groups (Table 14), contained much higher quantities of Severn Valley ware, which was not present in any great amount at Kingshill North (or, indeed, early Cirencester). Even among the Iron Age-style wares, Malvernian rock-tempered ware found a more significant place at Ditches compared with Kingshill North. The Ditches groups also included 'Bagendon black' grog-tempered fine ware, described at the oppidum (?equivalent to fabric R101), as well as samian and white wares. Overall, then, the Ditches groups show a supply network that linked more strongly with suppliers in the Severn basin and permitted a greater volume and range of continental wares. The similarities and differences in the pottery across these sites allow us to rank Kingshill North, Ditches, and Cirencester. The pottery from Kingshill North, focused on local, 'native', traditions, is consistent with a low-ranking agricultural settlement. The pottery from Ditches, with its mixture of fine and coarse local and traded wares, no doubt reflected the site's status as an elite centre (Trow *et al.* 2009, 67). Pottery supply to Cirencester at first had a military profile, but then changed as the town emerged to include the local aspects of Kingshill North and regional aspects of Ditches. This

Table 14: Inter-site comparison: Percentages of ware groups by site. Quantification by EVE, except Cirencester (CP1), which is based on vessel count. Data: Cotswold Community – Biddulph 2010, table 2.5; Cirencester defences – McSloy 2008, table 11; Cirencester (ceramic phase 1) – Cooper 1998, table 18; Cirencester (ceramic phase 2) – Cooper 1998, table 19; Ditches group A – Moore 2009, table 7 and Willis with Dannell 2009, 80; Ditches group B2 – Moore 2009, table 8 and Willis with Dannell 2009, 80-2.

Ware group	Cotswold Community	Kingshill North (Phase 4a/b)	Kingshill North (Phase 4c/d)	Cirencester defences	Cirencester (CP1)	Cirencester (CP2)	Ditches (Group A)	Ditches (Group B2)
A amphorae					4	5		
E 'Native' wares	59	87	69				39	41
F Fine wares					19	2		1
M Mortaria					1			
O Oxidised wares	3	1	2		17	26	32	24
R Reduced wares	34	12	30	98	14	53	26	34
S Samian wares	4			2	43	13	2	
W White wares					2		1	
Total EVE	11.6	2.73	6.88	2.5	206	8.4	15.25	13.39

phenomenon is not inconsistent with a population that accommodated both the high and the low born.

More sites are available for comparison using sherd count, rather than EVEs. On the whole this confirms the local outlook described at Kingshill North. Middle Duntisbourne, situated on Ermin Street north of Cirencester, produced groups dating to the 1st century AD. Wares of Iron Age tradition (E wares) were important, but their proportion was considerably lower than that recorded in Kingshill North's phase 4c/4d assemblage (Table 15). Even then, Malvernian rock-tempered wares were better represented than grog-tempered pottery (Timby 1999, table 7.10), a reverse of the relationship between those two wares recorded at Kingshill North. Another difference is the greater range and quantity of traded wares displayed at Middle Duntisbourne. Savernake grey ware, Severn Valley wares and continental imports take larger shares. Much of the site's ceramic needs, including supply of utilitarian coarse wares, were therefore being fulfilled by non-local suppliers. The pottery from the neighbouring site of Duntisbourne Grove had an understandably similar profile (Timby 1999, table 7.11); Malvernian rock-tempered wares, Severn Valley wares and Savernake grey ware were predominant. It is possible that the two sites benefited from their proximity to Ditches, which was 2.5 km to the north. The three sites generally had similar supply pattern. The pottery from Claydon Pike, south west of Cirencester, is more difficult to characterise. Its assemblage is different in a number of ways from Kingshill North; it saw lower proportions of Iron Age-style pottery, and higher proportions of fine and specialist wares, including white-slipped wares, samian and white wares (Table 15). The pottery also contrasted with Cotswold Community in these respects. On balance, the pottery appears to indicate that Claydon Pike was higher status than Kingshill North and Cotswold Community (Smith 2010, 92).

The relationships between these sites are illustrated by correspondence analysis. The resulting scattergrams show associations and disassociations between the assemblages; sites that are clustered or positioned reasonably close to each other tend to have similar assemblages in terms of ware groups. Figure 35, based on EVE data, confirms the pattern suggested by the percentages given in Table 14. In the top left corner of the plot, Cotswold Community and Kingshill North are both strongly associated with E wares. The assemblages from Ditches, shown below the axial intersection, form a second grouping; both appear to be strongly associated with oxidised wares, largely Severn Valley wares. The two Cirencester sites shown here are less homogeneous, but both fall into the top right portion of the chart and are linked by samian. Looking at assemblage data quantified by data based on weight, Figure 36 also indicates that assemblages from Cotswold Community and Kingshill North were very similar and again focused around coarse wares of Iron Age tradition. The almost identical groups from Ditches share space in the top right corner of the scattergram and are also relatively close to assemblages from Duntisbourne Grove and Middle Duntisbourne. All four appear to be strongly associated with oxidised wares. Claydon Pike contained a more diverse assemblage, and this is reflected in its position close to a variety of ware types.

The pottery from Kingshill North cannot be precise enough to pinpoint when in the second half of the 1st century AD the settlement was largely abandoned. However, the composition of the pottery does provide some clues. Apart from the dominance of wares of native tradition, the absence of South Gaulish samian in Phase 4d groups is especially telling. It is rare that the ware makes no appearance, even in a low-status site – samian took a 3% share of the early Roman assemblage at Cotswold Community (Biddulph 2010, table 2.5).

Table 15: Inter-site comparison: Percentages of ware groups by site. Quantification by sherd count. Data: Claydon Pike – Booth 2010, table 4.1; Cotswold Community – Biddulph 2010, archive data; Middle Duntisbourne – Timby 1999, table 7.10; Duntisbourne Grove – Timby 1999, table 7.11; Ditches group A – Moore 2009, table 7 and Willis with Dannell 2009, 80; Ditches group B2 – Moore 2009, table 8 and Willis with Dannell 2009, 80-2.

Ware group	Kingshill North (Phase 4c/d)	Claydon Pike (Phase 2)	Cotswold Community	Middle Duntisbourne	Duntisbourne Grove	Ditches (Group A)	Ditches (Group B2)
A Amphorae		1			1		
E 'Native' wares	75	40	62	18	37	40	49
F Fine wares		1		4		1	2
O Oxidised wares	3	10	8	51	34	24	18
Q White-slipped wares		1					
R Reduced wares	21	41	28	23	25	26	25
S Samian wares		1	1			3	3
W White wares		4		3	2	5	3
Total count	619	4970	1110	698	1401	649	853

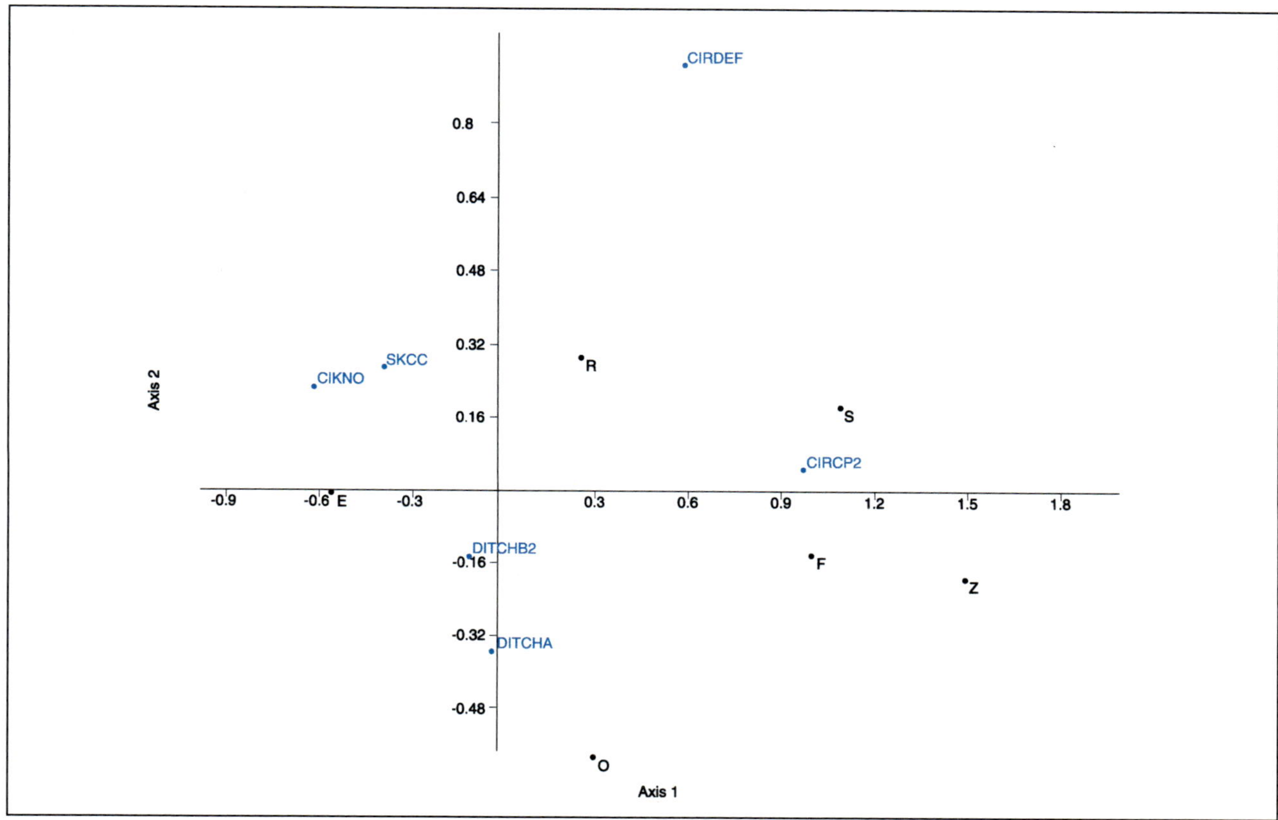

Fig. 35   Correspondence analysis plot showing the relationship between sites and ware groups. Data based on quantification by EVE.

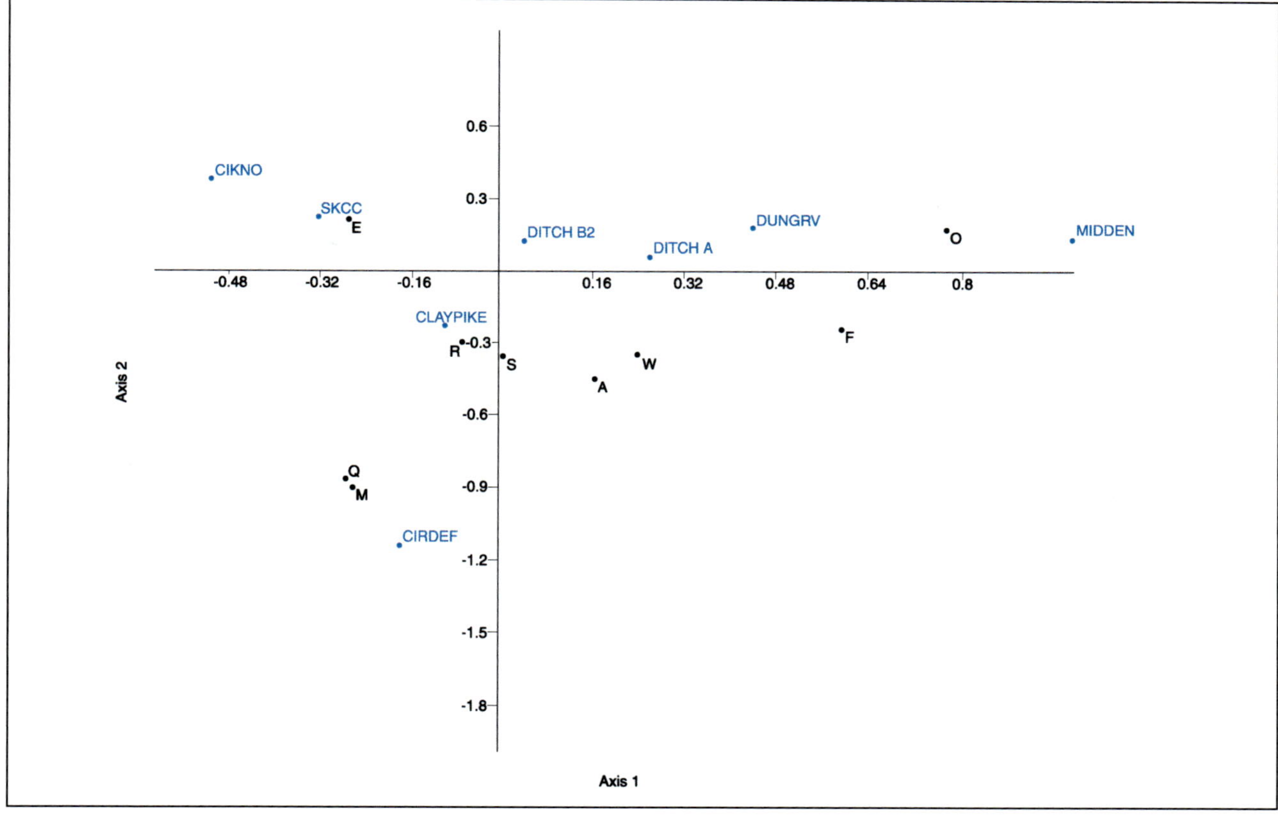

Fig. 36   Correspondence analysis plot showing the relationship between sites and ware groups. Data based on quantification by weight.

The reason could well be chronological. The importation of South Gaulish samian into Britain reached a peak in *c* AD 75/80 (cf. Dannell 1999, fig. 2.1), and it is in this period that we should expect small amounts of samian to arrive at the lower-ranking settlements. Its absence at Kingshill North (apart from a residual occurrence) suggests that the settlement was abandoned before this date. The chronology fits well with the inception of the civilian settlement at Cirencester. It is generally agreed that the military phase of Cirencester, which preceded the town, lasted from *c* AD 50/55 to 65/70 (Faulkner 1998, 377), and evidence from an early street surface at Trinity Road appears to confirm an early Flavian date for the laying out of the urban street system

(Holbrook 2008a, 138). If the inhabitants of the countryside around Cirencester did relocate (or were relocated) into the town in its earliest years (Faulkner 1998, 377), then the chronology of the post-conquest phase at Kingshill North, suggested by the pottery, is consistent with this.

Catalogue of illustrated pottery (Fig. 37)

Enclosure 8563 (Phase 4a)

1. **Barrel-shaped jar** (CB), fabric G21. Context 8730, posthole 8731
2. **Jar with footring base** (CP), fabric E80. Context 8720, ditch 8719

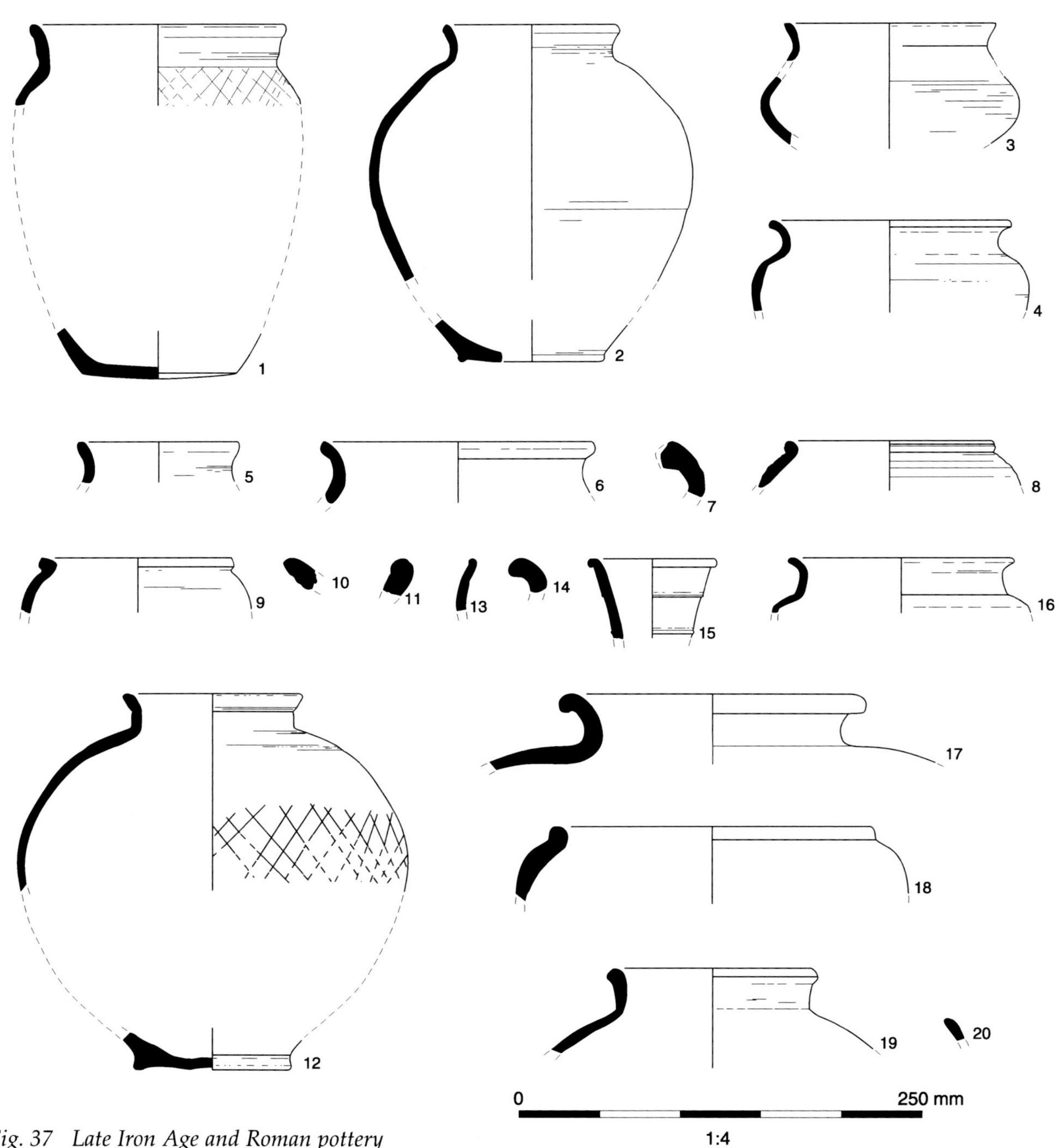

Fig. 37   Late Iron Age and Roman pottery

3. **High-shouldered, necked jar** (CE), fabric E80. Context 8720, ditch 8719
1. **High-shouldered necked jar** (CE), fabric R95. Context 9060, ditch 9059
4. **? Butt-beaker** (E), fabric E80. Context 9040, ditch 9038

Ditch group 8413 (Phase 4c)

6. **Narrow-necked jar** (CC), fabric O40. Context 8683, ditch 8684
7. **Storage jar** (CN), fabric R95. Context 8683, ditch 8684
8. **Globular jar** (CH), fabric E80. Context 8637, ditch 8628
9. **Bead-rimmed jar** (CH), fabric E80. Context 8498, ditch 8497
10. **Barrel-shaped jar** (CB), fabric G21. Context 8498, ditch 8497
11. **Globular jar** (CG), fabric E50. Context 8801, ditch 8789

? Structural slot 9028 (Phase 4c)

12. **Narrow-necked jar** (CC), fabric E80. Context 9030, slot 9028
13. **Barrel-shaped jar** (CB), fabric E80. Context 9030, slot 9028
14. **Barrel-shaped jar** (CB), fabric E50. Context 9030, slot 9028

Quarry group 8895 (Phase 4d)

15. **Carinated bowl** (HA), fabric E80. Context 8748, pit 8747
16. **High-shouldered necked jar** (CE), fabric R30 (sand and limestone fabric). Context 8902, pit 8900
17. **Storage jar** (CN), fabric R90. Context 8957, pit 8941

Ditch group 8537 (Phase 4d)

18. **Globular jar** (CG), fabric R95. Context 8566, ditch 8568
19. **Narrow-necked jar** (CC), fabric E80. Context 8567, ditch 8568
20. **Beaker** (E), fabric O40. Context 8465, ditch 8467

Fired clay *Cynthia Poole*

The assemblage comprised 193 fragments weighing 651g, with a mean fragment weight (MFW) of 3.4 g. The MFW reflects the poor preservation of the material with almost 66% (by weight) or 85% (by count) of fragments being unclassified (Table 16).

Table 16: Quantification of fired clay

	Count	% Count	Wt (g)	% Wt
Oven wall	1	0.52%	14.3	2.2%
Oven structure	1	0.52%	14	2.15%
Oven/hearth lining	17	8.81%	64.3	9.88%
Triangular brick	9	4.66%	105.5	16.21%
Utilised	82	42.49%	275.6	42.3%
Unidentified	82	42.49%	150.8	23.16%
Slingshot	1	0.52%	26.5	4.07%
Total	193		651	

Fabrics

Fabrics were characterised on visible macroscopic features and with the use of a x10 hand lens. Two fabrics were identified. Both were found in a range of colours and shades in combinations of red, yellow, brown and grey depending on the degree of firing levels of oxidisation or reduction during heating.

Fabric A was characterised by the presence of shell grits ranging in size from 0.5-4 mm. This was very similar to the local soil found adhering to some pieces of fired clay and it is likely that this fabric was obtained from the Oxford Clay or other clay soils and subsoils on or close to the site.

Fabric B was a fine sandy-silty clay containing no coarse inclusions visible macroscopically. A small number of samples were examined with a hand lens, and some variety was noted with medium-coarse quartz sand, occasional micaceous clay, and the fine shelly component. However, the majority of fragments in fabric B were not examined with a hand lens and have not been allocated to any sub-category. One sub-category visible macroscopically was designated as B/E3 on the basis of its similarity to the fabric E3 identified at Cotswold Community and used for fired clay and ceramic building material (Poole 2010, 153). This was a laminated clay with paler cream or brown streaks within the main matrix and no coarse inclusions. It was suggested that fabric E3 came from the Minety production area, though sources closer to Cirencester are possible. Fired clay normally derives from locally sourced clays and the probability is that the fired clay has utilised a number of local clay deposits or clay subsoils.

Forms

The number of diagnostic forms is extremely limited. Two fragments were identified as oven structure or wall on the basis of wattle impressions and possible straw impressions. A small quantity was identified as oven or hearth lining, having the appearance of *in situ* burnt soil or subsoil. One certain and one possible triangular perforated brick was found. The definite brick was pierced by a perforation 11 mm diameter widening to 14 mm at the edge. The full width of the brick was estimated to be c 50 mm, suggesting it falls into the lower end of the size range of this object type. The remainder of the structural fired clay was undiagnostic, consisting of fragments with a single surface or completely amorphous. The majority of the undiagnostic material is likely to derive from oven or hearth structure, though a few pieces had surface characteristics similar to the triangular brick. The triangular bricks were probably used as oven lining or oven/hearth furniture and normally date from the Iron Age or early Roman periods.

A complete slingshot of typical Iron Age ovoid form measured 41 mm long by 25-26 mm diameter and was made in fabric B/E3.

Table 17: Fired clay from phased contexts

Phase	Weight (g)
1	43
2	13.1
3	122
4	17.7
4a	48.1
4b	3.2
4c	88.3
4d	149.6
4f	3
6	7.5
Total	495.5

Discussion

This assemblage consists of hearth and oven structure, probably indicative of domestic (or agricultural) activity associated with cooking or crop processing. The presence of typical Iron Age forms suggests that the majority of the assemblage is likely to be contemporaneous, though the majority of pieces cannot be dated on their intrinsic characteristics. Relatively large quantifies of fired clay were recovered from Phase 3 pits and features dated to Phase 4d (Table 17), particularly ditch 8537 and pits 8742 and 8895.

Later prehistoric and Roman worked stone
Ruth Shaffrey

Iron Age

A single piece of worked stone recovered from middle Iron Age contexts is also the earliest chunk of perforated limestone with definite evidence for use (8310; Fig. 38). The hole is naturally occurring in the rock and although the rock demonstrates no signs of having been shaped or used, there is wear within the perforation indicating that it was suspended (see below).

Catalogue of Iron Age worked stone

Context 8310 **Possible weight** (Fig. 38). Shelly limestone. Large unworked chunk with natural perforation. The inside of the hole is slightly worn around the top edge. Measures 180 x 180 x max 45 mm thick. Fill of pit 8311 (8310). Phase 3: Iron Age.

Late Iron Age/Roman

This phase produced the largest assemblage of worked stone, including processors and a quern involved in food production, suggesting the presence of a dwelling or dwellings. Several weights were also recovered and are discussed in detail.

A single quartzite hammerstone was recovered from pit 8458 (fill 8457). One face is smoothed and the other is damaged, suggesting use as a multi-functional tool. Tools like this could have been put to a variety of uses, such as pounding and grinding organic or inorganic materials.

A single almost complete upper rotary quern of beehive style (SF 10073; Fig. 38) was recovered from phase 4c pit 8806 (8808), where it had been curated as part of a special deposit. It had been placed centrally in the pit, grinding surface upwards. Its deposition is extremely significant, but although other activity was occurring on site during the same phase, the pit cannot be related to any dwellings on site with certainty and little can thus be said about exactly what the deposition was intended to represent.

The quern was extremely well used with the grinding surface worn so close to the handle socket that the quern had broken across that area, rendering it unusable. The quern is made of Old Red Sandstone (ORS), almost certainly from the Wye Valley, which saw rotary quern production from the Iron Age onwards. It is a thick quern with concave grinding surface, convex upper surface and handle slot in the side, not piercing the feed pipe. It is of typical Iron Age design but not exactly like any illustrated by Curwen (1937, 141); nor does it match any examples recorded in an extensive survey of over 1200 Roman querns of the same lithology (Shaffrey 2006). It is classified as a beehive quern because of its overall shape and thickness, although it is not as exaggerated as Hunsbury or Yorkshire querns, the thickness of which can equal the diameter. A small number of beehive-style examples of ORS querns have been recovered from late Iron Age or very early Roman contexts (Shaffrey 2006, 37), but these are also so unusual that they can be confidently classified as being of pre-Roman origin. Thus it is likely that the initial period of use of this quern could be much earlier than its date of deposition, especially considering that it demonstrates extensive wear suggesting that it had seen long service and was first used in a much earlier phase.

Gloucestershire is one of the most likely places to find ORS querns of Iron Age date or form (Shaffrey 2006, 64). An example with a similar handle socket to this was recovered from a 1st-century AD context at Vineyards Farm, Charlton Kings, some 20 km to the north (Rawes 1991). Other examples of similar form have also been found at Cheltenham (West Drive), Cirencester (The Ditches), Fairford (Thornhill Farm) and Frocester (Shaffrey 2002; Shaffrey 2004; Price 2000).

Four chunks of limestone with naturally occurring holes were recovered from late Iron Age/early Roman phases. These are comparable with stones found in earlier phases, except that all the Roman examples demonstrate evidence of use. Two of the larger stones were shaped around at least one edge and were worn inside the perforation, suggesting suspension (SF 10082, not illustrated; context 8643, Fig. 38). One of the items is small and smooth with

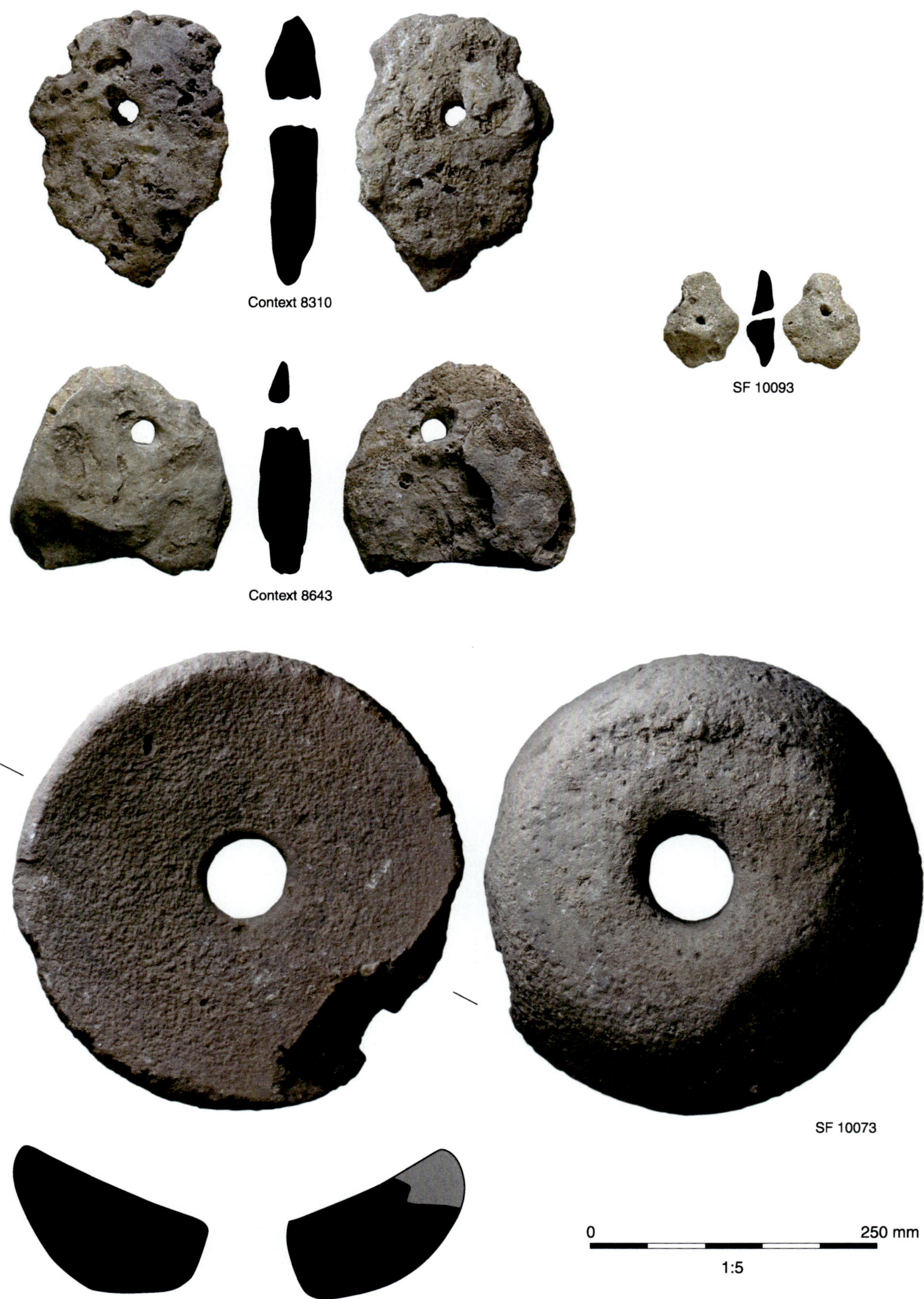

Fig. 38   Worked stone objects, phases 3 and 4

some possible wear from suspension (SF 10093); it weighs only 115 g. The remaining rock (context 8311) demonstrates no signs of having been shaped or used, but may have been collected with use in mind as all three items weigh between 1300 g and 1700 g and are of similar dimensions.

The four 'perforated' stones recovered from this phase are in addition to four from earlier phases. What appear to be perforations in the limestone are probably what remains of voids naturally formed in the rock when carbon dioxide dissolved the calcium carbonate of the rock fabric in joints up to tens of millimetres across (Sumbler *et al.* 2000, 7). Thus, naturally 'holey' rocks were taken advantage of; all the examples found at Kingshill North have a hole approximately in the middle, suggesting that stones were carefully selected. In earlier phases, these stones appear to have been collected but probably remained unused. In Iron Age and Roman phases, the stones were shaped and/or used. The natural availability of perforated stones is illustrated by an unworked example from a Phase 3 pit (8311).

Large stones were used as weights for a variety of functions throughout time, including as thatch weights, gate or door weights and most notably as fishing weights or net sinkers. Generally they are shaped and finished. Examples of weights that made use of stones left in a near natural state are known, however, for example at Horcott Pit (Shaffrey 2009), and it is reasonable to assume that this sort of artefact will be most commonly found on sites in areas where those types of stones occur

naturally. But the fact that they are naturally occurring also means that they are more difficult to identify in the field and may well be overlooked. It is therefore likely that practical weights like these may have more commonly in use than the archaeological record would currently suggest.

The assemblage also contains approximately 3 kg of burnt but otherwise unworked stone. This was recovered from 14 contexts, details of which can be found in the archive.

Catalogue of LIA/Roman artefacts

Context 8457 **Processor** (not illustrated). Quartzite pebble. Pebble, smoothed on one face and smashed on another indicating use as both a hammerstone and a smoother. Measures 60 x 62 x 51 mm. Fill of pit 8458 (8457). Phase 4: LIA/Roman.

SF 10093 **Pierced pebble** (Fig. 38). Shelly limestone pebble with natural perforation and some possible wear from suspension. Measures 80 x 60 x 22 mm. Fill of pit 8747 (8748). Phase 4d: LIA/ER (Early-mid 1st century AD).

SF 10073 **Incomplete upper rotary quern** (Fig. 38). Old Red Sandstone, Quartz Conglomerate. Pecked all over. Handle slot in the side measuring 60 mm long and 42 mm wide at the edge. Quern is overall slightly oval shaped. Measures 380 mm diameter x 90 mm maximum thickness. Fill of pit 8806 (8808). Phase 4c: LIA/ER (Early-mid 1st century AD).

Context 8643 **Possible weight** (Fig. 38). Limestone. Stone with a hole measuring 20 mm positioned roughly in the centre. The edges may be shaped and there is some possible suspension wear above the hole on one or both sides of the stone. Hole. Measures 240 x

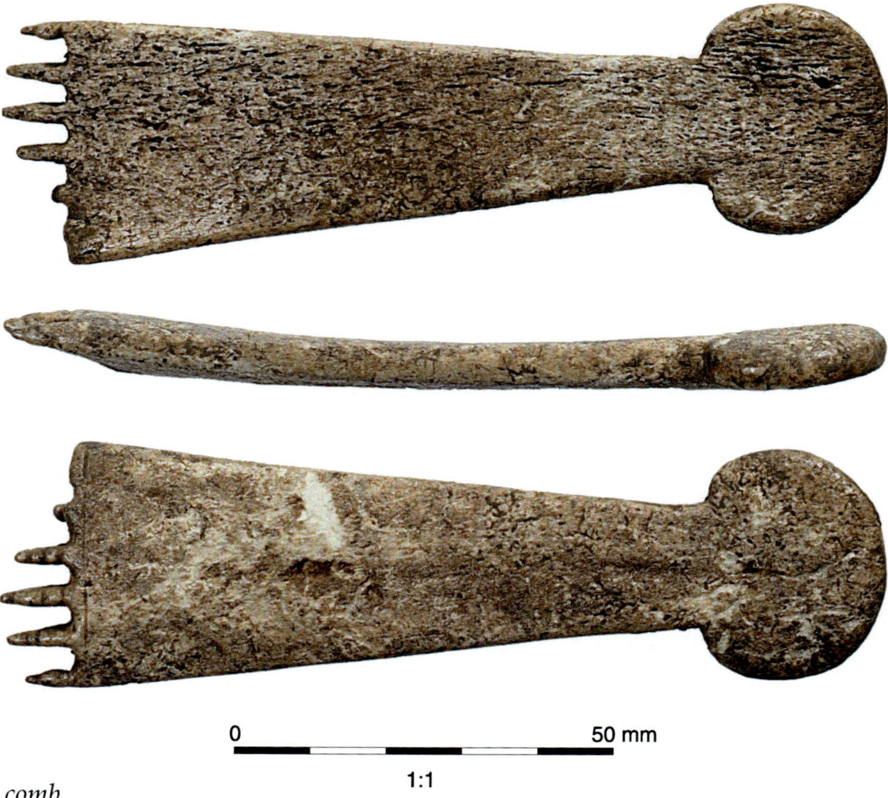

Fig. 39 Antler comb

150 x 50mm. Fill of pit 8642 (8643). Phase 4c: LIA/ER (Early-mid 1st century AD)..

SF 10082 **Possible weight** (not illustrated). Limestone. The edges look like they have been shaped and there is some possible suspension wear above the hole on one side of the stone only. Hole measures 30 mm diameter and is positioned roughly in the centre of the stone. Measures 200 x 150 x 40mm. Fill of pit 8900 (8903). Phase 4d: ER (mid-late 1st century AD).

Antler comb *Leigh Allen*

A complete antler comb (SF 10052) was recovered from the fill of Phase 3 middle Iron Age pit 8114 (Fig. 39). The comb is relatively small, measuring only 115 mm in length; the shaft is wider at the dentate end, narrowing towards the butt end, which is roughly circular. The comb is undecorated, apart from a single transverse groove just above the inter-dentate notches, but it does display a high degree of wear, particularly to the teeth.

The comb originally had six teeth, rectangular in section and tapering towards the tips. The inter-dentate notches are wide and U-shaped. Only four teeth remain; the tooth on the right-hand outside edge is missing and has been worn smooth almost to the level of the base of the inter-dentate notch. The tooth next to it survives only as a stump. The comb obviously underwent heavy use on this right-hand edge and continued to be used after these teeth had broken (or been worn away). The surviving teeth (including the stump) all have transverse grooves worn into them on the upper and lower surface. The narrow edges of the shaft are also highly polished through wear.

Combs of this type are fairly common finds on Iron Age sites. Large numbers have been recovered from Danebury (Cunliffe 1984), Meare Village East (Coles 1987), Maiden Castle (Sharples 1991), Glastonbury (Bulleid and St George Gray 1911-1917) and Cadbury Castle (Barrett *et al.* 2000). There remains considerable controversy about the possible use of this type of comb. There are arguments for and against their use as weaving tools, specifically in the pushing of the weft threads into position before they are beaten into position with a weaving sword, as discussed fully by Sellwood (1984, 371-378). Alternatively, they could have been used for combing sheep's wool during shearing or plucking, where the tips of the teeth would become worn through contact with the animals hide. Perhaps, with their careful manufacture and individual decoration, they were personalised hair combs (Coles 1987, 105-117).

Metal objects *Ian Scott, with a contribution by Paul Booth*

Composition of the assemblage

The metal finds assemblage comprises at least 1,236 objects or 1,716 fragments. (Each object was assigned a unique object or 'small find' number, prefixed below with SF.) Most of the metal finds are securely stratified and phased (Table 18). The assemblage consists almost exclusively of iron objects; there are six copper alloy objects, including three coins, and one lead object. The majority of identified objects are nails or nail fragments (91.2% by object count or 93.4% by fragment count). Two contexts (pit fills 8833 and 8799) produced numerous small unidentified fragments or crumbs of iron which have not been quantified, but no other metal finds. Context 8228, fill of grave 8227, produced some unquantified and unidentified small fragments, but also at least 1,092 nails (1,564 fragments), 68 hobnails and a single small miscellaneous fragment of iron. Indeed, context 8228 produced most of the metal finds from the site (93.9% by object count or 95.1 % by fragment count; Table 18).

Phase 1, unstratified and unphased

There are a few finds from natural features and from Neolithic layers and must be intrusive. The finds from natural features include a horseshoe nail

Table 18: Metalwork: Summary quantification by phase and function (object count)

Phase/Date	Coin	Transport	Personal	Structural	Nails	Misc	Query	Waste	Total
				Function					
Phase 0 - Natural		2			5	3		2	12
Phase 1 - Neolithic			1			1			2
Phase 3 - Mid Iron Age					1	2			3
Phase 4a - Late Iron Age			1		1	1			3
Phase 4c – Late Iron Age/early Roman		1	1	1	5	2		1	11
Phase 4d – Early Roman			1		5				6
Phase 4e - early/mid Roman			68		1092	1			1161
Phase 4f – Late Roman	1		3		5		1		10
Phase 6 - Post-medieval/modern		1	1		11	5			18
Unphased	2	2			2	2	1	1	10
Total	3	6	76	1	1127	17	2	4	1236

and three miscellaneous fragments. The finds from Neolithic deposits comprise a hobnail and a fragment of iron plate. In addition, there are ten objects from unstratified or unphased contexts. These include a copper alloy coin and an unidentified coin-sized disc (see below; SF 10015 and 10020).

Phase 3

Middle Iron Age contexts produced a single nail from the fill of pit 8826, and two fragments of iron rod or bar from the fill of pit 8382.

Phase 4a

Contexts of late Iron Age date produced three objects: one fragment of iron strip from context 8985, a nail from context 9040, and a fragment of a possible copper alloy buckle frame from context 9054. All contexts were deposits within ditch 8563.

Phase 4c

Contexts of late Iron Age/early Roman date produced 11 metal objects from nine contexts, and small unidentified iron fragments or crumbs from context 8833. The identified objects include a clearly intrusive horseshoe nail from context 8200 in ditch 8255; a fragment of copper alloy spring probably from a brooch, found in ditch 8413 deposit 9167, and a large spike or nail and two other nails from contexts 8412 and 8580, also from ditch 8413. Single nails were recovered from posthole 8702, and from pits 8808 and 8879. An eroded fragment of iron strip and a small piece of slag were collected from context 8637, a fill of ditch 8413, while ditch 8978 contained a bent and twisted fragment of iron strip.

Phase 4d

Contexts of early Roman date produced six metal finds from five contexts. These comprise a copper alloy spring fragment possible brooch, possibly partially melted, from pit 8747, and nails from ditch 8537 and pits 8575, 8741 and 8887.

Phase 4e

The majority of the metal finds came from a single context (8228) from early or mid Roman grave 8227. The grave fill produced at least 1062 nails, 68 hobnails and one small miscellaneous fragment of iron. Such a number of hobnails might indicate the presence of a nailed shoe. All the identifiable nails are Manning Type 1b wood nails with flat circular or near circular heads and tapering square section stems (Manning 1985, 134; fig. 32). The preservation of the nails ranges from very poor laminating examples to examples with no visible corrosion. It seems probable that the nails were buried in groups or heaps and that the outer nails corroded and eroded and protected the nails within the heaps or clumps from corrosion. Because many of the nails are extremely well-preserved and many are complete, or near-complete, it is possible to see that they have been bent or clenched. It seems certain that most if not all the nails had been used prior to burial.

A concentration of nails like this requires an explanation. As Manning (1985, 134) has noted, nails seem to span a range of lengths from under 20 mm long to 100 mm long, with a greater number of smaller nails. Complete nails from context 8228 were measured and allocated to length groups (Fig. 40). Only 165 of the at least 1062 nails could be measured with confidence. This gives a sample of 15.5 % of the nails. The suspicion is that larger nails are under-represented in the sample of complete nails, but the extent to which they may be under-represented has not been quantified. What the measurements show is that there is some clustering by length. There is a cluster of nails measuring between 20 mm and 30 mm long, with most examples measuring c 25 mm long. Only a small number of nails measured between 31 mm

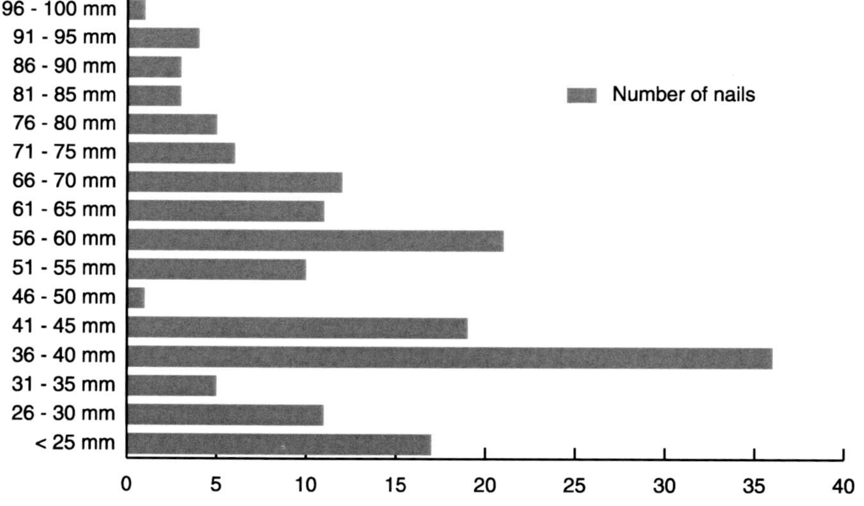

Fig. 40   Context 8228: Distribution of complete nails by length groups. Quantification by count (n = 165)

and 35 mm long. A second cluster measures between 35 mm and 45 mm long; again most examples in this group measure c 40 mm long. Only one nail measuring 46 mm to 50 mm long was recorded. The next cluster comprises nails measuring between 51 mm and 70 mm long with a definite peak of nails measuring 56 mm to 60 mm long. Longer nails occur in small numbers. Given that the majority of the complete nails were comparatively small and had been used before burial, it is suggested that the nails represent some form of wooden litter to support the body, which was burnt on the pyre and the remains gathered together and buried with the cremated bone and at least one shoe.

Phase 4f

There were just ten finds from 4th-century contexts. All were recovered from ditch 8203. There are five nails, three hobnails, and an iron fitting of uncertain function. The ditch also contained a Roman coin dated to AD 332-3 (see below).

Phase 6

Finds from post-medieval contexts number 18, including 11 nails. One of the nails is a modern wire nail from pit 8143. Among the other finds are a lead parcel seal and a rectangular iron buckle frame, both from the topsoil, and a number of miscellaneous pieces.

Coins *Paul Booth*

SF 10020 (unstratified): Incomplete AE3
Obverse: illegible
Reverse: Gloria exercitus (1 standard)
AD 335-341

SF 10080 (Fig. 41; context 8939, fill of ditch 8203): AE3 (17mm)
Obverse: FLIULCONSTANTIUSNOBC
Reverse: GLOR IAEXERC ITUS (2 standards), TRS* (Trier)
AD 332-3 (RIC VII Trier, 546)

SF 10015 (unstratified): unidentified copper alloy fragment; unlikely to be a Roman coin.

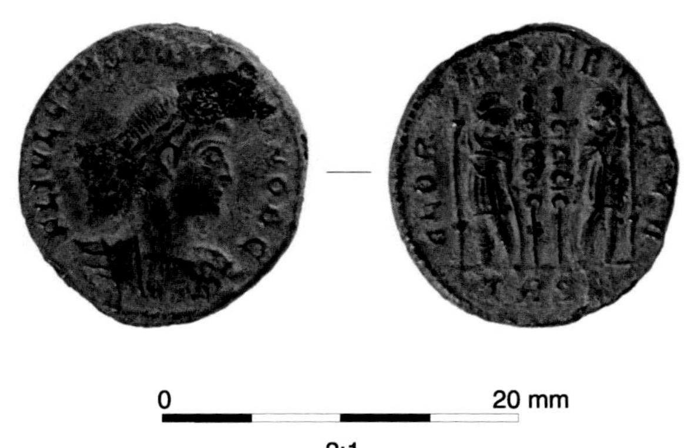

Fig. 41 Coin, SF 10080

Conclusions

The composition of the metalwork assemblage is very distinctive. It lacks any domestic or household element; personal items are limited to hobnails and two fragments of possible copper alloy brooch spring. The main component of the assemblage comprises the wood nails and hobnails from context 8228. It is suggested that the wood nails from this grave fill represent the remains of a litter burnt on the pyre.

Slag and related high temperature debris
Lynne Keys

A very tiny quantity (126g) of slag and heat-magnetised debris was recovered, mostly from soil samples. It was examined by eye and a magnet was used to test for magnetised material. Details are given in Table 19.

The diagnostic iron slags were produced by iron smithing. They are of two types: hammerscale from ordinary hot working of a piece of iron (making or repairing an object), and tiny spheres from high-temperature welding used to join or fuse two pieces of iron. Both are so small that they are invisible to the naked eye when in the soil, but they are virtually pure iron and highly magnetic. Once recovered by sampling they can be easily recognised and examined using a magnifying glass.

Their presence in small quantities in pit and ditch fills would normally pass without much comment, but some features containing iron microslags are of Neolithic or Bronze Age date. The features concerned are pits 8058, 8064, 8100, 8455, 8928 (Phase 1), and ring-ditch 8454 (Phase 2). The presence of iron working microslags in pre-Iron Age features raises questions that have to be addressed. No large iron slags were found in any Neolithic and Bronze Age features and, as the microslags are very tiny or fragmentary, it is likely that they were moved downwards from the Iron Age and later layers (which also contained iron working microslags) by worm action. For the Iron Age and later periods, virtually no bulk (larger) slags were present, so it may be that some smithing took place on the site during the past and the bulk slags produced were removed for recycling in roads or yard surfaces elsewhere.

Human remains from late Iron Age inhumation burials *Alistair Zochowski and Helen Webb*

Late Iron Age (Phase 4a/b)

Skeleton in grave 1104

This skeleton was between 50% and 75% complete. The cranium, mandible, vertebrae, ribs, the major long bones and hand and foot bones were all present, although none was entirely complete. No dentition had survived. These bones were in a good

Table 19: Summary of metalworking debris

Context	Sample	Slag identification	Weight (g)	Comment
8007	187	magnetic residue	1	fired clay & grit; 25pct iron microslags.
8031		iron-rich undiagnostic	17	
8057	33	magnetic residue	3	fired clay, grit, very, very occasional tiny frags. hammerscale flake & several tiny spheres.
8062	20	magnetic residue	2	fired clay, several tiny hammerscale spheres.
8063	21	magnetic residue	10	fired clay, charcoal, fired grit, one hammerscale sphere, one frag. iron microslag.
8089	22	magnetic residue	6	mostly fired clay, crushed charcoal.
8097	34	magnetic residue	4	fired clay, very occasional pieces broken hammerscale flake
8190	90	magnetic residue	1	tiny crushed material including one hammerscale sphere & bits of crushed flake, fired clay.
8212	91	magnetic residue	1	crushed fired clay & microslags, incl. two tiny hammerscale spheres.
8462	81	magnetic residue	1	mostly burnt, crushed material, occ. very tiny hammerscale spheres.
8474	76	magnetic residue	1	fired clay, broken hammerscale flake, one sphere & fragments of microslags.
8482	80	magnetic residue	3	some crushed hammerscale flake, occasional tiny spheres, crushed charcoal, fired clay.
8492	99	magnetic residue	1	fired clay & tiny undiagnostic slag.
8493	98	magnetic residue	6	fired clay, tiny charcoal bits and grit.
8494	100	magnetic residue	0.5	fired clay.
8498	94	magnetic residue	3	fired clay, charcoal bits, grit.
8530	86	magnetic residue	2	fired clay & grit; several tiny hammerscale spheres, one fragment of microslag splash.
8720	-	magnetic residue	0.5	fired clay
8793	192	magnetic residue	1	tiny crushed charcoal, fired clay, crushed hammerscale flake.
8793	192	undiagnostic	0.5	
8794	190	fuel ash slag	1	
8794	190	iron-rich undiagnostic	0.5	microslag fragment.
8808	186	magnetic residue	13	fired clay & grit; occ. microslags inc. one large and many small hammerscale spheres & lots broken flake.
8808	186	undiagnostic	0.5	microslag fragment.
8819	189	magnetic residue	11	fired clay, crushed charcoal, grit, very very occ. frags. broken hammerscale flake & occasional spheres.
8828	191	magnetic residue	0	crushed bits hammerscale flake & fired clay.
8833	195	magnetic residue	3	fired clay.
8833		iron-rich undiagnostic	5	
8920	248	magnetic residue	1.5	crushed bits fired clay & some broken hammerscale flake.
8929	228	magnetic residue	5	one tiny piece broken iron microslag, fired gravel & clay.
8938	232	magnetic residue	5	crushed fired clay & tiny stones, occ. hammerscale spheres.
9097	286	magnetic residue	5	fired clay; some pieces charcoal fragments etc.
9097	289	magnetic residue	3	fired clay & tiny stones.
9102	273	magnetic residue	2	fired clay & fired pea grit.
9142	300	magnetic residue	2	one large hammerscale sphere, some pieces broken flake, microslag pieces, tiny undiagnostic, iron bits, fired clay, crushed charcoal.
		TOTAL	122	

condition, or grade one (McKinley 2004, 16), with surfaces that showed slight, patchy erosion. No attempt was made to assess the sex of the individual in accordance with accepted practice. The skeleton was aged using diaphyseal lengths with reference to Scheuer *et al.* (1980) and Scheuer and Black (2000), and was estimated to have been between 38 and 44 weeks old. No pathology was observed.

Infant 1104 had been buried in the base of a ditch without grave goods. The presence of an unadorned burial within a ditch is typical for the Iron Age period (Whimster 1981, 10). A large limestone capping slab had been placed over the top of the burial. This is also not an uncommon feature of Iron Age inhumation burial. Other infant burials associated with capping stones include one at Winnall Down, Hampshire, where the infant had been buried within a posthole with flint packing, and at Maiden Castle, Dorset, where the infant had been buried in a rampart, and overlain with limestone blocks (Wilson 1981, 141). It has been suggested that in some cases, such blocks were used to keep the body in position during interment, but, particularly where they overlay the burial, they may have been to protect the body, perhaps against disturbance by animals, as suggested for the female rampart burial at Bury Hill, Hampshire (Wilson 1981, 141). Cunliffe (1995, 100) suggests that such burials may represent victims of ritual killings, their bodies placed as offerings to the earth deities.

Skeleton 8724, grave 8723

This skeleton was between 50% and 75% complete. Some of the elements were moderately fragmented, while the skull and pelvis were highly fragmented. The bones had suffered erosion and showed some root action, changes that are consistent with grade 2 of McKinley's (2004,16) condition categories.

Dental attrition suggested an age of over 30 years (Miles 1962), but this is based on an incomplete set of molar teeth (see above). Only fragments of sexually dimorphic skull features had survived. The supraorbital ridges of the skull were prominent, suggesting a male individual, and the mastoid processes were large and vertically aligned, which are also male traits. It was therefore concluded that the individual was male.

No long bones had survived intact to allow stature estimation. No non-metric traits were observed. Several teeth were present, but no mandible or maxilla had survived. The teeth included three left maxillary molars, three mandibular molars and three incisors. One of the incisors had a linear defect on the enamel surface. Such defects, known as enamel hypoplasia, are formed during periods of growth arrest when the enamel crown is developing. These periods of arrested growth have been linked to episodes of childhood disease, malnutrition and weaning (Hillson 1996, 166-167). Cribra orbitalia was present on the right orbit and was recorded as type 1 after Stuart-Macadam (1991, 109). Osteoarthritis, a joint disease that affects synovial joints, was present in the thoracic spine. Osteoarthritis is diagnosed on dry bone by the presence of eburnation (polishing) or at least two of either: pitting, bony contour change, and/or marginal osteophyte. The cause is multi-factorial, in which the advancement of age increasingly becomes a predisposing factor. There was also osteophytosis throughout the vertebral column.

Other pathology included hyperostosis frontalis interna (HFI) on the endocranial surface (inside surface) of the frontal bone. HFI is identified on dry bone as thickening and nodule formation and in the present skeleton the changes were slight. The condition has associations with virilism and obesity and is common amongst post-menopausal women. The cause of HFI is unknown but implies some sort of pituitary gland disorder in its aetiology (Aufderheide and Rodriguez-Martin 1998).

Prime adult male 8724 was buried in a small grave (8723) cut into a gully (8703). The gully and grave were aligned roughly north east-south west. The grave itself was just 1.02 m in length and 0.4 m in width, and the individual appeared to have been 'squeezed' into the grave. He had been placed on his left side, the side on which the majority of Iron Age inhumations are found, judging from other burials in southern Britain (Whimster 1981, 11). The head was at the very south-west end of the grave. Wilson (1981, 138) and Whimster (1981, 14) established that, while heads have been found towards almost every direction, there is a bias towards the heads being directed between north and east. The skull of skeleton 8724 faced upwards, but it is possible that the head had originally been placed with its left side up against the edge of the grave, it having tilted backwards (south-easterly) during decomposition. The arms were extended, the left arm underlying the body, and the right against the north west edge of the grave. The legs were flexed at the knees. The lower right leg (tibia and fibula) overlay the left femur, and the lower left leg was raised upwards against the bottom (north east) edge of the grave cut, with several foot bones outside the actual grave cut.

Crouched inhumation burials placed within pits and ditches in and around settlements are the principal archaeologically-visible burial rite of central southern England in the Iron Age (Whimster 1981), with antecedents in the late Bronze Age (Brück 1995). Burial 8724 indicates that the practice continued into the late Iron Age. The position of this burial, appearing as though it had been crammed into the grave, is perhaps not unusual for an Iron Age inhumation. Settlement burials run the gamut of contracted body positions, from very tightly crouched – the individuals probably having been bound – to loosely flexed (Wilson 1981, 136; Whimster 1981, 11). The fact that a grave had been specifically dug for skeleton 8724 is perhaps significant. Often Iron Age burials are found within pits or other features originally dug for a purpose other than disposal of the dead, for example, storage of grain, or for refuse (Whimster 1981, 10). Whether this was simply because when they went out of use they were convenient, ready-made graves, or whether there was some ritual significance is not clear. The cutting of a specific grave for skeleton 8724 may indicate therefore that this individual was different from the rest of the community in some way. Deposition in a specially dug grave implies more care, or investment of energy in the disposal rite, but it could simply be that no empty or half-filled pits were available (Wilson 1981, 143). The grave was possibly dug into the less compact ditch fill as it required less physical effort than cutting a grave through the natural, although it is perhaps more likely that the location was coincidental, the important factor being a location adjacent to the ditch bank. Recut pits have been recorded at Twywell, Hod Hill and Maiden Castle, Winterbourne Stoke and Beckford (Whimster 1981, 10). 'Scoops', and perhaps generally small graves, such as that belonging to skeleton 8724, may be regarded as less distinguished graves, possibly reflecting the status of the corpse, or the time and/or number of people available to perform the interment (Wilson 1981, 143).

Table 20: Summary of cremation burial 8228, grave 8227

Category	Value
Context	8228
Total weight (g)	673
<10mm weight (g)	103
10-4mm weight (g)	375
4-2mm weight (g)	194
Un-identified %	79
Skull %	5
Axial %	2
Upper limb %	3
Lower limb %	10
Maximum fragment size (mm)	20x12

Cremated human remains *Sharon Clough*

A single cremation burial (context 8228) comprising the remains of a single adult, probably of early-mid Roman date (Phase 4e), was recovered from grave 8227 (Table 20). The cremated remains were highly fragmented and were variable in colour and weighed in total 672 g

Methodology

The cremated bone was processed as environmental samples, which involved wet sieving at three fraction sizes, <10 mm, 10-4 mm and 4-2 mm. The human bone was extracted from the samples in the <10 mm and 10-4 mm fractions and the 4-2 mm fraction was retained for examination. The weight of the bone retained in each fraction and spit was recorded and its percentage of the total weight of the cremation calculated. This enabled the degree of fragmentation, which may indicate further processing of the cremated bone after the burning of the body on the pyre, to be quantified.

The bones retained from each sieve size were examined in detail and sorted into the following identifiable bone groups: skull (including mandible and dentition); axial (clavicle, scapula, ribs, vertebra and pelvic elements); upper limb and lower limb. The separation of the bone into these groups helps illuminate any deliberate bias in the skeletal elements collected for burial. Each sample was weighed on digital scales and details of colour and largest fragment were recorded. Where possible, the presence of individual bones within the defined bone groups was noted. Any unidentifiable fragments of long bone shafts or cancellous bone, which are often the majority recovered from cremations, were weighed and incorporated into any subsequent quantitative analysis. The prevalence of unidentifiable bone is largely dependent on the degree of fragmentation, since larger fragments are easier to identify than smaller ones.

It must also be taken into consideration that some skeletal elements are more diagnostic and more easily identifiable than others and, therefore, more often recorded. This may create bias in calculations of the relative quantities of skeletal elements collected for burial.

Age estimations from cremated remains are dependent on the survival of particular age diagnostic elements. In adult cremations, the most useful age indicators are degenerative changes to the auricular surface (Lovejoy *et al.* 1985), pubic symphysis and cranial suture closure (Meindl and Lovejoy 1985).

Weight

The cremation burial weighed 673 g in total. It is frequently found that 50% or less of the bone available after cremation is included in the burial (McKinley 2000). Experiments have found that it is fairly easy to collect all the bones from an undisturbed pyre, which often remain in anatomical order (McKinley 1997). McKinley (2000, 404) states that the weight of bone of an adult cremation from a modern crematorium varies from about 1000 to 3600 g. This would suggest that cremation deposit 8228 comprised only part of the individual. The identified elements were low in quantity, 79% remaining unidentified. The lower limbs were best represented, followed by the skull. Both these areas are more easily identified in very small fragments compared with other bones. Also identified were carpal bones, hand and foot phalanges and tooth roots. These are small bones, and low in weight, but their presence suggests that collection of bone from the pyre was not confined to large long bones and skull fragments.

Colour

The efficiency of a cremation is influenced by the following factors: the construction of the pyre, quantity of wood, position of the body, tending of the pyre, weather, duration of the cremation and pyre temperature (McKinley 2000, 407; McKinley 1994, 82-84). The colour of the cremated bone after cremation reflects the temperatures achieved during the cremation process (McKinley 2000, 405). The cremated bone of context 8228 varied considerably in colour: cranial fragments were largely white; long bone, especially lower leg bones were black or brown; higher up the leg the bone became whiter. Some of the distal phalanges were also noted to be black in colour. There was iron staining on some bone, assumed to be from close proximity to iron nails. A vertebral spinous process was brown and black in colour. From the distribution of colour changes observed it can be inferred that a range of temperature was achieved for the cremation. The pyre must have reached over 645°C some of the time, hence the white colour of, for example, cranial fragments. However, it appears the extremities and lower leg did not achieve temperatures above 285°C, suggesting that the entire body was not within the hottest part of the cremation pyre.

Fragmentation

The majority of fragmentation occurs after burial and then upon excavation (McKinley 1994), and predominantly occurs along the dehydration fissures which formed during the cremation process. McKinley (1994, 340-1) observed that in a sample of over 4000 cremations, over 50% of bone fragments were in excess of 10 mm in size, with the largest fragment being 134 mm and an average maximum fragment size of 45.2 mm (including immature and disturbed cremations). The largest fragment from Kingshill North was 20 x 12 mm, which is substantially smaller than this and the majority of fragments were within the 5-10 mm fraction. This suggests that there was more than average fragmentation of the cremated bone.

Skeletal biology and palaeopathology

The cremated bone deposit was found to be an adult and from a single individual. A distal femoral condyle fragment appeared to have eburnation on the surface, suggestive of osteoarthritis. A molar crown, unworn but burnt, was recovered and possibly survived the fire (the enamel of teeth usually explodes during the cremation process, leaving only the roots) because it had been impacted or unerupted within the mandible at the time.

Animal Bone

A single unfused cremated femoral head of a small mammal (for example pig, sheep, dog) was recovered from the deposit. It is possible this is an incidental intrusion, as so little of the animal was identifiable. However, it is also possible that a small mammal was included on the pyre. An additional sliver of unburnt animal tooth was also found.

Chapter 5: Medieval and Post-Medieval Finds (Phases 5 and 6)

Medieval and post-medieval pottery *John Cotter*

Introduction

A total of 290 sherds of pottery weighing 3.013 kg were recovered. Apart from just two residual medieval sherds, all the remainder is of post-medieval date, and mostly dates after *c* 1700. In general the pottery is in a very fragmentary and very worn condition apart from some of the more robust Victorian wares. No complete vessel profiles have survived and none of the material has been deemed worthy of illustration, particularly as most of the post-medieval types are commonplace across much of southern England, and better parallels exist. A very similar (though more extensive) range of post-medieval fabrics and vessel forms occur, for instance, at Oxford (Mellor and Oakley 1984). What follows, therefore, is a simply a quantified list of the various fabrics present and a summary report focusing on the more significant or interesting aspects of the assemblage.

Following standard procedures, an intermediate level catalogue of pottery types was constructed for the excavated assemblage and spot-dates produced for each context. The catalogue includes, per context and per pottery fabric, quantification by sherd count and weight. Quantification by rim EVEs (measurable rim percentage) was not considered worthwhile. Details of vessel form, part, decoration and any other features of note were recorded in a comments field. Full details remain in the archive.

Pottery Fabrics

Post-medieval pottery fabrics, which are in the majority here, were recorded using the codes of the Museum of London (LAARC 2007), which can be applied to most post-medieval types in southern England. The rare sherds of medieval pottery here are coded either to the Oxfordshire county type series (Mellor 1994) or the Southampton type series (Brown 2002). The types and quantities occurring at Kingshill North are listed below in roughly chronological order.

OXAM: Brill/Boarstall ware, *c* 1225-1625. Buckinghamshire (Mellor 1994, 111-140). 1 sherd, 5 g. A possible sherd of this identified from a modern topsoil context (8000). The sherd is worn and unglazed with a buff sandy fabric with cream surfaces. Possibly a late medieval example, perhaps 15th or 16th century, rather than earlier. Normally traded in the form of green-glazed jugs.

LV: Laverstock ware, *c* 1230-1350. Wiltshire (Brown 2002, 15). 1 sherd, 26 g. Possibly Laverstock, or something very similar, but not Brill/Boarstall owing to decorative differences. From a furrow containing 19th-century pottery (7523). The slightly worn sherd is from the lower handle junction of jug with part of a rod handle in a fine sandy cream-buff fabric with splashes of clear glaze with green speckles. Down the back of the handle is a vertical row of stabbed circular pits which join a possible horizontal row at the base of the handle.

FREC: Frechen stoneware, *c* 1525-1750. Import, Germany. 2 sherds, 10 g.

BORDB: Surrey/Hampshire white Border ware, brown-glazed, *c* 1650-1700. 1 sherd, 3 g.

PMR: Post-medieval red earthenwares, *c* 1550-1900. Mainly local. 109 sherds, 1779 g.

PMR FLP: Post-medieval red earthenware flowerpot, *c* 1675-2000. Mainly local. 35 sherds, 399 g.

WEST: Westerwald stoneware, *c* 1590-1750. Import, Germany. 4 sherds, 28 g.

TGW: English tin-glazed earthenware, *c* 1575-1825. London, Bristol etc. 1 sherd, 4 g.

CHPO: Chinese porcelain, *c* 1600-1900+ (mainly *c* 1725-1900). Import, China. 2 sherds, 4 g.

ENGS: English brown salt-glazed stoneware, *c* 1670-1900. Bristol, London, Staffordshire. 2 sherds, 29 g.

STMO: Staffordshire-type mottled brown-glazed earthenware, *c* 1680-1800. 3 sherds, 10 g.

STSL: Staffordshire-type combed slipware, *c* 1680-1900. 3 sherds, 6 g.

SWSG: Staffordshire-type white salt-glazed stoneware, *c* 1720-1780. 6 sherds, 18 g.

STBL: Staffordshire-type fine black-glazed earthenware (Jackfield-type), *c* 1740-1780. 1 sherd, 1 g.

ENPO: English porcelain, *c* 1745-1925+. 18 sherds, 79 g.

CREA: Later creamware, *c* 1770-1830. Staffordshire, Leeds, etc. 5 sherds, 7 g.

PEAR SLIP: Pearlware with slip decoration, *c* 1790-1830. Staffordshire etc. 1 sherd, 2 g.

ENGS BL: English salt-glazed stoneware blacking bottles, *c* 1820-1900. London, Bristol, Derbyshire. 5 sherds, 101 g.

ENGS BRST: English stoneware with Bristol glaze, *c* 1835-1900. Bristol, London, etc. 4 sherds, 63 g.

YELL: Yellow wares, *c* 1790-1900. Staffordshire, Derbyshire, etc. 8 sherds, 39 g.

REFW: Refined white earthenwares (including transfer-printed), *c* 1800-1900+. Staffordshire etc. 78 sherds, 400 g.

Summary of the pottery

The two worn and residual medieval sherds are the earliest post-Roman types present here. The Laverstock ware jug handle is of 13th- or 14th-century date; the Brill/Boarstall ware sherd (an import from Buckinghamshire) may be of 15th- or 16th-century date. Minety ware, which is perhaps the commonest medieval coarseware in neighbouring Wiltshire during the period *c* 1100-1550, is curiously absent, but given the very small size of the medieval assemblage this may not be so significant.

The rest of the assemblage is post-medieval and mostly, it would seem, of 18th- and 19th-century date. Although some pottery types (the red earthenwares and the few German stonewares) could in theory be as early as the 16th century, there is nothing in the assemblage here diagnostically earlier than *c* 1640 or *c* 1650. There are in fact only a handful of sherds datable to the 17th- and earlier 18th-centuries and nearly all of these are residual in their contexts, as they occur alongside 19th- or 20th-century wares. Among these are two sherds of German Frechen stoneware, including a rim and part of an applied facemask from a 'Bellarmine' bottle or jug which is probably of mid or later 17th-century date. Although the latter sherd occurs on its own in a pit (8100), its small size and isolation might suggest that it too is residual. A single sherd of brown-glazed Border ware from Surrey/Hampshire probably dates to *c* 1650-1700, but is also residual in a modern topsoil context (7500). The four sherds of German Westerwald stoneware are likewise residual in Victorian contexts. The ware was a common import of the period *c* 1650-1750 and the sherds belong to mugs and possibly jugs with moulded and blue painted decoration. Two small sherds of 18th-century Chinese porcelain and a few small sherds of Staffordshire products of similar date (STSL, STMO, STBL) are also likely to be residual.

The assemblage, however, is dominated by post-medieval red earthenwares (PMR, 109 sherds), mostly of fairly good quality and with a clear brown or greenish glaze internally and sometimes externally. Most vessels have a smooth creamy orange fabric, sometimes with fine streaks of white clay. Most of the surviving rim sherds are quite worn but include large storage jars, wide bowls and dishes, including one probably 18th-century example with traces of incised wavy line decoration on the rim. One or two sherds possibly from drinking vessels and jugs are also present. The most unusual item, probably of 17th- or 18th-century date and thinner and better made, is an enigmatic form, possibly a chafing dish (plate warmer) or a pomander, surviving as a small body sherd with several small perforations made before firing and with a narrow strap handle (8000). These ubiquitous glazed red earthenwares, which are probably of fairly local manufacture, are difficult to date precisely but most

of those here probably date to *c* 1650-1800 with a small number of vessels perhaps purely of 19th-century date. Flowerpots in red earthenware (PMR FLP) are also fairly common (35 sherds). Some of these are definitely 'Victorian' but some earlier-looking examples share the same fabric as the glazed redwares which suggests local manufacture. Two examples have a white slip band painted around or on top of the rim. This type of decoration occurs in a number of redware industries across south central England, including the post-medieval Brill redware industry where this feature is datable to *c* 1750-1830, although the examples here are probably local.

Refined white earthenwares (REFW), mainly from the Staffordshire potteries and dating to the 19th century, comprise the second largest fabric group from the site (78 sherds). These often have blue transfer-printed decoration and occur in the form of tablewares, such as plates, cups, saucers, dishes and jugs and so on. The latest datable item in this ware is part of a mug, possibly as late as *c* 1950-70, which has a polychrome transfer-printed design showing a railway train from around the 1930s or 1940s. There is also part of a late 19th-century pot lid from a preserve jar and part of a Keiller's Dundee marmalade jar, datable to *c* 1862 onwards. The base of a cream stoneware bottle with a clear 'Bristol' glaze bears the maker's stamp, 'POWELL BRISTOL' (*c* 1835-1906), suggesting that this part of Gloucestershire lay within the catchment area of the Bristol stoneware potteries rather than the dominating London potteries. Most of these Victorian and later wares were recovered from furrows and topsoil.

The character of the pre-19th century assemblage, dominated by local coarsewares and with few regional or foreign imports, points to low or, at best, middling prosperity. Given the very worn and mixed nature of the pottery, and the residuality of most earlier pieces, plus the presence of several flowerpots, it is quite likely that most of this material represents ordinary domestic rubbish, some of it perhaps further damaged by ploughing or horticultural activity. It is perhaps likely that most of it was dumped on the site from nearby households over a couple of centuries rather than actually used on the site.

Pipeclay objects and other tobacco pipes
John Cotter

The excavation produced a total of 42 pieces of clay pipe, weighing 103 g, from six contexts (Table 21). The pipes are mostly in a fairly worn condition with no particularly long stem fragments and only three very damaged bowl fragments surviving and three fairly fresh mouthpieces also present. The surviving pipe bowls and measurements of stem bores date the assemblage to between the 17th and the 19th century, but the Bakelite pipe mouthpiece from context (7500) must date after 1907 when this

Table 21: Clay and other pipes

Context	Date	Stem	Bowl	Mouth	Total count	Total weight (g)	Comments
7500	19th C	10	0	1	11	22	Short pieces of narrow stems and mouthpiece mostly with stem bores (SB) c1.5mm or slightly smaller. Some fairly worn
7500	1907-1950+	0	0	1	1	4	Not clay pipe. Damaged black Bakelite mouthpiece tapering at mouth end, socket at other end for attachment to wooden pipe shaft
7502	19th C	9	0	1	10	23	19C narrow stems mostly, with SBs 1.5-2mm. 1x thicker 17/18C stem with maker's mark on top of stem - incuse letters within milled circle 'ED HIGGENS' a Salibury pipemaker active c 1698-1710 (Oswald 1975, 198)
7514	19th C	1	0	0	1	2	Narrow stem with SB c1.5mm
7523	19th C	6	1	0	7	17	Mostly 19C narrow stems with SBs c1.5-2mm. 1 poss L18/E19C worn stem. 1x frag bowl rim prob L18/E19C?
8000	Late 18th/ Early 19th C	5	2	0	7	25	2x fairly narrow but worn stems with SBs c1.8-2mm. Rest of stems thicker with SBs c2.8-3mm incl 2 joining worn stems one with maker's mark 'ED HIGGENS' as in 7502. 2x bowls heels - both worn incl plain circ heel with attached stem prob L17/E18C and v worn bowl frag prob 17C with circular heel bearing traces of a stamp in relief - poss a star?
8031	Late 18th/ Early 19th C	5	0	0	5	10	All worn. Incl 2x fairly narrow stems with SBs c1.8-2mm. Rest very worn prob 17C or E18C with SBs c3mm
TOTAL		36	3	3	42	103	

material was invented. Most of the pipe stems are of narrow diameter and narrow bore and date to the 19th century.

The only significant pieces, residual in their contexts (7502 and 8000), were two identical maker's marks on the backs of two separate stems. These are within a milled circle containing the name 'ED HIGGENS' in incuse lettering. This pipemaker was active in Salisbury c 1698-1710 (Oswald 1975, 198). The three fragmentary pipe bowls include a rim fragment probably of late 18th/early 19th-century date, a heel fragment probably of late 17th/early 18th-century date and a very worn heel fragment bearing a mid-17th century-style stamp underneath, possibly a star in relief (8000).

A single worn piece of pipeclay wig curler, weighing 9 g, was recovered from a topsoil context (7500) containing a range of 17th- to early 20th-century material. The piece represents approximately half of the original object including a solid tapered stem and bulbous terminal (maximum diameter 17 mm) with a flattened end which bears no maker's mark. Wig curlers became popular during the second half of the 17th century (Mellor 1984, 262-3). A 17th- or 18th-century date for this piece seems likely (Fig. 42).

Ceramic building material *Dan Stansbie*

A total of 42 fragments of ceramic building material, weighing 617 g, were recovered during the course of the excavations. The vast majority of this material was recovered from the topsoil and subsoil. The assemblage is dominated by two main fabrics: CBM1 and CBM2, while a third fabric, CBM3, is present in minor amounts.

CBM1: orange poorly mixed sandy clay, containing occasional voids left by organic material

CBM2: orange brown sandy clay, containing occasional voids left by organic material and occasional small fragments *c* 1-2 mm of ironstone and shell

CBM3: orange sandy clay, containing moderate to frequent flecks of silver mica

The majority of the ceramic building material comprises small abraded unidentifiable fragments. However, some post-medieval brick and tile fragments are also present. Two fragments in CBM3 from the fill of plough furrow 7521 may have come from a modern land drain.

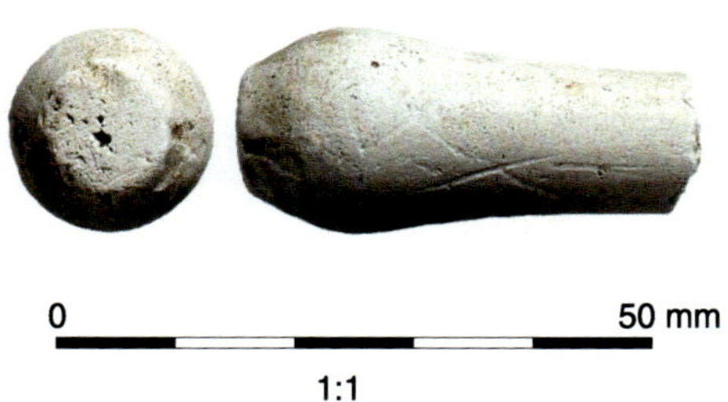

Fig. 42 Pipeclay wig curler

Table 22: Glass: Summary quantification by context and function (fragment count)

Context	wine bottle	bottle	tonic bottle	vessel	window	undiagnostic	Total
7500	1			1			2
7502	1			1			2
7506	1						1
7512	1						1
7514				1			1
7518				2			2
7523				1			1
8000	2	1					3
8035					1		1
8228						7	7
8378				1			1
8390			1				1
8825						1	1
8834						1	1
8844					2		2
8938						1	1
9110						1	1
9148	1						1
Total	7	1	1	7	3	11	30

Glass *Ian Scott*

There were 30 sherds of glass from the site, with no particular concentrations. Glass was found in 18 contexts (Table 22). Twelve contexts produced a single sherd of glass; five contexts produced two sherds and one context three sherds. Only context 8228 produced more than three sherds, but these were all very small and undiagnostic, and were recovered through sieving of soil samples. Altogether four contexts (8228, 8825, 8834 and 8938) produced only very small undiagnostic sherds from soil samples. A fifth context (9110) produced a single blue glass sherd with thick cordon or ridge. It is undiagnostic to form, but was possibly from a vessel.

Eleven of the 30 sherds of glass are undiagnostic, that is they cannot be assigned to window, vessel, or other class of glass find. The remaining 19 sherds include seven sherds from wine bottles. Most of these sherds were weathered and from thick-walled bottles dating before the later 19th century. The form of the bottles in most cases is unclear because the sherds are too small. One wine bottle sherd (context 8000) was not weathered and was probably from a modern wine bottle. The same context also produced a single body sherd from a bottle of oval section with moulded vertical reeded decoration. This was a machine-moulded bottle of late 19th-century or early 20th-century date. Context 8390 produced a base sherd from a moulded rectangular, or flattened octagonal, section tonic or medicine bottle.

None of the sherds identified as 'vessel' could be identified to form. Many of the sherds were heavily weathered with iridescent deposits on the surfaces and sometimes on the broken edges. None of the sherds, with the possible exception of two opaque white sherds from context 7518, need be later in date than the 19th century.

There were three sherds of window glass, none of them modern float glass. One small sherd of window glass (context 8035) is light olive green in colour. The other two sherds (context 8844) were darker olive green in colour and may have been from the same sheet of glass. The larger of the two sherds has a clear straight, thickened and rounded edge, which is diagnostic of cast glass. The smaller piece from context 8844 was slightly thinner but of the same colour. Again it is probably a piece of cast window glass. In Britain, cast window glass is found in contexts dating from the Roman period, but also from the 17th to 19th century contexts. The distinctive edge piece might be Roman in date, although Roman cast glass generally has one distinctly matt face and one glossy face. The sherd from context 8844 has a similar gloss on both faces, and is probably later in date. Given that 8844 was a Phase 4a occupation deposit, the glass is likely to have been intrusive even if it were of Roman date.

Chapter 6: Environmental Evidence

Animal bone *Lena Strid and Rebecca Nicholson*

Introduction

The animal bone assemblage consisted of a total of 8697 re-fitted fragments from securely dated contexts. Of these, 5539 fragments (63.7%) were hand collected and 3158 fragments (36.3%) were recovered from sieved bulk samples. The majority of the sieved remains were unidentifiable to taxa. While the site contained features from the late Neolithic up to the modern period, the bulk of the assemblage was late Neolithic and late Iron Age/early Roman. The scarcity of features more recent than early Roman suggests that the settlement was abandoned at the end of the early Roman period. The bones from later Roman and post-medieval features are included in overall tables, but will not be discussed further.

The bones were identified using a comparative skeletal reference collection in addition to standard osteological identification manuals, such as Bacher (1967), Cohen and Serjeantson (1996), Hillson (1992), Schmid (1972) and Woelfe (1967). All the animal remains were counted and weighed, and where possible identified to species, element, side and zone. For zoning, Serjeantson (1996) was used, with the addition of mandible zones by Worley (forthcoming). Sheep and goat were identified to species where possible, using Boessneck *et al.* (1964) and Prummel and Frisch (1986). They were otherwise classified as 'sheep/goat'. Long bone fragments, ribs and vertebrae, with the exception for atlas and axis, were classified by size, 'large mammal' representing cattle, horse and deer, 'medium mammal' representing sheep/goat, pig and large dog, 'small mammal' representing small dog, cat and hare, and 'microfauna' representing animals such as frog, rat and mice.

The general condition of the bones/context was graded on a 6-point system (0-5). Grade 0 equating to very well preserved bone, and grade 5 indicating that the bone had suffered such structural and attritional damage as to make it unrecognisable. For ageing, Habermehl's (1975) data on epiphyseal fusion was used. Cattle horn cores were aged according to Armitage (1982), using texture and appearance of the horn core surface. Tooth wear was recorded using Grant's tooth wear stages (Grant 1982), and correlated with tooth eruption (Habermehl 1975). In order to estimate an age for the animals, the methods of Halstead (1985), Payne (1973) and O'Connor (1988) were used for cattle, sheep/goat and pig respectively. Sexable elements, that is, cattle and sheep pelves, pig canine teeth and deer antlers were recorded, using data from Boessneck *et al.* (1964), Prummel and Frisch (1986), Schmid (1972) and Vretemark (1997). Observance of medullary bone in birds were used to indicate the presence of egg-laying hens. Measurements were taken according to von den Driesch (1976), using digital callipers with an accuracy of 0.01 mm. Large bones were measured using an osteometric board, with an accuracy of 1 mm.

Overview of assemblage

The assemblage is dominated by domestic mammals, mainly cattle, sheep/goat and pig. There was secure identification of sheep in the late Neolithic (Phase 1), mid-late Iron Age (Phase 3), late Iron Age/early Roman and early Roman assemblages (Phase 4). Goat was only identified in the Neolithic and the early Roman assemblages, in both cases from horn core fragments. Considering the general scarcity of goat compared with sheep in Iron Age and Roman assemblages (King 1991, 16), it is likely that the majority of the sheep/goat remains belong to sheep. Game is only found in the Neolithic phase. Bones from commensal microfauna were recovered from features of several periods. However, because these animals often burrow, they may be later inclusions. Bird bones are rare and with

Table 23: Animal bone: Preservation level for bones from all phases

Phase	n	0 Excellent	1 Good	2 Fair	3 Poor	4 Very poor	5 Extremely poor
Late Neolithic	5556	2.50%	5.00%	20.10%	47.80%	24.60%	-
Beaker-Bronze Age	298	-	2.70%	14.10%	79.50%	3.70%	-
Mid Iron Age	506	7.30%	25.30%	41.30%	24.10%	2.00%	-
Late Iron Age	256	1.20%	9.00%	35.20%	41.40%	13.30%	-
Late Iron Age / Early Roman	1137	0.90%	8.10%	28.30%	46.80%	15.90%	-
Early Roman	775	0.30%	3.90%	40.80%	45.30%	9.80%	-
Late Roman	73	4.10%	63.00%	12.30%	16.40%	4.10%	-

Table 24: Animal bone: Gnawed and burnt bones from all phases

Phase	n	Gnawed bones	Gnawed bones (%)	Burnt bones	Burnt bones (%)
Late Neolithic	5556	6	0.1%	613	11.0%
Beaker-Bronze Age	298			9	3.0%
Mid Iron Age	506	5	1.0%	93	18.4%
Late Iron Age	256	5	2.0%	24	9.4%
Late Iron Age / Early Roman	1137	13	1.1%	29	2.6%
Early Roman	775	4	0.5%	13	1.7%
Late Roman	73	1	1.4%		
Post-medieval - modern	23			3	1.3%
TOTAL	8624	34	0.4%	784	9.1%

Table 25: Animal bones by feature type from all phases

Phase	n	Pit	Ditch	Gully	Burial	Spread	Posthole
Late Neolithic	5556	5556					
Beaker-Bronze Age	298		26		273		
Mid Iron Age	506	506					
Late Iron Age	256		241	2		3	10
Late Iron Age / Early Roman	1137	300	834				1
Early Roman	775	590	163	12		10	
Late Roman	73		73				
Post-medieval - modern	23	18					
TOTAL	8624						

the exception of domestic fowl in the post-medieval assemblage, all avian remains are from wild birds. A single fish bone, an eel vomer, was recovered from a late Roman sieved sample. Eel is a very common fish in Roman assemblages (Locker 2007).

Overall, bone preservation level is fair to poor (Table 23), which has implications for the recognition of thin cut marks and minor pathologies. It is therefore highly likely that the relatively small number of recorded butchery marks and pathologies is due to the condition of the bone. Gnawed bones were rare (Table 24), but again this is likely to be skewed by bone condition in the Neolithic assemblage, where almost a quarter of all bones had no visible original surface. The frequency of gnawed bones in assemblages from other periods is more likely to be accurate, as there are few difficulties in observing traces from gnawing on bones which are fairly or moderately poorly preserved. Burnt bones are relatively abundant in the late Neolithic and the late Iron Age/early Roman assemblages. The fragments were fairly evenly distributed between features; no discrete bone dumps were identified (Table 25).

Phase 1 – Late Neolithic

The late Neolithic assemblage came from a range of pits spread across the site. Pig, followed by cattle,

was the most common animal in the assemblage, regardless of quantification method (Table 26). Since pigs are often under-represented in bone assemblages, particularly where bone preservation is poor, this suggests that pigs were indeed an important source of meat. The dominance of pig is in great contrast to the mid- and late-Neolithic site at Horcott Pit, some 15 km further east, where cattle dominate (Evans 2009, 108). Assemblages dominated by pig bones have often been interpreted as evidence for feasting, possibly indicating a display of wealth (Serjeantson 2006, 119). However, other important factors to consider include bone condition, local environment and feature type. Normally, denser bones such as those from large mammals and adult individuals survive better than bones from smaller mammals and juveniles, and the more porous pig bones are often under-represented (Lyman 1994, 289; Symmons 2005). Studies of Iron Age and Roman assemblages have shown that sites dominated by ditches are often dominated by bones from large mammals, whereas sites dominated by pits tend to be richer in medium mammal bones (Rielly 2009, 206). However, since the Neolithic assemblages from both Kingshill North and Horcott derive exclusively from pits, in this case it is probable that differences in the local environment may have been a significant factor determining the difference in species dominance. Sheep and goats are more suited than cattle to dry hill land with poorer pasture quality, whereas cattle prefer pastures on heavy wetland soils (Davis 1987, 181; Hamilakis 2000, 279). Pigs, on the other hand, can be fed exclusively on kitchen waste, but are traditionally associated with fattening on acorns and beech mast (Albarella 2006, 77). The site of Kingshill North lies on the border between the Cotswolds and the river valleys of the Thames and its tributaries, and the inhabitants could therefore use both the forested hills of the Cotswolds for pannage and sheep pasture and the Churn river valley for cattle pasture. In contrast, Horcott, which lies further from the Cotswolds and near the river Coln, lies in a catchment area more suited to the grazing of cattle.

In contrast to later periods, where sheep are more commonly found than goat (Hambleton 1999, 14), there is little evidence for the inter-species relationship between sheep and goats on the British mainland in the Neolithic (Clutton-Brock 1989). The fact that four horn core fragments were recovered from pit (8058), possibly from the same individual, would therefore be a useful addition to the existing data.

Epiphyseal fusion data is largely consistent with ageing data from dental eruption and wear; cattle and sheep/goat were mainly slaughtered as adults, whereas most pigs were younger than 1.5 years when slaughtered (Tables 27-30). This is also the case at Horcott, suggesting that despite a focus on different species, the actual animal husbandry in this region was very similar. Pigs, with their great fecundity, were kept solely for meat and slaughtered young. Cattle were mostly used for pulling ards and milking, while sheep/goat provided milk and, in the case of sheep, wool. At this date, wool would have been removed by plucking or combing rather than by clipping; Neolithic sheep are thought to have been similar to the Soay, which have an annual moult (Ryder 1964). Surplus animals were probably culled as sub-adults. The dental evidence for ageing caprines is scant at both sites, but suggest that sheep/goats were not kept to advanced ages.

Table 26: Number of identified bones/taxon by chronological phase. MNI is within parentheses.

Species	Neolithic	Beaker-Bronze Age	Middle Iron Age	Late Iron Age	Late Iron Age Early Roman	Early Roman	Late Roman	Post-med - Modern
Cattle	121 (4)	271 (1)	11(2)	30 (2)	69 (3)	70 (3)	1 (1)	
Sheep/goat	93 (3)		40 (4)	22 (1)	142 (7)	118 (4)	1 (1)	2 (1)
Sheep	2		3		2	7		
Goat	4					1		
Pig	538 (10)	1 (1)	2 (1)	3 (1)	8 (2)	5 (1)		
Horse			2 (1)	3 (1)	24 (2)	18 (2)	2 (1)	
Dog	2 (1)		93 (2)		4 (1)	1 (1)	1 (1)	
Dog/fox	1							
Rabbit								1 (1)
?Aurochs	2 (1)							
Red deer	1 (1)							
Roe deer	9 (1)							
Deer sp.	63	1						
House mouse								
Mouse sp.	2							
Field vole	13 (2)		1 (1)					
Bank vole / Field vole	5		1					
Shrew sp.	1							
Domestic fowl								3 (1)
Crow / Rook			25 (2)					
Raven					1 (1)			
Indet. bird	2				1			5
Amphibian	1				3			
Eel							1 (1)	
Microfauna	61		10		4		1	
Small mammal	20				1	1		
Medium mammal	441		95	30	76	85	3	
Large mammal	211	2	16	15	112	101	53	
Indeterminate	3963	23	207	153	690	368	10	12
Total fragment count (NISP)	5556	298	506	256	1137	775	73	23
Total weight (g)	14015	2449	1122	1404	9047	6901	344	23

Table 27. Animal bons, all phases: dental analysis of cattle, using Halstead (1985)

Phase	n	0-1 months	1-8 months	8-18 months	18-30 months	30-36 months	Young adult	Adult	Old adult	Senile
Neolithic	1							1		
Bronze Age	2								2	
MIA										
LIA										
LIA/ER	3			1		1		1		
ER	4			1		2		1		

Table 28. Animal boes, all phases: dental analysis of sheep/goat, using Payne (1973)

Phase	n	0-2 months	2-6 months	6-12 months	1-2 years	2-3 years	3-4 years	4-6 years	6-8 years	8-10 years
Neolithic	3				1		2			
EIA-MIA	1						1			
LIA	1								1	
LIA/ER	9		2	1	3	2		1		
ER	8			1	1	1	1	3	1	

Table 29. Animal bones, all phases: dental analysis of pig, using O'Connor (1988)

Phase	n	Juvenile	Immature	Sub-adult	Adult	Elderly
Neolithic	11	3	7	1		
MIA	1		1			
LIA						
LIA/ER	1				1	
ER						

Deliberate slaughter of juvenile animals for meat or to free milk for dairy production is tentatively suggested by several neonatal and juvenile bones from cattle, sheep/goat and pig. However, these may represent natural mortalities, implying that breeding animals were kept close to, or within, the settlement. The other domesticated species, dog, is present in small numbers. Judging by epiphyseal fusion and bone surface structure, all dogs were fully grown at the time of their death. While butchery marks were absent, the use of dog meat for human consumption cannot be excluded.

Game is represented by aurochs, red deer and roe deer bones. A further 47 antler fragments were also present. The aurochs bones consist of one second phalanx (9101) and one femur fragment (8814). The femur is unfused and therefore cannot be measured. It is, however, of a similar size as a modern fused cattle femur, which is far larger than domestic Neolithic cattle. Measurements from the phalanx (Table 31) fall in between measurements from male and female aurochsen from Denmark (Degerbøl 1970, 124-125). Generally, animals on islands are smaller than their continental counterparts due to genetic isolation (Magnell 2006, 58-59). This suggests that the aurochs from Kingshill North may have been male, although due to the scarcity of comparative measurements from British aurochsen, this must be regarded as a tentative interpretation. Aurochs (*Bos primigenius*) bones are rarely found on sites in England which post-date the Neolithic and they seem to have become extinct in Britain by the end of the second millennium BC (Lynch *et al.* 2008; Yalden 1999, 128-129). Stable isotope analysis of aurochs and cattle bones from British Neolithic sites supports the hypothesis that aurochs inhabited a forested landscape while domestic cattle lived on open grassland, although the authors note that the results could also indicate that aurochs inhabited wetland rather than forest (Lynch *et al.* 2008, 1033). Six red deer antlers and one roe deer antler included a shed burr, indicating that they had been collected in spring for antler working or to be used as pickaxes or hoes (cf. Clutton-Brock 1982). One pig third metatarsal (9151) and one pig third phalanx (9101) were noted during recording as being very large and could possibly be from wild boar. However, as these were not measurable, it was not possible to confirm or reject this hypothesis. The small number of bones from wild mammals indicates that hunting would have provided a minor supplement to a diet focused on dairy products and meat from domestic mammals together with grain and vegetable-based produce (Serjeantson 2006, 121-122).

Deposits of articulated animal remains from Neolithic sites are rare (Morris 2008, 66-67). Kingshill North included one such deposit, that of a neonatal pig. The pig was found in the single fill (8819) of pit 8455 together with a mixture of disar-

Table 30. Animal bones, all phases: Epiphyseal closure of cattle, sheep/goat, pig and horse. Articulated skeletons excluded.

| | Neolithic | | BA | | EIA-MIA | | LIA | | LIA/ER | | ER | |
	n%	unfused	n%	unfused	n%	unfused	n%	unfused	n%	unfused	n%	unfused
CATTLE												
Early fusion	13	7.7%	2	0.0%			2	0.0%	11	0.0%	3	0.0%
Mid fusion	14	14.3%					2	50.0%	9	33.3%	4	25.0%
Late fusion	3	33.3%							2	0.0%	6	16.7%
SHEEP/GOAT												
Early fusion	5	20.0%			2	0%	1	0.0%	8	25.0%	3	33.3%
Mid fusion	2	0.0%							2	50.0%	7	28.6%
Late fusion	9	0.0%			1	0%			4	50.0%		
PIG												
Early fusion	17	41.2%							1	0.0%		
Mid fusion	52	94.2%									2	100.0%
Late fusion	9	67.7%							1	100.0%		
HORSE												
Early fusion							1	0.0%	7	0.0%	3	0.0%
Mid fusion							1	0.0%				
Late fusion									2	0.0%	3	33.3%

Table 31. Measurements of the second phalanx from aurochs in the Neolithic Kingshill North assemblage compared with aurochsen from Denmark (Degerbøl 1970)

Site	Species	Bone	Measurement	n	Mean	Min	Max
Kingshill North	Aurochs	Phalanx 2		1	53.4		
Kingshill North	Aurochs	Phalanx 2	Bp	1	37.1		
Denmark (male)	Aurochs	Phalanx 2	Bp	7	40.9	39.0	43.0
Demark (female)	Aurochs	Phalanx 2	Bp	6	33.8	32.0	36.0
Kingshill North	Aurochs	Phalanx 2	Bd (estimated)	1	(30.2)		
Denmark (male)	Aurochs	Phalanx 2	Bd	6	35.2	33.0	38.0
Demark (female)	Aurochs	Phalanx 2	Bd	6	28.9	27.0	31.0
Kingshill North	Aurochs	Phalanx 2	SD	1	28.1		
Denmark (male)	Aurochs	Phalanx 2	SD	8	32.4	31.0	34.0
Demark (female)	Aurochs	Phalanx 2	SD	9	26.6	26.0	28.0

Table 32. Greatest length and greatest distal width of cattle and sheep/goat bones in the Neolithic Kingshill North assemblage and contemporary sites in Britain (ABMAP)

Site	Species	Bone	Measurement	n	Mean	Min	Max
Kingshill North	Cattle	Metatarsal	Bd	4	53.3	52.1	54.4
ABMAP (E-L Neolithic)		Metatarsal	Bd	4	57.8	53.5	63.2
Kingshill North	Cattle	Tibia	Bd	3	64.3	62.5	67.2
ABMAP (E-L Neolithic)		Tibia	Bd	6	66.8	59.6	72.5
Kingshill North	Sheep/goat	Tibia	Bd	2	25.5	25.3	25.7
ABMAP (E-L Bronze Age)		Tibia	Bd	4	22.6	21.2	23.5
ABMAP (E-L Iron Age)		Tibia	Bd	54	22.7	19.9	25.4
ABMAP (Early Roman)		Tibia	Bd	67	23.1	20.0	29.8
ABMAP (Late Roman)		Tibia	Bd	101	25.4	20.1	29.8

ticulated animal bone, pottery sherds and flint sherds. The context record does not note whether the pig was fully articulated in the pit or not, but most body parts were present. While butchery marks were absent, this should not be regarded as evidence that the piglet was not eaten, as experiments have shown that butchery marks may be absent on bones from carcasses that were butchered and filleted (Strid 2000, 37).

The measurable bones were few, but some tentative conclusions can be made from inter-site comparisons. The Kingshill North cattle were within the same size range as animals from contemporary sites in south-western England (Table 32). There were no comparable sheep/goat measurements from Neolithic sites. A comparison with British sites from later periods showed that the Kingshill North sheep were the same as late Roman sheep. Whether this size difference is attributable to a difference in breed or (more likely at this date) in sex composition is unclear, owing to the small numbers of bones.

Butchery marks were recorded on bones from cattle, pig and indeterminate medium mammal. Cut marks on tarsal bones and proximal metapodials, indicating disarticulation of the lower legs, occurred on both cattle and pig. Cut marks from skinning were only found on one distal cattle metacarpal. Longitudinal splitting to facilitate marrow extraction was recorded on two cattle long bones. Evidence of filleting was noted on one pig radius and on two ribs from medium mammal. One rib from a piglet or lamb had been chopped off near the vertebral column. Taken as a group, the butchery marks provide evidence of skinning, disarticulation, portioning and filleting of the carcass. The scarcity of butchery marks is not surprising, partly because of the poor bone condition in this phase, and partly because even with good bone preservation, not all bones from food waste display butchery marks (Magnell 2003).

An articulating radius and ulna from sheep/goat were the only bones in the Neolithic assemblage that displayed pathological conditions. A smooth bone growth was recorded on the lateral edge of ulna/radius joint surface of the radius and on the corresponding part of the ulna; the aetiology is uncertain. The ulna can fuse naturally to the radius, and it may be the beginning of this process which is observed here.

Phase 2 – Beaker to Bronze Age

The Phase 2 assemblage derives from three features: a Beaker burial (8588), its associated ring ditch (8454), and middle Bronze Age burial 1905 (Table 26).

A total of 270 cattle bone fragments were recovered from contexts 8589 and 8641, the upper fills of burial 8588. With the exception of a distal scapula fragment, the cattle remains derived exclusively from the head and lower feet, but it is not possible

to tell whether the head and feet belong to the same animal. However, while such an assemblage would normally suggest butchery waste, the position on top of a human burial makes it more likely that the bones represent a hide with these elements intact. Using Halstead's interpretation of dental wear, the cattle falls in the age range Old Adult (Table 27). The metapodials were too fragmented to be measured for withers' height or calculation of the animal's sex (cf. Mennerich 1968). Transverse cutmarks were observed on a lateral metapodial, traces from the disarticulation of the metapodial from the upper leg. The lack of pathologies suggests that the animal may not have been used intensively for heavy traction.

There are no other similar 'head and hooves' deposits of animal bones in association with human burials at Kingshill North. Neolithic and Bronze Age 'head and hooves' burials are relatively common in continental Europe, but they occur only rarely in Britain (Piggott 1962; Pollex 1999). Three known British examples are Fussell's Lodge, a Neolithic long barrow in Wiltshire (Ashbee 1966), Bishop's Cannings (Robertson-Mackay 1980) and Barrow Hills (Barclay and Halpin 1999), two early Bronze Age barrow mounds in Wiltshire and Oxfordshire respectively. Fussell's Lodge contained one set of cattle head and hooves within the burial chamber. Unfortunately, it is again not possible to say with certainty that the skull and foot bones came from the same animal, as they were not immediately adjacent. The metapodials in this case were fused, and would thus derive from an animal of at least two years of age. Butchery marks were not noted, but whether this is due to poor recording or genuine absence is not certain (Morris 2008, 78-79). The cattle remains at Bishop's Cannings comprised a skull, four metapodials and associated phalanges, which were placed together in the fill at the edge of the burial cut. All teeth were well worn, and the incisor wear suggested an age of 6-10 years. A metric analysis of skull and horncore suggested that the animal was female. Butchery marks were not noted (Morris 2008, 87; Grigson 1980, 164-167). The cattle remains at Barrow Hills comprised one horn core and one metatarsus, which were placed in the ditch around the barrow, thus removed from the main burial. There was no information regarding the age of the animal (Barclay and Halpin 1999, 156; Williams 1948).

The rarity of head and hooves burials in Britain is intriguing. Were these burial goods the exclusive privilege of a certain group in society, connected to religious beliefs or social status? It has been argued that the hide in itself may have been the valuable item, and burials with cattle hides that did not contain attached skeletal elements would be invisible in the archaeological material (Morris 2008, 87).

A small number of animal bones, which included one cattle molar, one cattle second phalanx, one pig calcaneus and one deer antler fragment, derived from the ring-ditch that surrounded burial 8588 (group 8454). Apart from the fragmented piece of shed deer antler, possibly waste from antler working, the remains suggest butchery waste and kitchen waste disposal.

The second burial with animal grave goods was 1905. This middle Bronze Age burial included the lower torso of a sheep placed on the deceased's left side near the head. The sacrum was complete, indicating that this was not two separate leg joints being placed in the grave. Context records show that parts of the context had been excavated before it was discovered that it was an articulate animal burial. The presence of further sheep remains in the burial fill – one axis, one left mandible, one right radius, one left ulna and one right metacarpal – suggests that an entire sheep/goat that was deposited in the grave originally. The burial cut was rather shallow, only 0.39 m deep, suggesting that plough damage may have been responsible for the disarticulation of the remains. All sheep bones were fused, indicating an age-at-death of more than 3.5 years. Morphological traits on the pelvis indicated that the animal was female. The bone condition was poor and butchery marks could not be observed. The burial fill also contained one cattle metatarsal fragment, which may be an accidental inclusion. Middle Bronze Age burials are very rare in Britain (Healy pers.comm.) and it is therefore difficult to compare this animal deposit with similar contexts. Animals have been deposited in graves from both earlier and later periods (Mannermaa 2008; Whimster 1981, 106); they may have been remains from a funeral feast or may have been intended as food for the afterlife.

Phases 3 and 4 – Iron Age and early Roman

The Iron Age and early Roman group consists of four phased assemblages (Phases 3 and 4a-d). Each contains fewer than 300 fragments in total from the three major domesticates, as well as fewer than a minimum of 30 individuals (MNI), thus rendering any comparison between these taxa and groups tentative regardless of quantification method (Hambleton 1999, 39). Nevertheless, with the exception of the late Iron Age assemblage (Phase 4a/b), where cattle dominated slightly, sheep/goat was consistently the most common taxa (see Table 26). This was particularly true for the late Iron Age/early Roman (Phase 4c) and early Roman (Phase 4d) assemblages, where sheep/goat were strongly dominant. As the Phase 4c assemblage is dominated by bones recovered from ditches and the Phase 4d assemblage mostly derived from pits, assemblage differentiation between feature types is not likely to be a major reason for the sheep/goat dominance in the later phases.

Livestock

In general, a predominance of sheep/goat has been seen as typical of native British sites, whereas cattle and pig dominated Romanised settlements (King 1991, 17). This is, however, a simplified definition. Apart from the possible bias from feature type representation (see above), the local environment may favour different species. Dry hill land is, for example, more suitable for sheep than cattle (Davis 1987, 181). Neither of these hypotheses takes into account trade in live animals, which may skew the remaining animal bone assemblages.

Nearby contemporary sites show a great variation in species frequency. The dominance of cattle at the Iron Age settlement of Duntisbourne Grove may be caused by skewed recovery, since over 95% of the bones came from ditches. The intra-site ratio of sheep and pig is probably more accurate, as environmental studies indicate a woodland environment, more suited for pig than sheep (Powell 1999, 431-433). A similar environment is suggested for Middle Duntisbourne, which is consistent with its relatively high ratio of pig (Powell 1999, 437). The other Cotswold site, the Ditches enclosure, is also dominated by cattle, although there is a large intra-site variation in species abundance between different areas of the excavation area (Rielly 2009, 196-197).

All the comparative sites in the region – Ashton Keynes, Longdoles Field and Warrens Field (Cotswold Water Park), Latton Lands, Cotswold Community – were dominated by cattle, except for the small mid-late Iron Age phase of Cotswold Community, where sheep were most frequent (Knight 2007; Poole 2009; Strid 2010; Sykes 2007a; Sykes 2007b). The consistent abundance of cattle and scarcity of pig suggests a landscape with open fields and few, if any, large areas of woodland. The predominance of sheep/goat for at Cotswold Community may be due to a decrease of wetland pastures or an increased importance of wool production (Strid 2010, 237).

Dental ageing data for cattle and pig from Kingshill North were scarce, a reflection of the small assemblages sizes, and no particular age-at-death pattern could be discerned Tables 27 & 29). Ageable sheep/goat mandibles were more common and displayed a wide range of slaughter ages. Phase 4c shows a peak in young sheep/goats, whereas Phase 4d was dominated by slightly older animals. It is, however, unclear whether this reflects a true change of emphasis in sheep/goat husbandry, or whether the imprecise dating of Phase 4c has generated a false data pattern (Table 28). Epiphyseal fusion suggests that most cattle and sheep/goats were slaughtered as sub-adults or adults. In contrast, as is usually the case, pigs were generally slaughtered before they were fully skeletally matured (Table 30). The lack of older cattle may suggest cattle husbandry to a larger extent focused on meat production and less on the use of cattle for traction. However, the sample size is small and, in Phase 4d, there is a distinct possibility that live cattle were sold to the Roman military fort at Cirencester. Most cattle in the early levels of Cirencester were 1-5 years of age, representing prime meat (Thawley

1982, 214). Most sheep/goats were killed as sub-adult and young adults, which suggests a sheep/goat husbandry which was mostly focused on a combined meat-, dairy- and wool-production. As such, the sheep would yield one or two years' worth of wool clips before slaughter, as well as provide two to four lambs to replenish the herd. The dental data from the Phase 4d provide evidence that several individuals were kept past four years of age, suggesting that wool production became an increasingly important part of a sheep husbandry. It would be tempting to connect this to developments in Cirencester, which would be a market for several types of goods that the military itself could not produce.

Juvenile animals were relatively uncommon. A total of 48 lamb bones were deposited in Phase 4c enclosure ditch 8413. Three astragali displayed cut marks from disarticulation of the lower limbs or from skinning. Skinning cut marks are on their own not necessarily an indication that the animals were eaten, but as no articulated remains were noted during excavation of the ditch, it would suggest that the lamb remains represented food waste. In contrast, only one calf bone was recovered. A total of four bones in the Phase 4c assemblage could be sexed: one cattle and two sheep/goat pelves, and one pig maxillary canine, all deriving from females. However, the sample size was too small to yield any useful information regarding animal husbandry.

From the above we can tentatively conclude that during the Iron Age and early Roman periods, animal husbandry at Kingshill North functioned at subsistence level, where surplus young animals were culled for meat, and the remainder were kept for a few more years during which they yielded wool and milk. Cattle were also used for traction. This kind of strategy appears to have been fairly typical for contemporary rural settlements in the Cotswolds as well as in the Thames valley, although a variation of this strategy is suggested for late Iron Age/early Roman sites such as Longdoles Field, Cotswold Community and Ditches. Longdoles Field

and Cotswold Community have an almost equal amount of young and old cattle (Sykes 2007a; Strid 2010), suggesting that here the use of secondary products became more important.

It has been argued that the increase of cattle that was associated with Romanisation was not so much related to the increase of beef consumption, but rather reflected the increased use of cattle for traction following an expansion in arable land needed to feed a growing population (Grant 1989, 138). At the Ditches, north of Cirencester, the bone assemblage contained a large number of old cattle, almost 70% being five years or older (Rielly 2009, 201). Most of the sexable cattle were female, suggesting that an important focus of the Ditches economy was dairy products. Rielly hypothesises that cheese could have been sold to the Roman military fort in Cirencester (Rielly 2009, 207). Similar trade has not been observable for Kingshill North, but since the settlement was abandoned after or during the early Roman period, there may have been little time for any changes in animal husbandry to leave traces in the bone assemblage.

Although the number of measureable bones was small, the Kingshill North cattle and sheep/goats appear to be within the same size range as animals from contemporary sites in the region (Table 33). Elsewhere, a size increase in domestic livestock has been reported from other parts of Britain and the Netherlands during the Roman period (Dobney 2001, 38-39).

Butchery marks were recorded on a total of 13 bones from cattle, sheep/goat, large and medium mammal. As expected in a rural Iron Age and early Roman settlement, the main disarticulation of the carcass was carried out with knives (Maltby 2007, 60-61). Cut marks were mainly placed at long bone ends, although cut marks also occurred on the shaft of one sheep/goat humerus and one long bone from a large mammal, the latter consistent with filleting. Chop marks were only noted twice, both on the coronoid process of two cattle mandibles, indicating disarticulation of the jaw.

Table 33. Greatest length and greatest distal width of cattle and sheep/goat bones in the late Iron Age - early Roman Kingshill North assemblage and contemporary sites in Britain (ABMAP 2003)

Site	Species	Bone	Measurement	n	Mean	Min	Max
Kingshill North	Cattle	Metatarsal	GL	1	219.5		
ABMAP (LIA-ER)		Metatarsal	GL	18	207.0	188.4	234.2
Kingshill North	Cattle	Tibia	Bd	3	57.7	53.3	61.2
ABMAP (LIA-ER)		Tibia	Bd	101	55.6	47.2	76.0
Kingshill North	Sheep/goat	Metatarsal	GL	1	126.9		
ABMAP (LIA-ER)		Metatarsal	GL	8	130.6	110.0	147.5
Kingshill North	Sheep/goat	Metatarsal	Bd	1	20.2		
ABMAP (LIA-ER)		Metatarsal	Bd	18	20.8	16.5	24.1
Kingshill North	Sheep/goat	Tibia	Bd	1	21.2		
ABMAP (LIA-ER)		Tibia	Bd	100	23.0	19.9	29.8

Pathological conditions were rarely observed in the material. Infected molar roots (Baker and Brothwell 1980, 150) were recorded on one Phase 4a/b and one Phase 4c sheep/goat mandible, while bone absorption at the fourth premolar and first molar was seen on one Phase 4d sheep/goat mandible. The last case suggests infection of the gum, possibly from food lodged between its teeth (Baker and Brothwell 1980, 153).

Other animals

Apart from possibly intrusive microfauna, other animals in the Kingshill North assemblage included only horse, dog and corvid. Notably, articulated skeletons of a dog and a corvid were recovered from the base of middle Iron Age pit 8851 (see below); otherwise, dog remains were rare. Judging by epiphyseal fusion and bone surface structure, all dogs were adult or sub-adult at the time of death, and the absence of pathologies suggests that they were not obviously maltreated. Horse remains were more common in the assemblage, and were more frequent than pig in the later phases. Apart from an unfused distal radius, indicating an age at death of less than 3.5 years, all bones were from skeletally mature animals. This supports Harcourt's hypothesis that in the Iron Age, horses were kept in feral free-ranging herds, and captured and broken in as adults when the need arose (Harcourt 1979, 158). Cut marks were not observed on either dog or horse remains, and probably neither animal was eaten. A few examples of cut marks from disarticulation and/or filleting on horse and dog bones have been observed on contemporary sites (Knight 2007; Wilson *et al.* 1978, 125), although when viewing Iron Age and early Roman assemblages overall, these are clearly rare incidents, possibly connected to hunger periods or ritual/medicinal use of the meat (Maltby 1996, 23-24). One Phase 4c horse atlas had ossified ligament attachments at the dorsal side of the cranial joint surface, which may be a sign of muscle strain. Perhaps the animal had been used to power a quern, preventing it from moving its head freely. The absence of game at Kingshill North is consistent with other Iron Age and early Roman assemblages in the Cirencester region, suggesting that hunting was a rare pastime.

A deposit of particular interest is the articulated skeletons of a dog and a corvid (crow/rook, *Corvus corone/frugilegus*) in the base of Phase 3 pit 8851. A radiocarbon date on the corvid distal humerus and carpometacarpus gave a date of 394-209 cal BC (95%; NZA-33476). The dog and corvid skeletons were mostly complete and the lack of some skeletal elements is probably due to retrieval or taphonomic factors. Despite using Tomek and Bochenski's (2000) manual for species identification of corvid bones, the morphological traits were inconclusive regarding crow or rook. Measurement of the dog bones provided an estimated withers' height of 52 cm, which is in the average range for Iron Age dogs (Harcourt 1974, 162). Specialised physical types of

dog seem not to have been available in Britain until the Roman period (Harcourt 1974), and we may assume that this was an all-round working dog, possible bred for herding or guarding purposes.

Deposition of complete animals in pits are commonly found in Britain throughout the Iron Age, although the interpretation has varied between disposal of a dead animal not fit for consumption to deposit of a ritual nature (Hill 1995, 28). Cunliffe has argued that the placement of sacrifices in the bottom of storage pits was connected to the appeasement of chthonic spirits and deities (Cunliffe 2003, 146-147). This hypothesis fits well into the symbol of the dog as a guardian, thus extending its role in living society to the spirit world (cf. Smith 2006, 12-13). Dogs are indeed rather common in Iron Age articulated burial groups, whereas birds are relatively rare (Morris 2008, 103, 110; Smith 2006, 13). Of the wild birds, raven is the most frequent species, although one complete and two partial crows/rook skeletons were found at Owslebury (Morris 2008, 103-104, 169). Corvids have in many cultures, including Celtic and Roman, been linked to death and the underworld, and it may be in this aspect that they were considered suitable for sacrifice (Serjeantson and Morris 2011, 99-102).

Conclusions

The late Neolithic settlement at Kingshill North was focused on cattle and pig husbandry. The high incidence of pig suggests that woodland was locally available, together with open fields for cattle pasture and arable cultivation. The presence of local forest may also be implied by the presence of aurochs, red deer and roe deer. Ageing data suggest that cattle and sheep/goat were mainly kept for secondary products, such as milk, wool and traction, with surplus animals slaughtered as sub-adults for meat. Pigs were kept exclusively for meat. Game was rare, which suggests that hunting was a relatively rare pastime which contributed very little to the everyday diet.

The Beaker/Bronze Age assemblage was dominated by a 'head and hooves' burial, that is, cattle skull, metapodials and phalanges from inhumation grave 8588. The cattle bones are probably the remains of a hide with head and feet attached. While 'head and hooves' burials are not very common in Britain, as opposed to continental Europe, it is possible that hides without skeletal remains were relatively common grave goods, but generally have not survived.

The Iron Age/early Roman assemblage derives from the last phase of the Kingshill North settlement. The Iron Age animal bone assemblage is rather small, but tentatively suggests that sheep/goat was more common in the middle Iron Age, whereas cattle increased in importance in the late Iron Age. The late Iron Age-early Roman assemblages were dominated by sheep/goat. It is unclear whether this is connected to changes in the local environment favouring sheep/goat, increased wool production or trade in cattle to the military fort in Cirencester. Pigs were scarce and game absent, indicating that the forested landscape of the Neolithic had been transformed into an open landscape by the Iron Age.

Articulated burial groups of a possible ritual nature were identified in the middle Iron Age assemblage, which contained the skeletons of one crow/rook and one dog in the base fill of a pit. It is not possible to say with certainty why the animals were deposited but it has been suggested that dogs may have been seen as guardians against under-world spirits and deities or sacrificed as appeasement to such.

Land snails *Carl Champness*

Thirty samples were examined from the excavations at Kingshill North. These derived from a variety of settlement feature types – pits and ditches dating to the Neolithic, Bronze Age, Iron Age and Roman periods. An initial assessment of the samples indicated preservation and abundance of molluscan remains was highly variable across the site (Stafford, in OA 2009). The richest assemblages derived from pits dated to the late Neolithic and features assigned to the late Iron Age/early Roman period. Preservation was otherwise quite poor, particularly in those features dated to the early Bronze Age. Detailed analysis was carried out on samples from 11 features in order to provide a comprehensive species list for these periods. The results of this analysis, along with a summary of the assessment results from the remaining samples, are presented below. Further details of the assessment, including supporting tables can be found in the site archive.

Method

All samples were processed during the assessment stage at Oxford Archaeology. Samples processed specifically for molluscan remains consisted of 2 litres of sediment, disaggregated in water, floated onto 0.5mm nylon mesh and air-dried. The residues were also retained to 0.5 mm. For the purpose of assessment the flots were then scanned under a binocular microscope at magnifications of x10 and x20 and an estimate of abundance recorded. The flots of larger bulk samples (10-40 litres) from other features, primarily allocated for the retrieval of charred plant remains, were also examined in order to provide a comprehensive assessment for all the periods represented across the site.

The flots and residues of samples selected for further analysis were systematically picked for identifiable mollusc fragments. Due to the large volumes of sediment processed, only a proportion of the finer grade (1-0.5 mm) residues from the bulk samples were sorted. Flotation in these samples appears to have been good with only very occasional items retained in the residues. The species present in each assemblage were identified and whole shells and apical fragments counted. Shells of *Cecilioides acicula* were excluded because this species burrows deeply and provides no useful information on conditions as a sediment or soil formed. *C acicula* can be extremely numerous and its inclusion in the total tends to obscure the results from the other species. Nomenclature follows Kerney (1999). Habitat groupings follow the scheme of Evans (1972, 1984).

Phase 1: Late Neolithic pits 8058, 8064, 8392 and 8813

The flots from eleven samples were examined from four Neolithic pits containing early Grooved Ware pottery. The artefact-rich feature fills and stratigraphic evidence would suggest that the majority of the pits were deliberately backfilled during short periods of activity. The pit samples therefore provide snap-shots of the environments surrounding the pits during a particular phase of activity, but do not contain a sequence to provide evidence of environmental change.

Preservation of molluscan remains was generally poor. The assemblages were all very similar and of low diversity, dominated mostly by open country species, *Vallonia excentrica*, the obligate xerophile *Helicella itala*, and to a lesser extent *Vallonia costata* and *Pupilla muscorum* (Table 34). This suggests that the soil used to backfill the pits formed in a dry open landscape, probably rough grassland. Smaller numbers of shade-loving species were present in two sequences, particularly context 8063 from pit 8064 and 8815 from pit 8813. These included *Discus rotundatus*, *Carychium tridentatum* and *Oxychilus cellarius*, which suggest more enclosed conditions, perhaps scrub or some form of woodland, were, or had previously been, present in the area.

One cautionary note to be made regarding the assemblages is the very low numbers of shells compared with the large volume of processed sediment, together with the consistent presence of *Candidula intersecta* and *C gigaxii*, considered to be Roman introductions in the Upper Thames Valley (Kerney 1999). This suggests that a component of these assemblages may consist of intrusive elements and are therefore not wholly representative of the environment prevailing at the site during the Neolithic period.

Phase 2: Beaker to Bronze Age

Only one feature dated to the late Neolithic/early Bronze Age period (Phase 2) was sampled and this was exclusively funerary in character. Five samples were taken from the early Bronze Age barrow ditch (group 8454). This produced a predominantly open-country assemblage, but included both shade-loving and open-country species, along with a small

Table 34: Land snails (Phase 1). Key: C – catholic species, O – open-country, S – shade-loving.

Period		Neolithic	Neolithic	Neolithic	Neolithic	Neolithic	Neolithic	Neolithic	Neolithic	Neolithic	Neolithic	Neolithic
Feature Type		Phase 1	Phase 1	Phase 1	Phase 1	Phase 1	Phase 1	Phase 1	Phase 1	Phase 1	Phase 1	Phase 1
Fill of		Pit	Pit	Pit	Pit	Pit	Pit	Pit	Pit	Pit	Pit	Pit
Group Number		8058	8058	8064	8064	8064	8392	8392	8392	8813	8813	8813
context		8056	8057	8062	8063	8089	8393	8394	8424	8815	8816	8817
Sample No		32	33	20	21	22	57	58	101	197	198	199
Depth												
Vol.		37	18	30	27	27	39	28	10	9	9	9
Taxa	Habitat											
Carychium tridentatum (Risso)	S			1								
Cochlicopa spp.	C									6	2	
Vertigo pygmaea (Draparnaud)	O		1		2						1	
Vertigo pusilla (Müller)	S											
Pupilla muscorum (Linné)	O	6	4	8	10	2	2	2		2	6	5
Vallonia costata (Müller)	O			8	10	3	2	1		2	5	5
Vallonia excentrica (Sterki)	O	8	7	12	12	5	4	2		9	20	20
Vallonia spp.	O			3	2		3	5				
Acanthinula aculeata (Müller)	S											
Ena obscura (Müller)	S											
Punctum pygmaea (Draparnaud)	C									2		
Discus rotundatus (Müller)	S		2	9	3	2		2		16	8	7
Vitrina pellucida (Müller)	C							1				
Vitrea spp.	S			5	2					2		
Nesovitrea hammonis (Ström)	C			1								
Aegopinella pura (Alder)	S											
Aegopinella nitidula (Draparnaud)	S			1								
Oxychilus cellarius (Müller)	S	2		7	7	5		10		3		
Zonitidae indet.	S										1	
Euconulus fulvus	C											
Clausiliidae indet.	S											
Clausilia bidentata (Ström)	S				2							
Helicidae indet.	O											1
Candidula spp.	O	6										
Candidula gigaxii (Pfeiffer)	O		4	5	5		9	5		3		3
Candidula intersecta (Poiret)	O				1							
Cernuella virgata (da Costa)	O	7				4						
Helicella itala (Linné)	O	1	2		4	1						1
Trichia hispida (Linné)	C	3	5	3	3	6		1	4	3		
Cepea / Arianta sp.	C			1	1							1
Total		33	25	64	64	28	20	29	4	48	44	47
per litre		1	2	2	2	1	1	1	0.4	5	5	5

number of catholic species (Table 35). On the whole, the barrow assemblage was one of the better preserved assemblages and consisted of 152 individuals. Similar to the Neolithic samples, the open-country component was dominated by xerophile species *V excentrica* and *H itala*, with lesser quantities of *P muscorum* and *Vertigo pygmaea*. Of the more restricted shade-loving species present, *Vitrea contracta* and *Oxychilus cellarius* dominated. The open-country component is indicative of a dry open environment, probably grassland. *V contracta* and *O cellarius*, although classified as shade-loving, has rather more catholic habitat preferences than *D rotundatus* and thrives in well-vegetated places, including tall grassland and scrub.

Phase 4: Late Iron Age and Roman

Ten samples from pits and ditches dated to the Iron Age and Roman periods were examined during the analysis. The assemblages were among the better preserved, though unexceptional, and consisted of a restricted range of open-country species (*H itala, V excentrica, P muscorum, V pygmaea*), indicating that dry open conditions and well-established grassland and/or arable prevailed at the site (Table 36). Groups from Phase 4c enclosure ditch 8413 (context 8705) and a broadly-dated pit (context 8795; Phase 4) were dominated by open-country species. There is a significant increase in a very limited range of open-county species (*V excentrica* and *H itala*) that

Table 35: Land snails (Phase 2). Key: C – catholic species, O – open-country, S – shade-loving.

Period		BA	BA	BA	BA	BA
Feature Type		Phase 2	Phase 2	Phase 2	Phase 2	Phase 2
Fill of		Ring ditch	Ring ditch	Ring ditch	Ring ditch	Ring ditch
Group Number		8439	8441	8452	8528	8597
context		8440	8442	8451	8530	8640
Sample No		68	69	70	86	163
Depth						
Vol.		10	10	10	23	10
Taxa	Habitat					
Carychium tridentatum (Risso)	S			1		
Cochlicopa spp.	C					2
Vertigo pygmaea (Draparnaud)	O	1		1	2	2
Vertigo pusilla (Müller)	S					
Pupilla muscorum (Linné)	O	2			4	7
Vallonia costata (Müller)	O	3	2	8	2	9
Vallonia excentrica (Sterki)	O	3	6	8	3	20
Vallonia spp.	O					
Acanthinula aculeata (Müller)	S					
Ena obscura (Müller)	S					
Punctum pygmaea (Draparnaud)	C		1			
Discus rotundatus (Müller)	S			2	3	3
Vitrina pellucida (Müller)	C					1
Vitrea spp.	S				2	16
Nesovitrea hammonis (Ström)	C					
Aegopinella pura (Alder)	S			1		
Aegopinella nitidula (Draparnaud)	S	1			2	2
Oxychilus cellarius (Müller)	S					6
Zonitidae indet.	S					
Euconulus fulvus	C					
Clausiliidae indet.	S				1	
Clausilia bidentata (Ström)	S					
Helicidae indet.	O					
Candidula spp.	O		5	4		
Candidula gigaxii (Pfeiffer)	O	5				
Candidula intersecta (Poiret)	O					
Cernuella virgata (da Costa)	O					
Helicella itala (Linné)	O		1	2	5	4
Trichia hispida (Linné)	C				2	3
Cepea/Arianta sp.	C			1	1	
Total		15	15	25	23	72
per litre		2	2	3	1	7

Table 36: Land snails (Phase 4). Key: C – catholic species, O – open-country, S – shade-loving.

Period		LIA-Rom	LIA-Rom	LIA-Rom	LIA-Rom	LIA-Rom	LIA-Rom	LIA-ER	LIA-ER	LIA-ER	LR	LR	LR	LR
		Phase 4	Phase 4	Phase 4	Phase 4	Phase 4	Phase 4	Phase 4c	Phase 4c	Phase 4c	Phase 4f	Phase 4f	Phase 4f	Phase 4f
Feature type		Pit	Pit	Pit	Pit	Pit	Pit	Ditch	Ditch	Ditch	Ditch	Ditch	Ditch	Ditch
Group Number		8795	8795	8795	8102	8102	8102	8705	8705	8705	9013	9013	9013	9013
context		8793	8794	8828	8106	8107	8108	8707	8707	8706	8939	8939	9012	9012
Sample No		192	190	191	27	28	29	297	298	299	293	294	295	296
Depth								0.00-0.20	0.20-0.30	0.30-0.50	0.00-0.20	0.20-0.45	0.45-0.65	0.65-0.85
Vol.		20	36	20	27	28	29	17	13	15	15	17	16	16
Taxa	Habitat													
Carychium tridentatum (Risso)	S				6	44								
Cochlicopa spp.	C		2		1	2					1	4		
Vertigo pygmaea (Draparnaud)	O		2	1	3						10	36	9	43
Vertigo pusilla (Müller)	S					2								
Pupilla muscorum (Linné)	O		22	3	3	3	2	2	1		12	26	6	3
Vallonia costata (Müller)	O		6	1	6	8						22		
Vallonia excentrica (Sterki)	O	14	25	12		6	7	39	20	3	65	190	44	74
Vallonia spp.	O					1								
Acanthinula aculeata (Müller)	S				1									
Ena obscura (Müller)	S					1								1
Punctum pygmaea (Draparnaud)	C					6					2	9		3
Discus rotundatus (Müller)	S				18	75								
Vitrina pellucida (Müller)	C													
Vitrea spp.	S				9	15								
Nesovitrea hammonis (Ström)	C					1								
Aegopinella pura (Alder)	S				3	18								
Aegopinella nitidula (Draparnaud)	S				2	6					8	33	20	36
Oxychilus cellarius (Müller)	S		2		5	4								
Zonitidae indet.	S							1						
Euconulus fulvus	C					1								
Clausiliidae indet.	S													
Clausilia bidentata (Ström)	S				2	4								
Helicidae indet.	O													
Candidula spp.	O						2	1						
Candidula gigaxii (Pfeiffer)	O		4	1	4	2								
Candidula intersecta (Poiret)	O													
Cernuella virgata (da Costa)	O							1		1				
Helicella itala (Linné)	O		5	2	2			2			5	20	6	8
Trichia hispida (Linné)	C	8	3	2		5		30	11	3	89	168	31	60
Cepea/Arianta sp.	C										1			2
Total		22	71	22	66	203	20	75	33	6	193	508	116	230
per litre		1	3	1	2	7	1	4	3	0.4	13	30	7	14

are representative of open dry short grassland. This corresponds with significant decreases in shade-loving species and an increase in the percentage of catholic species. Both *H itala* and *P muscorum* favour short open grassland environments, but can tolerate disturbed ground. *P muscorum* is less tolerant of arable cultivation, but is often found associated with bare open ground within short grassland, and potentially associated with intense grazing.

The assemblage from pit 8102 (Phase 4) showed a marked contrast to those of the other late Iron Age and Roman features in that they were significantly more diverse and abundant. The pit was dominated by shade-loving species, which reached up to 74% of the totals. The most abundant species were *D rotundatus*, *C tridentatum* and various zonitids, indicating leaf litter and the presence of broad-leaf deciduous woodland. Lesser numbers of rupestral species that live on and under tree trunks (*Clausilia bidentata* and *Acanthinula aculeata*) were also present along with occasional specimens of *Vertigo pusilla* and *Acicula fusca*. The latter species is generally rare on archaeological sites, never occurring in great numbers, and is considered to be a good indicator of wooded conditions (Evans 1972, 141-142). Open-country species were present in lesser quantities, averaging 25-30%. This component of the assemblage, however, was dominated by *V costata*, representing between 10% and 4%. Although *V costata* is essentially considered to be an open grassland species, it has been recorded in lesser numbers in more enclosed environments. Evans (1972) suggested it could achieve up to 12% abundance in open woodland and 6% in closed canopy. *V costata's* ability to inhabit woodland environments means it is essentially one of the first of the open-country species to take advantage or colonize disturbed or newly cleared areas. Open country xerophile species (*V excentrica*, *H itala*, *P muscorum*) were present in insignificant numbers. However, the presence of *Candidula* sp, does indicate that more recent material has contaminated the assemblage. Overall, the pit assemblage suggests that deciduous woodland existed in the late Iron Age or Roman landscape, or at the very least this feature was back-filled with soil that had formed under woodland conditions. There is some evidence to indicate an open aspect to the woodland canopy, perhaps grassy clearings, or that the land had recently been cleared with open-country species beginning to colonize. This is in stark contrast to the assemblages associated with the main settlement enclosure that indicated disturbed open conditions.

The late Roman field boundary ditch 8203 (Phase 4f) produced the richest assemblage of all the samples (context 9013). The assemblage was very similar in nature to the main settlement enclosure ditch, being dominated by open-country species, but with the two notable exceptions of the shade loving *Aegopinella nitidula* and dry open country *Vertigo pygmaea*. The latter is not found in woodland, whereas *A nitidula* inhabits a wider variety of shaded environments that include moist grassland, and can tolerate bare ground and arable fields. The increased numbers of *A nitidula* may indicate the presence of arable fields close to the boundary.

Discussion

The results of the molluscan analysis from the late Neolithic features at Cirencester are somewhat inconclusive. The assemblages were dominated by species indicative of dry open conditions, probably tall grassland, perhaps with localized scrub/woodland surrounding. However, molluscan preservation was extremely poor and there are signs of later intrusion. Indeed, the number of individuals per litre from the majority of the features would not have produced useful assemblages, particularly for the late Neolithic, had the samples been the more usual two-litre sized samples.

From the late Neolithic period onwards at Cirencester there is evidence for the development of much more open environments of dry short grassland/scrub which appear to have prevailed into the Bronze Age. This is consistent with an open landscape associated with funeral monuments and practices, which may have originally been intended to be viewed from some distance.

The establishment of the late Iron Age/early Roman ditch 8413 within the site marks a transition to more disturbed ground conditions, although still in a predominantly open short grassland environment, with evidence of grazing and bare ground. However, the woodland assemblage located in pit 8102, located to the north of the main settlement, indicates a possible phase of secondary woodland regeneration away from areas of intense activity. By the mid to late Roman period, large arable fields were present to the south of the site.

There is a general lack of palaeo-environmental sequences around Cirencester to indicate past environmental change. Previous work has tended to focus on the identification of waterlogged and peat deposits in particular to provide a sequence of vegetational change. This has been provided by pollen, insects, and plant remains from palaeochannels, fen deposits and a growing number of waterlogged deposits from waterholes and deep features associated with settlement. These studies generally suggest extensively open conditions by the early-mid Bronze Age, with an intensification of grazing and arable cultivation during the Iron Age and Roman periods (Lambrick 2009).

Within the wider context of the Upper Thames Valley, sites such as Gravelly Guy and Horcott Pit on the River gravels suggest that during the early Bronze Age at least part of the second gravel terrace was being used for permanent pasture (Lambrick and Allen 2004). The area around the Devil's Quoits was also predominantly open grassland during the later Neolithic and early Bronze Age (ibid). Further afield, evidence from Barrow Hills, Radley, suggested that Mesolithic woodland had given way to grassland by the middle Neolithic and that conditions on the site remained open until the Late Bronze Age when a phase of local vegetation regeneration took place (Robinson 1999). A similar phase of woodland survival (or regeneration) was recorded in the mid to late Iron Age at Duntisbourne, on the upper slopes of the Cotswolds (Mudd *et al.* 1999, 77-97). Further evidence of land abandonment and woodland regeneration has been recorded after the Neolithic at other sites, mainly on the chalklands. This regeneration occurred at various periods in later prehistory and may be related to a countrywide trend as seen in pollen diagrams (Evans 1993). Locally, however, there appears to be much variation within the area regarding the timing of woodland clearance and periods of secondary woodland regeneration. This may have been partly in response to shifting settlement patterns and abandonment of areas within the uplands during the Iron Age and Roman periods.

Charred plant remains *Wendy Smith*

Introduction and methodology

In total, 117 bulk samples from a variety of features were assessed. The assessment results were fairly unproductive, with most samples producing little or no charred plant remains. However, several samples merited further analysis because of their date and/or archaeological significance, even though the samples were not particularly rich. These include four late Neolithic pit samples, two middle Iron Age pit samples, one late Iron Age sample from within a ditch and one Roman cremation sample. The samples were analysed in order to explore what plants were in use during the Neolithic, what cultivated cereals were in use during the Iron Age and Roman periods, and to determine whether ritual selection of plants was evident.

Samples were processed by flotation using a modified Siraf-style flotation machine. The resulting flot was sieved to 250μm and the heavy residue, which does not float, was sieved to 500μm. The dried heavy residue was sorted by eye for charred plant remains.

The present author sorted charred plant remains from flots and from unsorted heavy residue fractions using a low-power binocular microscope at magnifications between x12 and x30. The entire flot and heavy residue fractions were sorted for charred plant remains. Identification of plant remains (including charcoal) was made by direct comparison to the Oxford Archaeology reference collection, as well as standard identification keys (eg Cappers *et al.* 2006). Nomenclature for the plant remains follows Stace (1997) for indigenous species, and Zohary and Hopf (2000) for cultivated species. The traditional binomial system for the cereals is maintained here, following Zohary and Hopf (2000, tables 3 and table 5).

Quantifications of most seeds (in the broadest sense) were made on embryos, except in the case of hazel (*Corylus avellana* L.) nutshell fragments, and crab apple (*Malus sylvestris* L.) hypanthium (fruit) fragments. In the case of the crab apple fragments, it is unlikely in any case that these would total more than one individual crab apple. Fragments of hazel nutshells were weighed and then equated to complete hazel nutshells. The estimate count of complete hazel nutshells used here is based on a calculation presented by Wendy Carruthers in Mithen *et al.* 2001, whereby 42 g of charred hazel nutshell fragments are equivalent to 100 hazelnuts.

Results

Phase 1 – Late Neolithic

A total of four samples from three late Neolithic pits produced small quantities of plant remains (Table 37). Pit 9096 produced one possible cereal grain, and both pit 9096 and pit 9100 produced small quantities of indeterminate cereal/ large grass caryopses. Unfortunately, these were poorly preserved, often fragmented remains of cereal/grass caryopses, so more secure identification was not possible. All three pits produced hazel (*Corylus avellana* L.) nutshell fragments, but only pit 9100 produce crab apple (*Malus sylvestris* L.) pips and fruit wall (hypanthium) fragments. In general, the hazel nutshell results were extremely poor for pits 8100 and 9096 (that is, fewer than two whole hazelnuts). Although these could conceivably be the remains of food preparation, it is also possible that these are merely nuts inadvertently burned with hazel wood fuel. Unfortunately, charcoal from both samples 35 and 286 was primarily less than 2 mm and, therefore, unlikely to be identifiable, so this possibility can only be suggested without testing. However, the samples from pit 9100 are significantly richer, with 23.4 hazel nutshells estimated from the fragments recovered from sample 272. The recovery of crab apple pips and fruit wall (hypanthium) fragments from this sample as well as charred hazel nutshells could also imply preparation of another wild foodstuff. Nevertheless, it is unlikely that this amounts to more than one individual crab apple and, therefore, it also could simply have been burned inadvertently with apple-wood fuel. Again, charcoal recovered from samples 272 and 273 were relatively small-sized (<2 mm) and, therefore, were not recommended for further analysis. As a result, it is not possible to ascertain if apple wood fuel was in use or not.

Unfortunately, the limited quantity of charred plant remains (fewer than or equal to two seeds per litre of sediment sampled – see Table 37) means that it is difficult to ascertain if these remains represent accidentally charred tree fruits or nuts inadvertently burned with wood fuel, or if they are indeed background noise from processing or disposal of wild foodstuffs. The limited recovery of charred

Table 37: Neolithic plant remains

Sample No	35	272	273	286	
Context No	8098	9101	9102	9097	
Feature No	8100	9100	9100	9096	
Feature Type	pit	pit	pit	pit	
Sample Volume (L)	10 L	20 L	40 L	40 L	
Flot Volume (ml)	14 ml	85 ml	70 ml	90 ml	
Seeds per litre of sediment (excluding ?ancient seeds)	1.77	2.02	0.16	1.55	
Latin binomial					*English Common Name*
FLOT					
Cereals					
Cereal - indeterminate	-	-	- ·	1	
Cereal / POACAEAE - indeterminate	-	4	-	2E	
Tree/ Shrub					
Corylus avellana L. - nutshell fragments (no [weight (g)] = conversion)	98 [0.7g] = 1.7 HNS	>1000 [8.0g] = 19 HNS	72 [0.3g] = 0.7 HNS	121 121 [0.6g] = 1.4 HNS	hazel
Malus sylvestris L. - hypanthium fragment (with flower remnant)	-	1	-	-	crab apple
Malus sylvestris L. - hypanthium fragment	-	3	-	-	crab apple
Malus sylvestris L. - pip	-	9E	-	-	crab apple
cf. *Malus sylvestris* L. - pip (?immature)	-	-	2	-	possible crab apple
Weed/ Wild					
Chenopodium spp.	-	-	-	3†	goosefoot
Atriplex spp.	++†	+++†	26†	12†	orache
Rumex sp.	-	1	-	-	dock
Veronica hederifolia L.	-	-	-	2†	ivy-leaved speedwell
Unidentified - fruit stone fragment	-	-	-	-	-
Unidentified - ?tuber fragment	-	-	2	1	-
Unidentified - highly vitrified, amorphous fragments	17	-	+++	57	-
Unidentified - highly vitrified, amorphous ?fruit fragments	-	+++	-	-	-
Unidentified	-	-	-	1	-
HEAVY RESIDUE FRACTIONS					
>10 mm Heavy Residue					
Corylus avellana L. - nutshell fragments (no [weight (g)] = conversion)	-	10 [1.2g] = 2.9 HNS	-	-	hazel
10 – 4 mm Heavy Residue					
Corylus avellana L. - nutshell fragments (no [weight (g)] = conversion)	-	-	3 [0.3g] = 0.7 HNS	-	hazel
4 - 2 mm Heavy Residue					
Corylus avellana L. - nutshell fragments (no [weight (g)] = conversion)	-	99 [0.2g] = 0.5 HNS	38 [0.3g] = 0.7 HNS	-	hazel
Unidentified - highly vitrified, amorphous fragments (<4mm)	-	-	+	-	-
2 - 0.5 mm Heavy Residue					
Corylus avellana L. - nutshell fragments (no [weight (g)] - conversion)	-	-	48 [0.1g] = 0.2HNS	-	hazel
Unidentified - highly vitrified, amorphous fragments (<2mm)	-	-	++++	-	
TOTAL IDENTIFICATIONS (excluding ?ancient seeds)	17.7	40.4	6.3	62	
Other Remains					
cf. Oyster shell fragment (most likely decayed from oolitic limestone)	-	1	-	-	-
Bone fragments (?human) - <4mm	-	+++	-	-	-
Molluscs (land snails - especially *Cecilioides acicula*)	-	++++	-	-	-

Nomenclature follows Stace (1997). Key: + = <5, ++ = 5 - 10, +++ = 10 - 50, ++++ = 50 - 100 and +++++ = >100. NE = estimate count of whole items based on fragments and N† = items which may not be ancient. In all cases 100% of the flot or heavy residue fraction was sorted.

Table 38: Middle Iron Age plant remains

Sample No	25	278	
Context No	8142	9084	
Feature No	8143	9083	
Feature Type	pit	pit	
Sample Volume (L)	29 L	8 L	
Flot Volume (ml)	160 ml	35 ml	
Seeds per litre of sediment	2.86	31.25	
Latin Binomial			*English Common Name*
Cereal Grain			
Hordeum spp.	11	9	barley
Triticum spp. - indeterminate	10	8	wheat
Cereal - indeterminate	9E	12E	cereal
Cereal/ POACEAE - detached embryo		6	cereal/ large grass
Cereal/ POACEAE - indeterminate	15E	24E	cereal/ large grass
Cereal Chaff			
Hordeum spp. - six-rowed type rachis node	-	2	barley
Hordeum spp. - indeterminate rachis node	-	3	barley
cf. *Hordeum* spp. - indeterminate rachis node	-	2	possible barley
Triticum dicoccum Schübl. - glume base	5	18	emmer
Triticum dicoccum Schübl./ *spelta* L. - indeterminate spikelet fork	-	1	emmer/ spelt
Triticum dicoccum Schübl./ *spelta* L. - indeterminate, glume base	9	2	emmer/ spelt
Triticum spelta L. - spikelet fork	-	1	spelt
Triticum spelta L. - indeterminate glume base	-	2	spelt
Triticum spp. - indeterminate rachis node	3E	23E	wheat
Triticum spp. - indeterminate glume fragment	+	+	wheat
Cereal/ POACEAE - indeterminate culm node	1	1	cereal/ large grass
Tree/ Shrub			
cf. *Prunus spinosa* L. - thorn	-	1	blackthorn/ sloe
Weed/ Wild Plants			
Chenopodium spp.	-	15E	goosefoot
Atriplex spp.	-	15E	orache
Silene spp.	-	2	campion
Fallopia convolvulus (L.) Á. Löve	-	2	black-bindweed
Rumex spp.	-	2	dock
Malva spp.	-	2	mallow
cf. *Thlaspi arvense* L.	-	1	possible field penny-cress
Medicago spp./ *Melilotus* spp./ *Trifolium* spp.	-	2	medick/ melilot/ clover
cf. *Veronica hederifolia* L.	-	1	possible ivy-leaved speedwell
Galium spp.	3	8E	bedstraw
Valerianella dentata (L.) Pollich	-	3	narrow-fruited cornsalad
Eleocharis uniglumis (Link) Schult./ *palustris* (L.) Roem. & Schult.	-	1	common/ slender spike-rush
cf. *Eleocharis uniglumis* (Link) Schult./ *palustris* (L.) Roem. & Schult.	-	1	possible common/ slender spike-rush
Avena sp.	-	1	oat
Avena spp. - awn fragments	-	+	oat/ brome
Avena spp./ *Bromus* spp.	7	1	brome
Bromus spp.	4	-	annual meadow-grass- type
Poa annua L. - type	-	3	Grass Family
POACEAE - small-sized caryopsis	-	45	Grass Family
POACEAE - medium-sized caryopsis	-	22	-
Unidentified	-	3	-
Unidentified - bud	1	-	-
Unidentified - bud scar (? Herbaceous plant)	1	1	-
Unidentified - ?bud/ ?catkin fragment	1	-	-
Unidentified - highly vitrified, amorphous clumps	+++	-	-
Unidentified - high vitreous objects (?plant)	-	4	-
Indeterminate	3	-	-
TOTAL IDENTIFICATIONS	83	250	

Nomenclature follows Zohary and Hopf (2000) for cultivated plants and Stace (1997). Key: + = <5, ++ = 5 - 10, +++ = 10 - 50, ++++ = 50 - 100 and +++++ = >100. NE = estimate count of whole items based on fragments. Data based entirely on the flot and in all cases 100% of the flot was sorted.

plant remains and the dominance of tree fruits and nuts is quite typical of Neolithic deposits (Moffett *et al.* 1989), especially in Gloucestershire (eg Nympsfield chambered tomb – Arthur and Pardine 1975; Hazelton North – Straker 1990).

Phase 3 – Middle Iron Age

Two middle Iron Age pit samples were fully analysed (Table 38). Sample 25 was fairly poor, producing only 83 identifications equivalent to 2.86 seeds per litre of sediment sampled. Some 54% of identifications from sample 25 were of cereal grain. Unfortunately, preservation of cereal grain was relatively poor and identification was only made to barley (*Hordeum* spp.) or wheat (*Triticum* spp.). Cereal chaff was not particularly abundant (21.7% of all identifications). However, glume wheat chaff was present and where possible to make identification to species level, only emmer (*Triticum dicoccum* Schübl.) was identified. A limited number of weed or wild taxa were recovered, dominated by indeterminate cultivated or wild oat (*Avena* spp.)/brome grass (*Bromus* spp.).

Sample 278 was much richer, producing 250 identifications in total. Weed or wild plants account for 50.8% of all identifications from sample 278. Many of the weed/wild taxa are typical weeds of cereal crops such as goosefoot (*Chenopodium* spp.), orache (*Atriplex* spp.), dock (*Rumex* spp.), narrow-fruited cornsalad (*Valerianella dentata* (L.) Pollich) and indeterminate wild/ cultivated oat/ brome grass (*Avena* spp./ *Bromus* spp.). Indeterminate small, medium or large wild grasses (POACEAE) were abundant, accounting for 28% of all identifications from this sample. Like sample 25, cereal grain was relatively poorly preserved and identification was only made to barley (*Hordeum* spp.) or wheat (*Triticum* spp.). Cereal chaff was not particularly abundant (22% of all identifications). However, glume wheat chaff was present and where possible, most glume bases were identified as emmer (*Triticum dicoccum* Schübl. – n = 18). Two spelt (*Triticum spelta* L.) glume bases were also identified, which could either indicate that spelt was a contaminant of this crop (either in the field or in storage) or that both crops were cultivated and cereal crop processing waste was subsequently mixed on deposition into this pit feature.

These results were consistent with late Bronze Age/early Iron Age results by Pelling (1999) and late Bronze Age results by Ede (2000) from Shorncote Quarry, especially in terms of the abundance of brome (*Bromus* spp./ *Bromopsis* spp. – reported by Pelling (1999) as *Bromus*/ *Eubromis*) and other indeterminate wild grasses. Early Iron Age charred plant remains from Bampton in Oxfordshire (approximately 20 miles east of Cirencester) also were poorly preserved and present only in low concentrations (Pelling 2000).

Brome (*Bromus* spp.) grass (also known as 'chess' or 'rye brome', although specifically this refers to *Bromus secalinus* L.) was recovered from the Kingshill North samples, although in relatively low concentrations. Both brome grasses and wild and cultivated species of oat are native to the British Isles and, therefore, can occur naturally in the wild. At present, both brome and the indeterminate wild/cultivated oat are classified as a weed/wild plants primarily because we cannot assume they were cultivated intentionally. However, given their relative abundance in some samples, perhaps they are better regarded as a crop in their own right, even if not necessarily grown for human consumption. Certainly, Campbell (2000, 50) has speculated that brome was cultivated for fodder at early Iron Age Danebury (and environs) and was then replaced by oat in the late Iron Age. The development of hay meadows for the intentional cultivation of grass feed for livestock also dates to sometime in the Iron Age (eg Hodgson *et al.* 1999)

Phase 4a – Late Iron Age

A layer (8985) within an intervention (8907) through ditch 8563 was sampled (Table 39). The sample was relatively poor with only 143 items quantified. However, the sample's volume was relatively small, only 2.5 litres, and therefore produced a relatively abundant assemblage of 53 items per litre of sediment sampled, which means this was the richest sample encountered at the site. Approximately 10% (n = 15) of all identifications were cereal grain. Only indeterminate cereal and indeterminate wheat (*Triticum* spp.) grains were identified. Cereal chaff accounted for 26% of all identifications (n = 37); unfortunately, due to poor preservation glume bases could not be identified to species level. Weed/wild taxa dominated this sample, accounting for 57% (n = 82) of all identifications. Indeterminate medium grass (POACEAE) caryopses and rye-grass (*Lolium* spp.) caryopsis were most frequently encountered.

The poor preservation and low density of charred plant remains is similar to other prehistoric charred plant remains from the upper Thames terrace and in Gloucestershire in particular (eg Ede 1999; Pelling 1999; Pelling 2001). Poor preservation means that it is not possible to determine what role emmer (*Triticum dicoccum* Schübl.) or spelt (*Triticum spelta* L.) played in late prehistoric Cirencester.

Phase 4e – Early-mid Roman

One relatively poor sample from cremation burial 8227 was analysed (Table 39). In total, only 104 identifications were made from this 15 litre sample, producing just under seven seeds or items per litre of sediment sampled. The majority of plant remains recovered were weed/wild taxa (n = 91 or 87.5% of all identifications), with indeterminate medick/ melilot/clover (*Medicago* spp./ *Melilotus* spp./ *Trifolium* spp.) seeds accounting for a third of the weed/wild assemblage. Again, cereal grain was poorly preserved and identifications could only be pushed as far as genus level, eg barley – *Hordeum* spp. or wheat – *Triticum* spp. Only a few fragments

Table 39: Late Iron Age/early Roman plant remains

	239	42	
Sample No	239	42	
Context No	8985	8228	
Feature No	8907	8227	
Feature Type	? cremation/?ash layer within ditch	cremation pit	
Phase	Phase 4a LIA (mid 1C BC– early 1C AD)	Phase 4e EROM-MROM (late 1–3C AD)	
Sample Volume (L)	2.5 L	15 L	
Flot Volume (ml)	< 5 ml	120 ml	
Seeds per litre of sediment	57.2	6.93	
Latin Binomial			English Common Name
Cereal Grain			
Hordeum spp.	-	1	barley
Triticum spp. - indeterminate	4	1	wheat
Cereal - indeterminate	5E	3	cereal
Cereal/ POACEAE - detached embryo	1	-	cereal/ large grass
Cereal/ POACEAE - indeterminate	5E	5E	cereal/ large grass
Cereal Chaff			
Triticum dicoccum Schübl./ *spelta* L. - indeterminate, glume base	12	-	emmer/ spelt
Triticum spelta L. - spikelet fork	-	1	spelt
Triticum spelta L. - indeterminate glume base	1	-	spelt
Triticum spp. - indeterminate rachis node	23E	1	wheat
Triticum spp. - indeterminate glume fragment	+	-	wheat
Cereal - indeterminate internode	1	-	cereal
Tree/ Shrub			
Corylus avellana L. - nutshell fragment	1	1	hazel
Unidentified - nutshell fragments (<2mm)	8	-	-
Weed/ Wild Plants			
Chenopodium spp.	4	7E	goosefoot
Chenopodium spp./ *Atriplex* spp. - internal structure	1	-	goosefoot/ orache
Atriplex spp.	1	6	orache
Polygonum sp./ *Fallopia* sp./ *Rumex* sp./ *Carex* sp. - indet. internal structure	-	1	knotgrass/ black-bindweed/ dock/ sedge
Fallopia convolvulus (L.) Á. Löve	-	2E	black-bindweed
Rumex spp.	2	2	dock
Vicia spp./ *Lathyrus* spp.	-	30E	vetch/ vetchling
Medicago sp./ *Melilotus* sp./ *Trifolium* sp.	-	1	medick/ melilot/ clover
cf. *Conopodium majus* (Gouan) Loret - tuber	-	1	possible pignut
cf. *Daucus carota* L.	1	-	possible carrot
cf. *Torillus* sp.	1	-	possible hedge-parsley
Galium spp.	-	17E	bedstraw
ASTERACEAE - *Anthemis* sp./ *Tripleurospermum* sp. - sized internal structure	1	-	Daisy Family – chamomile/ mayweed type
Avena sp. - floret base	-	1	oat
Avena spp. - awn fragments	+	+	oat
Bromus spp.	-	1	brome
cf. *Lolium* spp. type	27E	-	possible rye-grass type
POACEAE - small-sized caryopsis	6	11	Grass Family
POACEAE - medium-sized caryopsis	24	1	Grass Family
POACEAE - large-sized caryopsis	-	6	Grass Family
cf. POACEAE - stalk	1	+	Possible Grass Family
Unidentified	13E	2	-
Unidentified - bud scar (? Herbaceous plant)	-	-	-
Unidentified - tuber fragments	-	2	-
Unidentified - highly vitreous objects (? Clinker)	-	++++	-
Unidentified - high vitreous objects (?plant)	+	-	-
TOTAL	143	104	

Nomenclature follows Zohary and Hopf (2000) for cultivated plants and Stace (1997). Key: + = <5, ++ = 5 - 10, +++ = 10 - 50, ++++ = 50 - 100 and +++++ = >100. NE = estimate count of whole items based on fragments. Data based entirely on the flot and in all cases 100% of the flot was sorted.

of cereal chaff were recovered. However, a complete spelt (*Triticum spelta* L.) spikelet fork was noted.

These results are quite different from those elsewhere in Cirencester where cereal grain often dominates (eg the Kingscote corn-drier (Giorgi 1998); *Corinium* (Connolly 1982); Frocester Court Roman villa (Clarke 1970); or Upton St Leonards (Clarke 1971)), all of which had very distinct weed floras. However, it is likely that if this sample was indeed related to a funerary pyre, then this is in fact a sample of burnt grass or turves rather than weeds of crop and could explain the discrepancy with other Roman samples, which are frequently associated with corn-driers or crop processing wastes.

Conclusions

Sampling for archaeobotanical remains was relatively intensive at Kingshill North, with 117 samples collected from the 4.5 hectare excavations. Only eight samples, containing moderate densities of plant remains and of archaeological significance, merited further analysis. In general, preservation was poor, but this may be related to the shallow deposition of charred plant remains on agricultural or gardening lands that were likely to be subjected to ploughing or tilling action. Certainly the majority of samples assessed from the site contained modern root, which suggests that they were located at or immediately below modern topsoil levels. However, this trend for poorly preserved plant remains recovered in low densities clearly is not limited to the site and appears to be the case for the immediate region.

One question that remains is whether the cultivation of spelt wheat replaced the cultivation of emmer in this region during later prehistory or whether spelt was merely cultivated alongside emmer. To have a chance of addressing this, it is strongly recommended that samples of no less than 40 litres in volume are collected from any future excavations in this region. The limited evidence from Roman Cirencester, with only one or two samples examined from earlier excavations, means that data gathered from the Roman periods as well as prehistoric periods is of regional importance for this area. Indeed, van der Veen (2007, 204) recommends that a minimum sample volume of 40-60 litres of sediment should be collected and this certainly seems appropriate in cases where a region has produced relatively little Roman archaeobotanical data.

Table 40: Radiocarbon dates

Phase	Feature	Material	Lab code	$\delta^{13}C$ (‰)	C14 Age BP	Calibrated date (2σ)
1	Context 8089, pit 8064	Antler fragment	NZA-33477	-23.3	4096 ± 25	2856 cal BC-2809 cal BC (20.8%)
						2748 cal BC-2721 cal BC (6.3%)
						2698 cal BC-2571 cal BC (67.4%)
1	Context 9102, pit 9100	Charred nutshell	NZA-33150	-23.6	4096 ± 30	2859 cal BC-2807 cal BC (20.8%)
						2755 cal BC-2718 cal BC (8.6%)
						2703 cal BC-2568 cal BC (63.8%)
						2513 cal BC-2500 cal BC (1.9%)
1	Context 8098, pit 8100	Charred nutshell	NZA-33140	-25.1	4109 ± 30	2863 cal BC-2804 cal BC (23.7%)
						2759 cal BC-2673 cal BC (71.3%)
1	Context 9097, pit 9096	Charred nutshell	NZA-33151	-26.9	4182 ± 30	2886 cal BC-2834 cal BC (22%)
						2815 cal BC-2665 cal BC (72.9%)
1	Context 9101, pit 9100	Charred nutshell	NZA-33224	-23	4415 ± 25	3261 cal BC-3244 cal BC (3.6%)
						3100 cal BC-2922 cal BC (91.2%)
2	Skeleton 1903	Human bone	OxA-20188	-20.21	3187 ± 26	1502 cal BC-1415 cal BC (95.4%)
2	Skeleton 1403	Human bone	OxA-20186	-21.53	3718 ± 29	2201 cal BC-2031 cal BC (95.4%)
2	Skeleton 8656, grave 8588	Human bone	OxA-20184	-21.29	3830 ± 29	2458 cal BC-2418 cal BC (5.3%)
						2407 cal BC-2376 cal BC (6.3%)
						2367 cal BC-2363 cal BC (0.4%)
						2351 cal BC-2198 cal BC (82.1%)
						2163 cal BC-2152 cal BC (1.4%)
3	Context 8948, pit 8851	Bird bone	NZA-33476	-20.2	2264 ± 25	394 cal BC-349 cal BC (46.3%)
						296 cal BC-209 cal BC (48.8%)
3	Context 8142, pit 8143	Charred grain	NZA-33147	-22.6	2266 ± 30	396 cal BC-348 cal BC (43.5%)
						302 cal BC-208 cal BC (51.3%)
4a	Skeleton 1104, grave 1102	Human bone	OxA-20187	-20.82	1976 ± 26	41 cal BC-cal AD 75 (95.4%)
4a	Context 8985, ditch 8907, group 8563	Charred grain	NZA-33149	-22.6	2012 ± 30	90 cal BC-cal AD 64 (95.1%)
4b	Skeleton 8724, grave 8723	Human bone	OxA-20185	-20.1	2083 ± 26	181 cal BC-41 cal BC (95.4%)
4e	Context 8228, grave 8227	Charred grain	NZA-33144	-24.3	1834 ± 30	cal AD 86-247 (95%)

Radiocarbon dating *Edward Biddulph*

A total of five radiocarbon dates were initially obtained from skeletons uncovered during the evaluation and excavation. These dates were calculated by the University of Oxford Radiocarbon Accelerator Unit (lab code OxA), and the results are presented above by phase (Table 40). Nine further dates, also shown in Table 40, were obtained from seeds, animal bone and nutshell by the Rafter Radiocarbon Laboratory, Institute of Geological and Nuclear Sciences Ltd (lab code NZA). The uncalibrated dates are in radiocarbon years BP (Before Present – AD 1950) using the half life of 5568 years. Calibration was achieved using IntCal04 atmospheric data (Reimer *et al.* 2004).

Chapter 7: Discussion

Archaeology and topography *Edward Biddulph*

An examination of the distribution of archaeological features at Kingshill North suggests that to a great extent the topography of the site determined the location of features. Overall, features were located across the gentler-sloping central part of the site, with the flatter and higher area to the north and the steeper and lower ground to the south remaining largely unoccupied throughout the prehistoric and Roman periods (see Fig. 5). The Grooved Ware pits (Phase 1) extended in a band that occupied the relatively gentle slope and broadly followed the contours of the slope. The pits appeared to be contemporaneous in terms of their radiocarbon dating, but were not necessarily dug at the same time. If people were returning the site on a regular basis, possibly to take part in a midwinter gathering or ceremony (see Roe, Chapter 3 above, and Mullin below), then some years, potentially up to 60 years, may have separated the first and last pits. The first Neolithic people would have carefully considered the topography, but subsequent visitors needed only to copy their predecessors, as the work of establishing the best location for the pits had already been done. Eventually tradition, rather than topography alone, dictated where new pits were dug.

As Mullin argues below, the location of the Beaker burials (Phase 2) may have been influenced by the presence of the Neolithic pits, and generally there seems to be a good case for the co-occurrence of Grooved Ware pits and round barrows in the Upper Thames Valley. At Kingshill North, the co-occurrence reinforced the apparent correlation between features and the topography, although it is notable that round barrow 8454 overlooked the steeper slope to the south, undoubtedly giving the monument prominence. Beaker burial 1402 was positioned further north on the gentler slope, but middle Bronze Age grave, like the round barrow, was on the break of slope and had the steeper part of the hillside below it.

The distribution of pits assigned to the middle Iron Age (Phase 3) is similar to that of the Grooved Ware pits in that the pits occupied the southern part of the site, but a number of the features were dug into the steeper ground a few metres to the south of the earlier prehistoric pits. Habit and tradition may have brought the Iron Age inhabitants to the same area time after time to dig their pits, although pits were also situated on the gentler slope to the north. The late Iron Age and Roman settlement (Phase 4) was concentrated in the centre of the excavated area and occupied the gentle slope. The Iron Age and Roman farmers were presumably attracted by the benefits of a south-facing slope brought by increased sunlight, although the settlement's proximity to the round barrow, if still a visible monument by the late 1st-century BC, may have provided a further inducement to settle there.

Neolithic to Bronze Age (Fig. 43) *David Mullin*

The Late Neolithic

Seventeen pits were assigned a late Neolithic date: 11 contained Grooved Ware of the Woodlands sub-style and worked flint, a further three contained Neolithic worked flint. All the pits containing either Grooved Ware or worked flint also contained animal bone and ten of these contained charred plant remains or charcoal (see Table 1). A further three pits had similar morphology and occurred in close proximity to definite late Neolithic pits and were therefore grouped with them.

The pits occupy a roughly linear zone across the centre of the site, and they appear to be broadly contemporary. The radiocarbon dates overlap and all fall within a relatively short period spanning 2900 to 2550 cal BC. This is well within the range for Grooved Ware in Britain and contemporary with the main period of Clacton and Durrington Walls sub-styles (Garwood 1999). The dates conform well with those from the Upper Thames Valley, which appear to relate to a coherent tradition of material deposition (Garwood 1999), but are early within the sequence for the Woodlands sub-style. It is a possibility that the Woodlands and the Clacton sub-styles of pottery are actually part of one tradition. Garwood (1999) suggests a degree of chronological patterning, with Clacton tending to be earlier in date than the Woodlands sub-style. The dates from Kingshill North do not support this, however, and it should be noted that the chronology for the Clacton and Woodlands sub-styles proposed by Garwood is based only on a total sample of eight dates from six sites.

The 'lattice lozenge' motif on the Grooved Ware from Kingshill North is exceptionally rare; indeed Cleal (1999) goes as far as to suggest that the known examples may be the work of a single potter. The material has been recovered from sites in the Upper Thames Valley, at Barrow Hills, Radley; Roughground Farm, Lechlade and Tolleys Pit, Cassington, and the material from Kingshill North adds to this limited distribution, extending it out of the Thames Valley and onto the Cotswolds, where Grooved Ware is infrequently found. The 'mesh' design is

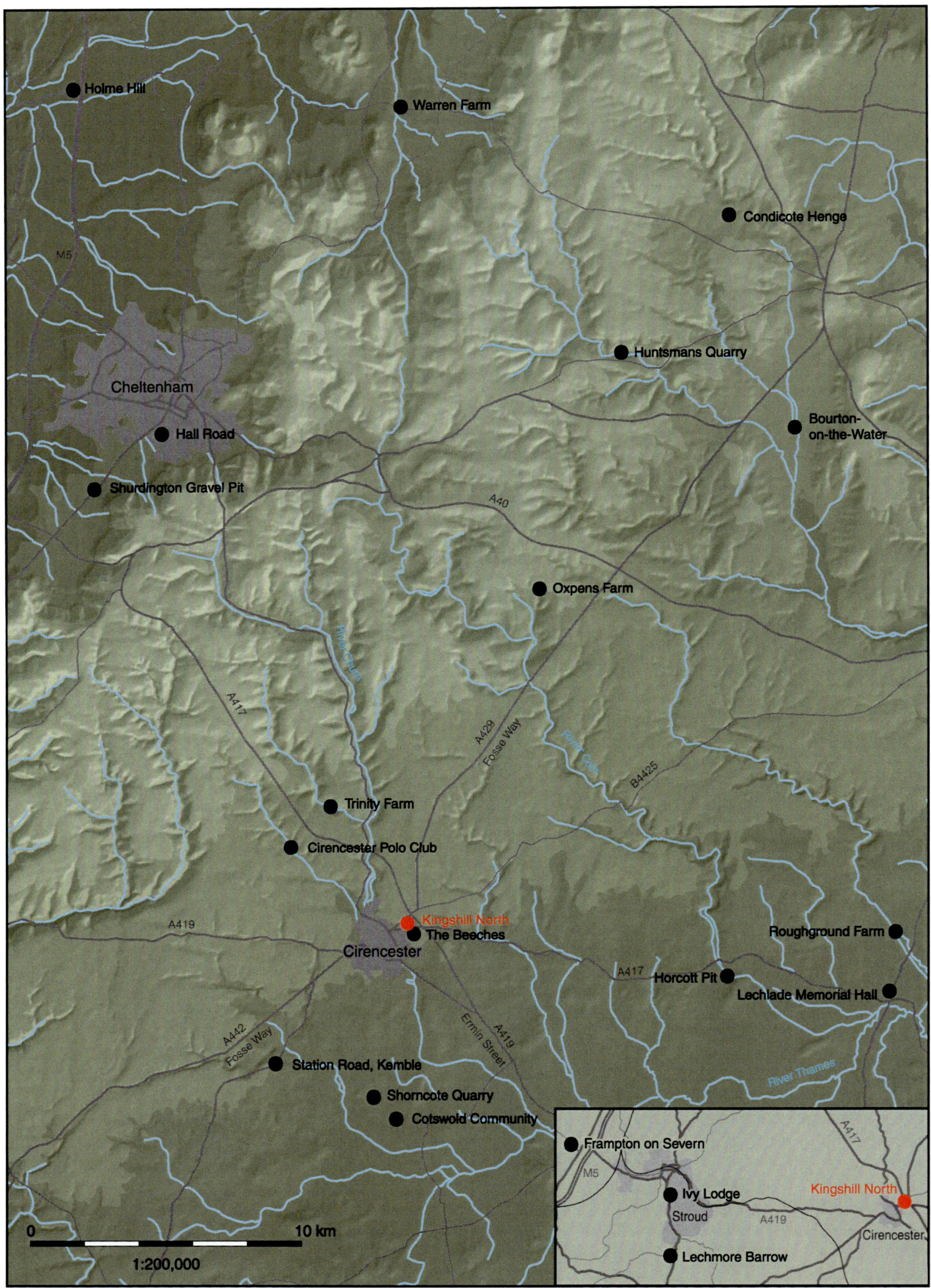

Fig. 43   *Phases 1 and 2 – locations of sites mentioned in discussion*

also found on other items of material culture, such as late Neolithic 'Maesmore' style maceheads, but also occurs on Grooved Ware of the Clacton sub-style (Cleal 1999, 4), further strengthening the links between the two styles. This distinctive design has variously been described as referring to fishing nets (Garwood 1999) and to basketry (Cleal 1999), but it also bears a striking resemblance to the bark of ash and willow trees (see Fig. 28), which have particular properties. Ash is an excellent fuel wood, while the willow can be used for basketry. It may also be noted that willow bark has traditionally been used for pain relief, and indeed the active ingredient, *salicin*, is used in modified form in aspirin (Singh and Ernst 2009, 238). The design of this particular style of Grooved Ware may, then, go beyond skeuomorphism and potentially refer to qualities of particular kinds of tree. Specific parts of the landscape may also be referred to in the use of limestone containing large amounts of fossil shell in the fabric of the pottery. While this may occur relatively locally, in particular to the south of Cirencester, the choice of this material appears to have been deliberate and not related to mechanical or technical properties of the rock. Indeed, this material is used in the fabric of Grooved Ware vessels in the Upper Thames Valley (Barclay 1999) and Worcestershire (Edwards 2007) where it is not immediately available locally, and the extensive use of shelly fabrics in Woodlands sub-style Grooved Ware also suggests that it carried symbolic meaning.

The Grooved Ware pit containing the largest amount of material at Kingshill North was 8813, which contained a complete stone axe and the fragment of an axe made of flint, a total of 505 worked flints (including 21 flint scrapers), five bone pins, a worked rib fragment and the rounded-end of a bone spatula. An antler was also recovered from the fill, alongside pig, cattle and deer bone, and burnt hazelnuts. While this is a fairly standard repertoire for Grooved Ware pits, the richness and treatment of the objects is unusual; although most of the items are fragmentary, there is no sign of deliberate breakage or burning. The pit can best be paralleled with pit 3196 at Barrow Hills, Radley, which also contained large amounts of worked flint, bone awls, animal bone, utilised antler and fragments of three Woodlands sub-style Grooved Ware vessels, including one with lattice lozenge decoration (Barclay and Halpin 1999).

The occurrence of spatulae in Grooved Ware contexts at Kingshill North is noteworthy, as these objects usually occur in Beaker graves. Fragmentary spatulae were recovered from two pits (8813 and 8064), where they occurred alongside Grooved Ware, worked flint, other worked bone and charred plant remains. The nearest site where spatulae were present is again Barrow Hills, Radley (Barclay and Halpin 1999), where two spatulae were recovered, although both came from Beaker graves. All the other local examples summarised by Barclay *et al.*

(1999, 235) were recovered from Beaker graves and none is recorded in the most up-to-date gazetteer of Grooved Ware associated finds in Britain (Longworth and Cleal 1999). While it is tempting to suggest that the spatulae were later additions to the pits, this is unlikely since there was no evidence for recutting and all were found securely stratified with other late Neolithic material.

While the animal and plant remains in the Grooved Ware pits occurred in relatively modest quantities, an articulated neonatal pig was recovered from pit 8455 and the remains of a dog from pit 8392. Bird bone was also identified in pit 8930. The majority of the assemblage was, however, dominated by cattle and pig remains, with a fairly high incidence of deer bone and antler. The plant remains included small amounts of cereal, crab apple and hazelnut shells. The most striking aspect of the animal and plant remains recovered from the pits is the occurrence of both wild and domestic species in the same contexts. Again, this is a fairly common occurrence and has been explained as the retention of a semi-nomadic lifestyle through into the later Neolithic, although Thomas (2010, 11) has recently drawn attention to the possibility that Grooved Ware pit assemblages relate to the preparation, presentation and consumption of food. This argument may receive support from the presence of a large number of scrapers within the worked flint assemblage, as well as from the evidence for butchery at Kingshill North.

The predominance of young pig within the animal bone assemblage is also suggestive of feasting, pig being commonly found associated with Grooved Ware, although this is more common at sites such as henges, rather than within pits (Mukherjee *et al.* 2008). The faunal and plant remains point to the continued exploitation of wild resources in the late Neolithic, alongside domesticated species.

The special nature of the deposits should not be overlooked, however, and the material is strongly suggestive of the bringing together of both wild and domestic species in the context of conspicuous consumption, potentially bringing to mind the management and control of the landscape to the participants. This may have more commonly occurred within a monumental context, such as within a henge, but recent work at Durrington Walls (M Parker Pearson, pers. comm.) is demonstrating the presence of pits containing 'special deposits' of Grooved Ware, worked flint and animal bone prior to the construction of such monuments.

The consumption of 'exotic' items can also be seen at Kingshill North in the deposition of fragments of Cornish axe heads and the high quality and quantity of the bone pins and awls recovered from the pits. The worked flint is also imported, as it does not occur naturally on the limestone of the Cotswolds and was probably brought from the chalk around the Avebury area, although it is not possible to be certain of its precise origins. The consumption of 'exotics' again appears to relate to the ability of the community which dug the pits to mobilise a wide range of resources from a variety of locations both local and distant and to dispose of them in a highly visible way.

Beaker/Bronze Age

Beaker burials are rare in Gloucestershire and the two examples from Kingshill North add significant new information for this part of Britain. It is worthy of note that, where skeletal remains from Beaker burials have been examined and the sex of the buried body has been determined, only one other Beaker burial in Gloucestershire has contained female remains. This is a common pattern; Clarke (1970) records nearly twice as many men as women from Beaker burials and the Gloucestershire examples fit into this pattern well. The reasons why males appear to have been selected over females remains unclear, however, but may be related to status or social roles in life.

Neither of the individuals buried at Kingshill North were locals. Both originated from the chalk areas, but one was from the south or east, the other from the south-west (see Lamb and Evans, above). The earliest individual was a female, buried within a pit enclosed by a ring ditch and the Beaker which accompanied her was mostly complete and tempered with grog and limestone. This fabric is more commonly found within Gloucestershire and Somerset and is almost certainly of local manufacture. It is tempting to suggest that the woman buried within the ring ditch may have been 'assimilated' into local society, were it not for the remarkable grave in which she was buried. Although there were no other grave goods apart from the Beaker and a worked bone object, the body was deposited within a deep rectangular grave, above which was deposited cattle head and hooves. The most obvious parallel for this practice is the burial from Hemp Knoll, near Avebury, Wiltshire (Robertson Mackay 1980), where an adult male was buried in a wooden coffin within a deep, rectangular pit below a round barrow. This burial was accompanied by a Langdale stone bracer and a bone belt ring and a Beaker was placed by the body's feet. An ox skull and hooves had been placed outside the coffin, but within the burial pit. The coffin was radiocarbon dated to 2190-1620 cal BC and 2860-1640 cal BC, but given that the material dated was oak and the large margin of error in the dates, these are not helpful in assessing the relative dates of this site and that at Kingshill North. The Beaker from Hemp Knoll was classified by Needham (2005, 192) as belonging to the 'Short-Necked' class, which has its origins in or before the 23rd century BC, but which appears to overlap with the S-profile Beakers, of which that from Kingshill North is an example. The 'head and hooves' burial rite occurs across northern Europe and has been noted in Britain in at least nine long barrows, all within Wessex (Robertson Mackay 1980, 147). The

practice has also been found with Beaker burials, notably at Amesbury, Wiltshire, where a crouched inhumation may have been accompanied by an ox skull and hooves (Ashbee 1978). It is also noteworthy that a cattle skull was recovered from a grave at Barrow Hills, Radley (Barclay and Halpin 1999, 122), although this grave was of early Bronze Age date and also contained unshed antler tines. The presence of a head and hooves burial outside Wessex is unusual and it is perhaps significant that the person to whom this rite was afforded at Kingshill North was non-local and probably came from the chalklands of southern England.

The second burial (1404) was very different. It was deposited within an apparently unmarked flat grave and accompanied by a Beaker which had inclusions of flint and grog, inclusions which are more common in Beakers from Wiltshire and southern England than in those from the Midlands and South West. As noted above, flint does not occur naturally on the Cotswold limestone and the inclusion of flint within the fabric of this Beaker suggests either the importation of raw materials or the use of waste from flint knapping. Although Beakers with flint in their fabrics have been found elsewhere in Gloucestershire, notably at Roughground Farm (Allen *et al.* 1993) and Cirencester Polo Club (Nichols 2004), these are rare. The presence at Kingshill North of a flint-tempered Beaker with an individual from the chalklands is at the very least suggestive of a deliberate referencing of their geographical origin in the fabric of the pot. This vessel also contained grog-in-grog which is was also flint tempered and likely to represent the recycling of fabric from a flint tempered Beaker. The vessel was deposited in the grave as worn sherds, again suggesting that it had had an extended life, perhaps the fragments which were not deposited going on to be incorporated as grog in yet another Beaker.

The radiocarbon dates from the site suggest a period of at least a hundred years between the deposition of the Grooved Ware and the Beaker burials, although a period of 400 or more years may be more likely. It does not appear that the Grooved Ware pits were marked by posts, and it is not certain that they were visible above ground after this period, but the positioning of the Beaker ring ditch between two groups of pits may be more than mere coincidence. Cleal (1999) has previously noted the co-occurrence of Grooved Ware pits and round barrows, but this has not previously been observed in Gloucestershire, despite a degree of barrow excavation (Grinsell 1961). The probable reason for this is that these excavations were undertaken, on the whole, by antiquarians more interested in the contents of the barrows than their local environs and setting. The relative lack of Grooved Ware pits in the county may, then, be more apparent than real and due to the lack of detailed examination of the spaces between round barrows. The co-occurrence of pits containing Grooved Ware and Beaker pottery has been noted at other sites in the county such as

Roughground Farm (Allen *et al.* 1993) and Horcott Pit (Lamdin-Whymark *et al.* 2009), but the question of why this pattern is so common – sites previously used for one purpose being reused several hundred years later in a different way, while apparently respecting the original site plan – has not be addressed. It is tempting to suggest that the activities which took place here in the late Neolithic were somehow remembered, or that they made an impact on the landscape which was still visible many years later, but neither of these interpretations are particularly satisfying.

Needham (2005) suggests that the Beaker phenomenon in Britain started around 2500 cal BC. Only seven radiocarbon dates for Beaker contexts are known from sites other than Kingshill North in Gloucestershire, all but one from sites in the Upper Thames Valley (Table 41). The one date from the Cotswolds from a henge at Condicote (Saville 1983) is from mature wood and should be regarded as unreliable. The other dates are from samples from short-lived species or human bone in direct association with Beakers. Although the dates for the Beakers from Trinity Farm (Mudd *et al.* 1999) and Roughground Farm (Allen *et al.* 1993) fall relatively early within the Beaker sequence, the remaining dates are late and overlap with the period of use of Food Vessels and Collared Urns elsewhere in Britain. The dates from Kingshill North fall between these earlier and later dates. The Beaker from Shorncote (Hearne and Heaton 1994) was placed by Needham (2005) in his 'Weak Carinated Beaker' class, which spans the period 2200 to 1900 cal BC, although, again, this particular vessel seems to be very late in the sequence. The later dated Beaker from the Memorial Hall, Lechlade (Thomas and Holbrook 1998) falls into Needham's 'Long Necked Beaker' classification, which occurs early in the Beaker sequence, but is also associated with late dates, between 3520 and 3360 BP. The earlier dated Beaker from Memorial Hall is classed as an 'S-profile Beaker'. Needham (2005, 200) suggested that this Beaker may have been old when placed in the burial. This draws attention to one of the major problems with Beaker chronology and the general failure of dating schemes to confirm models of Beaker development based on stylistic traits. As

Ann Woodward (2002) has pointed out, Beakers may have circulated as heirlooms before finally being deposited, leading to a confusion of late dates for stylistically early Beakers.

As can be seen in Table 41, the dates from Kingshill North and from Gloucestershire in general are not particularly early, those from Kingshill North falling within the 'Fission Horizon' between the 'pioneer' use of Beakers and their more widespread acceptance (Needham 2005). The date of the Beaker within the ring ditch is identical to the date from a 'mass grave' containing seven individuals and Beaker pottery from Boscombe Down, Wiltshire. Some of the individuals in the grave were not local to Wiltshire and probably originated in the west of Britain (Needham 2005; Evans *et al.* 2006). The Beakers from Boscombe Down are very different to those from Kingshill North, however, and have more in common with European All Over Cord Beakers. The date from the flat grave at Kingshill North is identical to that from a burial at Radley, Oxfordshire, which was accompanied by a tall, mid-carinated Beaker (Needham 2005, 187) and to a series of Beaker burials from Scotland, including skeleton 1 at Thurston Mains, East Lothian and cist 1 at Broomend of Critchie (Needham 2005).

The isotopes from the individuals buried at Kingshill North indicate that they were not local, and probably originated from chalkland regions of England. As such they fit within an emerging picture of population mobility in the later Neolithic, with an individual from continental Europe found in the Stonehenge environs and good evidence now available for the movement of individuals at a regional and national level (Jay *et al.* forthcoming). Needham (2007) has suggested that mobility was part of the Beaker way of life and that after initial movement of small groups from the Continent, the budding-off of groups who then moved into new areas was responsible for the widespread uptake of Beakers and the collapse of the Grooved Ware 'culture' in the 22nd century BC. Kingshill North finds fit within this pattern of the movement of individuals over relatively short distances into an area already known to Grooved Ware using groups. These sorts of connections were already present in

Table 41: Radiocarbon dates from contexts associated with Beakers in Gloucestershire

Site	Radiocarbon date	Calibrated date	Material dated
Trinity Farm	3876 + 57BP	2490 to 2150 cal BC	hazelnut shells
Trinity Farm	3836 + 58BP	2470 to 2140 cal BC	hazelnut shells
Roughground Farm	3710 + 100BP	2460 to 1880 cal BC	bone
Condicote Henge	3720 + 80BP	2430 to 1890 cal BC	mature wood
Kingshill North skeleton 8656	3830 ± 29BP	2351 to 2198 cal BC	human bone
Kingshill North skeleton 1403	3718 ± 29BP	2201 to 2031 cal BC	human bone
Lechlade Memorial Hall	3530 + 50BP	2020 to 1740 cal BC	human bone
Shorncote	3480 + 60 BP	1950 to 1640 cal BC	human bone
Lechlade Memorial Hall	3460 + 50BP	1920 to 1630 cal BC	human bone

the late Neolithic and are clear from the exchange between the Cotswolds and regions beyond, as seen in the presence of flint and Cornish axe heads in the Grooved Ware pits. Indeed, although Beaker burial practices appear to represent a 'clean break' from the practices of the later part of the Neolithic, when formal burial was relatively rare, deposits continued to be made in pits and these are, in fact, more common and include more Beaker vessels than burials, especially in the western part of Britain (see Lewis and Mullin forthcoming). Two examples close to Cirencester illustrate the point. At Cirencester Polo Club, to the north of Cirencester at Daglingworth, a single pit contained sherds of Beaker, representing a minimum of eight vessels, alongside animal bone, including cattle and possible wild boar (Nichols 2004). At Trinity Farm, Bagendon (Mudd *et al.* 1999), a total of three pits contained 164 sherds of Beaker pottery, from at least 14 vessels, alongside worked flint, hazelnut shells and burnt stone. The contents of the pits, and the treatment of this material, often deliberately broken and burnt, has much in common with the material from pits containing Grooved Ware. Alex Gibson (2007) has argued that the change in burial practices seen in the Beaker period has its origins in the later Neolithic and is not such a clean break as has previously been thought. When the evidence from pits is considered, the division between Grooved Ware and Beaker practices is even less clear-cut.

Middle Bronze Age

The single feature of middle Bronze Age date from the site was burial 1905. Such inhumations are rare, with few other recorded examples dating to this period. The usual rite in the middle Bronze Age is cremation, usually with a Deverel-Rimbury vessel, or local variant. Examples of this rite have been recorded in Gloucestershire at Bevans Quarry, Temple Guiting (O'Neil 1967) and also at Shorncote Quarry (Barclay and Glass 1995), but is generally rarer in the west of Britain than in the south and east. A middle Bronze Age inhumation is known from Cotswold Community (Powell *et al.* 2010, 41-42), where an adult female buried in a rectangular grave was radiocarbon dated to 1510 to 1400 cal BC (95%; SUERC-18831), contemporary with the date of 1502 to 1415 cal BC (95%; OxA-20188) from Kingshill North. The burials were in different positions, however: that from Kingshill North being on its back with its legs crossed, and the burial from Cotswold Community being tightly crouched on its right side. Other burials placed on their backs are known from Appleford Sidings, Oxfordshire (Booth and Simmonds 2009), where a young woman was buried in a roughly oval grave pit in a tightly crouched position, on her back with arms folded across her stomach, and knees drawn up to her chest. Although the burial was not scientifically dated, a middle Bronze Age globular urn had been placed at the left side of her body. At Mount Farm

near Dorchester-on-Thames, Oxfordshire (Lambrick 2010), the latest burial on the site was the inhumation of a young woman dated to 1680-1220 cal BC, while at Watkins Farm, Oxfordshire (Allen 1990), a body was placed in an extended position at the bottom of a ramped well which contained wood radiocarbon dated to 1400-1250 cal BC (HAR-8253).

The burial from Kingshill North was also accompanied by a joint of meat. At the Beeches, immediately to the south of the site (Young 2001), an animal burial was found in a pit inside an enclosure, the burial was dated to 1400 to 1120 cal BC (NZA-12281) and further animal bone from this area was dated to 1510 to 1310 cal BC (NZA-12282). Significantly, a piece of human skull, associated with fragments of Globular Urn, also gave a middle Bronze Age date of 1400 to 1130 cal BC (NZA-12280). All these dates overlap with that from Kingshill North and possibly indicate that the main focus of middle Bronze Age activity was in this area, where, incidentally, there was little evidence for earlier occupation.

Within the wider area, there is evidence for middle Bronze Age occupation at Roughground Farm (Allen *et al.* 1993) and Horcott Pit (Lamdin-Whymark *et al.* 2009), where Middle Bronze Age pottery appears to be associated with domestic activity. Deverel Rimbury pottery was also present at Cotswold Community (Powell *et al.* 2010), where a relatively large assemblage was recovered from a series of pits and a waterhole. These sites appear to represent the first 'organised' agricultural settlements and belong to the period when the first field systems and land divisions emerge (Yates 2007). However, Gloucestershire lies at the edge of the distribution of field systems: they are focused in the Upper Thames Valley and there is a paucity of evidence from the Cotswolds. Quite why this is the case is open to question, but may represent a difference in land use – the high Cotswold being used for summer pasture, while the valleys were exploited for arable and seasonal grazing.

Iron Age to Roman (Fig. 44) *Edward Biddulph*

The middle Iron Age activity

There was a gap of at least 1000 years after the middle Bronze Age burial (1905) was interred. The absence of early Iron Age activity at Kingshill North is unsurprising, as evidence for early Iron Age settlement around Cirencester is sparse. Residual early Iron Age pottery was recovered from a section across the Lynches trackway, a route of Roman origin that extended alongside the River Churn from Cirencester. The pottery from the section, located about 4 km north-west of Kingshill North, pointed to a settlement in the vicinity, though no features were detected (Mudd 1999, 517). At the Beeches, about 500 m south of Kingshill North, excavation revealed an enclosure ditch, whose filling was dated by pottery to the early Iron Age. Its width and depth led the excavator to speculate on a possible defensive

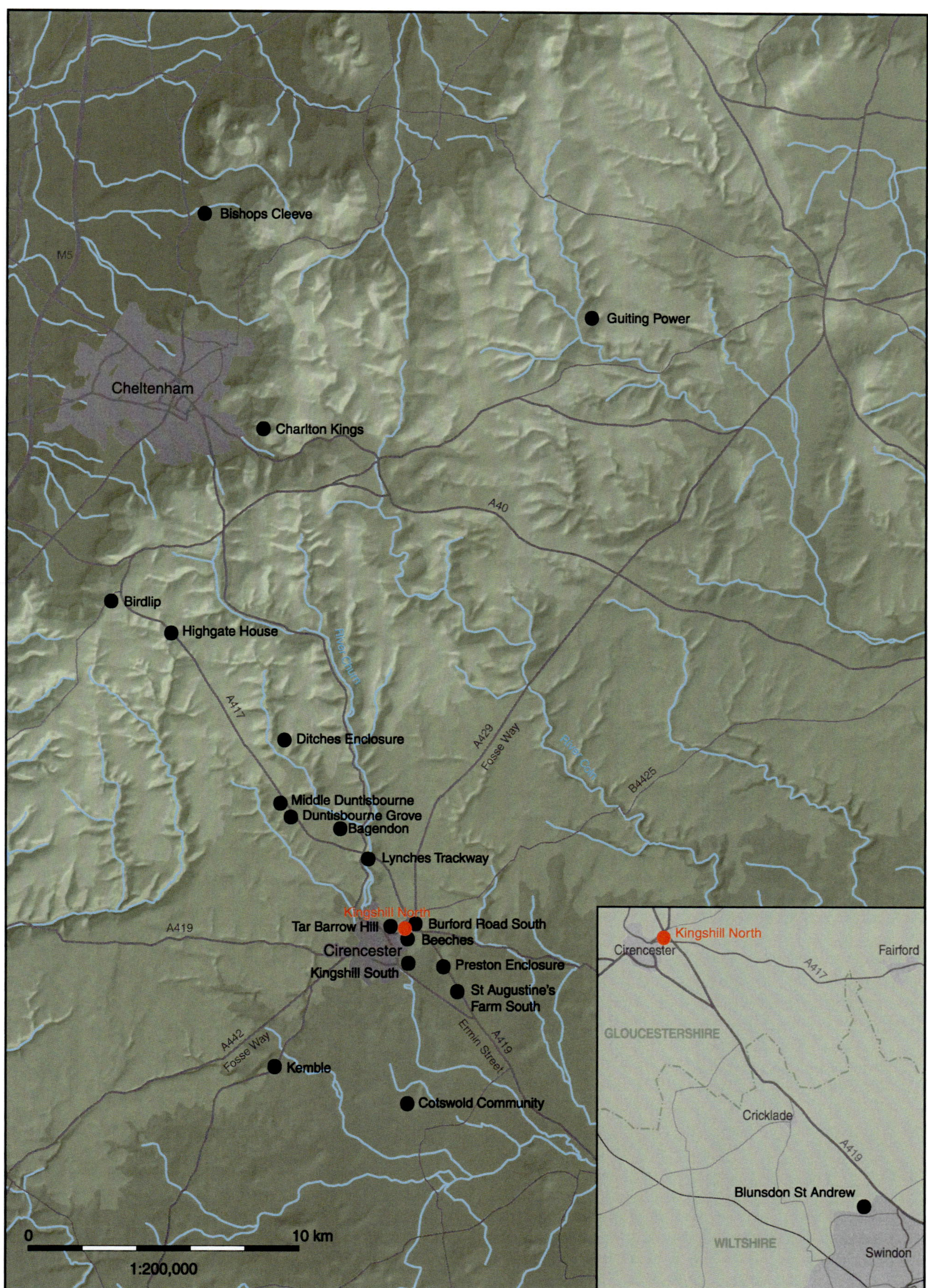

Fig. 44   Phases 3 and 4 – locations of sites mentioned in discussion

function, though without further evidence, the matter remained unresolved. Postholes nearby suggested the presence of associated structures, although the features were undated (Young 2001, 38). Further afield, extensive settlement evidence broadly dated to the late Bronze/early Iron Age was recorded at the Cotswold Community site, 5 km south of Kingshill North. Excavations uncovered dispersed areas of unenclosed settlement set within a pastoral and agricultural landscape (Powell *et al.* 2010, 71, fig. 2.31). Further east, at Roughground Farm, Lechlade, a roundhouse, pits and boundary ditches were assigned to the early Iron Age (Allen *et al.* 1993, 36-40).

The next phase of activity at Kingshill North began in the middle Iron Age (Phase 3). The phase is characterised by pits dug across the southern part of the site. The frequency, form and distribution of the pits appear to be a curious repetition of the late Neolithic phase, but the pits can be placed in the Iron Age with certainty. Radiocarbon dates the filling of two pits between the 4th and 3rd centuries BC (for example, 394-209 cal BC – 95%; NZA-33476), and all pits contained pottery that dated to the middle Iron Age, or was at least consistent with that period. Additionally, the range of animal bones recovered from the Iron Age pits, with its emphasis on sheep or goat, was different from the cattle and pig profile of the Neolithic assemblage. As for function, the profiles of the pits – generally vertical-sided, flat-based and, in some cases, undercut – are consistent with Iron Age features typically identified as storage pits, with grain being the likely primary content (cf. Bersu 1940; Reynolds 1979; Whittle 1984, 128-37; Lambrick 2009, 274-77). A relatively rich sample of charred plant remains recovered from the bottom fill of pit 9083 may represent the remains of the final use of the pit for storage, in this case the storage of fodder (see W Smith, above), although the assemblage also contained elements that suggested secondary deposition of crop-processing waste. The shallower pits, such as 8143 and 8138, are less easily identified as storage pits. Some of these may originally have been deeper, being located at the top of the hillside and therefore more prone to truncation than those further down the slope, although shallow pits were found there too. These pits may alternatively be viewed as water-storage pits (cf. Parry 1998, 45). Where shallow pits were cut into or lined with clay, Parry (1998, 45) also suggests a possible role in pottery production, potentially serving as clay-puddling tanks.

Other middle Iron Age sites in the region were similarly characterised by groups of storage pits. A group of 19 pits set within two principal enclosures, were recorded at Birdlip, Cowley, some 20 km north-west of Cirencester. The pits there were largely cylindrical, with barrel-shaped pits also represented. Overall the pits were deeper and narrower than those at Kingshill North, measuring on average 1.3 m across and 0.93 m deep, although there was overlap in the ranges (Parry 1998, 39). A middle Iron Age date was ascribed to most of them, but pottery suggested that some pits were filled or dug as late as the 1st-century AD (Parry 1998, 44). A mass of pits, dated to the middle Iron Age and associated with postholes, was excavated at Guiting Power, located on the higher hills of the Cotswolds some 25 km north of Cirencester. The pits there, however, were generally shallower than those at Kingshill North and Birdlip, with the range extending to 0.6 m in depth, and a water-storage function, rather than grain storage, was preferred (Saville 1979, 127, 136). Two pits, one of middle to late Iron Age in date, the other dating to the 1st century AD, were uncovered in excavations at Vineyards Farm, Charlton Kings (Rawes 1991). At Bishop's Cleeve, seven pits, associated with roundhouses and spreads of occupation soil, were recorded. These measured on average 1.6 m in diameter and 0.8 m deep (Lovell *et al.* 2007, 99). Thirteen middle Iron Age pits, along with soil-marks, were excavated at Gilder's Paddock, another site in Bishop's Cleeve. The pits formed two clusters; the pits in one group were cylindrical, measuring up to 1.48 m wide and 0.57 m deep (Parry 1999, 93), while those in the second group were shallower and wider – up to 1.64 m in diameter and 0.35 m deep (Parry 1999, 96). The difference, recalling the separation of shallow and deep pits at Kingshill North, may have been one of function. An investigation at a site at Kemble, *c* 5 km south-west of Cirencester, produced five steep-sided pits with an average diameter of 1.1 m and depth of 0.6 m (King *et al.* 1996, 19). Closer still to Kingshill North, investigation of an area at Burford Road South just a few hundred metres east of the site revealed four pits broadly dated to the later prehistoric period (Mudd *et al.* 1999a, 72). Two of the pits were relatively large at over 4 m wide, but shallow at up to 0.3 m deep, and they are unlikely to have functioned as grain-storage pits. Material characteristic of 'burnt mound' deposits were recovered from them (Mudd *et al.* 1999a, 74), and the pits, like those at Kingshill North, appear to have been peripheral to, even isolated from, roundhouses and the focus of habitation. Where more extensive remains of middle Iron Age settlement are known, the evidence points to enclosed nucleated settlements with associated field systems (Moore 2006, 85). A number of such sites have been recorded in the Cotswolds and the Upper Thames Valley. The enclosed settlement at Birdlip comprised a roughly square enclosure that surrounded a ten-metre wide ring-gully. This enclosure was connected by ditches to a boundary ditch that was semi-circular in plan and enclosed the pits alluded to above (Parry 1998, fig. 3). An enclosure with associated pits was seen at Highgate House, close to Birdlip and *c* 13 km north of Cirencester (Mudd and Lupton 1999, 59-64), while a segmented ditch system was recorded at St Augustine's Farm South, 2 km south of Kingshill North (Mudd and Muir 1999, 35-8). A hexagonal enclosure uncovered at Preston, a short distance north of St Augustine's

Farm South, contained pits and ditches and the curving gully segments of roundhouses (Mudd and Mortimer 1999, fig. 3.9). A cluster of roundhouses attached to an enclosure was recorded at Cotswold Community (Powell *et al.* 2010, 74-82), and similar evidence – roundhouses and associated pits and ditches – was uncovered at Thornhill Farm, Fairford (Jennings *et al.* 2004, 21-30).

Once the middle Iron Age pits at Kingshill North were abandoned, they were available for further deposition. Much of the material recovered from the pits, typically pottery and animal bone, is likely to derive from domestic waste, with the level of fragmentation suggesting that the finds had undergone episodes of disturbance and weathering, for example from exposure on a midden or through ploughing, before final deposition. There was, however, evidence of deliberate, structured deposits in the form of the skeletons of a crow or rook and dog in pit 8851. The skeletons were deposited along with limestone rubble and stony soil into an essentially empty pit – there had been a degree of erosion at the side of the pit before deposition. The deposit therefore represents an event enacted after the pit had served its primary storage function. An antler comb, retrieved from pit 8114, is also of interest. Though a single item, the deposit may be of the same tradition that induced the middle Iron Age inhabitants of Bishop's Cleeve to place a group of weaving equipment – an antler comb, up to three antler needles, a triangular loomweight and a spindle whorl – into a storage pit (Lovell 2007, 99).

Chronological overview of the late Iron Age and Roman settlement

The archaeology assigned to phases 4a to 4c essentially falls into a single period, the late Iron Age. Potentially this spans the 1st century BC to first half of the 1st century AD, although the pottery and radiocarbon determinations from features in this period lean towards the later part of this range. There is virtually nothing among the pottery and other datable artefacts to separate the remains into sub-phases. Division was possible, however, on stratigraphic and spatial grounds. Ditch 8563, which partially enclosed a group of postholes that formed the outline of a roughly rectangular building some 10 m long by 5 m wide, was attributed to Phase 4a. A radiocarbon date (90 cal BC-cal AD 64 – 95%; NZA-33149) obtained from charred grain from the ditch, along with pottery including grog-tempered pedestal vessels and high-shouldered necked jars, suggests that the ditch was filled at the end of the 1st century BC or the early 1st century AD. A burial (1104) was interred within the fill of the enclosure ditch probably during the first half of the 1st century; the skeleton gave a radiocarbon date of 41 cal BC to 75 cal AD (95%; OxA-20187). Though the ditch had been filled, the burial suggests that it remained visible, perhaps as a slight dip or area of taller vegetation.

Pottery collected from features assigned to Phase 4b was identical in form and fabric to that from phase 4a features – but in stratigraphical terms represents a development of the landscape. Ditch 8918 cut the termini of the infilled ditch, 8563, and extended through the structure, now abandoned, that 8563 enclosed. Ditch 8918 was not designed to enclose. It defines a boundary, but its shape, in plan resembling the shape of an archer's composite bow, may also have facilitated the herding of livestock or allowed temporary enclosures to be erected. Postholes cut into the fill of ditch 8563 may have been positioned with reference to ditch 8918, creating a small enclosure or palisade. Like 8563, ditch 8918 was associated with a structure; postholes at its northern end loosely defined a roundhouse that overlay the northern part of 8563. The dating of a burial (8723) inserted into the northern terminus of ditch 8918 is problematic. That it post-dated the ditch is certain. A radiocarbon determination obtained from the skeleton, however, provided a date of 181 to 41 cal BC (95%; OxA-20185), potentially making it earlier than the Phase 4a features. This is a matter not easily resolved. We could suggest that the skeleton of an individual alive in the first half of the 1st century BC or earlier was re-buried at the end of the 1st century BC or early 1st century AD, or that the dating of the skeleton and phases 4a and 4b all coincide in the narrowest of chronological overlaps, but both suggestions have the signs of special pleading. The radiocarbon date could, of course, be at fault, although there was no obvious means of contamination.

Ditch 8918 was in turn replaced by ditch 8413, which was substantially larger in width and length (Phase 4c). Ditch 8413 formed a significant boundary, and its semi-circular form in plan, enhanced further by recuts and extensions. A possible roundhouse was erected close to the southern terminus of 8413, while two slots (9028 and 9076/8) may mark the position of a rectangular structure. Internal sub-division is suggested by two rows of postholes; one extends ENE-WSE immediately south of the roundhouse, while another, orientated NNW-SSE, was located nearer the northern end of the ditch. A narrower boundary ditch (8255) extended along the southern edge of the excavation area. The pottery recovered from ditch 8413 included Severn Valley ware and Savernake ware, suggesting that the ditch received material after the mid-1st century AD. The other features assigned to this phase – ditch 8255, the structures, postholes, and extensions and recuts to 8413 – in contrast lacked the post-conquest wares, comprising instead wares of late Iron Age type, suggesting that deposition was confined to the first half of the 1st century AD. If these were indeed associated with ditch 8413, as seems reasonable on spatial grounds, then ditch 8413 may well have been dug during the final decades of the late Iron Age but continued to receive material into the Roman period.

In Phase 4d, ditch 8413 was extended at its northern end, and two short gullies or ditches defined a small enclosure extending from the southern end of the ditch. An intercutting sequence of probable quarry pits, and other, larger, pits were dug within the area enclosed by 8413 to extract clay and limestone. Pottery retrieved from a number of these features usually comprised late Iron Age wares – typically limestone-tempered and grog-tempered pottery – associated with Roman-period material, such as grey wares, Savernake ware and Severn Valley ware. How far into the second half of the 1st century such assemblages can be pushed is a matter of debate. Comparison with the earliest (military) phase of Roman Cirencester is potentially misleading, since the pottery supply to the fort was shaped by the specific requirements of the soldiers, which depended to a larger extent than neighbouring settlements on regional and continental sources (cf. Cooper 1998, 327; for discussion, see Biddulph, late Iron Age and Roman pottery, Chapter 4, above). However, on the basis of assemblages from nearby sites, for instance Ditches (Moore 2009, 114), a date for deposition within the third quarter of the 1st century is not unreasonable.

The site saw very little activity from the late 1st century onwards (phases 4e and 4f). A cremation grave (8227), radiocarbon dated to cal AD 86-247 (95%; NZA-33144), was inserted into the fill of ditch 8918. A ditch (8203) in the southern part of the site, containing late Roman pottery and a coin of Constantine, was filled during the 4th century. Pottery of 2nd-century date, including Central Gaulish samian, was also recovered, though this is likely to have been incorporated as residual occurrences in later deposits through agricultural activity. The site remained available for farming into modern times.

Production and economy

The evidence of land snails indicates that the landscape around the settlement was largely open (see Champness, Chapter 6, above). The grassland environment, though with some provision for woodland and arable land, provided pasture and harvested fodder for livestock. The animal bone evidence and the composition of the plant assemblage are also consistent with an economy based predominantly on livestock (see Strid and Nicholson, Chapter 6, above). Sheep (or goat) made the largest contribution to the assemblage recovered from middle Iron Age pits. Cattle were also represented in this phase, but were less important than sheep, and remained so throughout the Iron Age and early Roman period, except in Phase 4a/b, when the species briefly made a larger contribution to the animal bone assemblage than sheep.

This predominance of sheep is typical of 'native' British settlements, rather than those with a Roman character, which are weighted more towards pigs and cattle (King 1991, 17). The open countryside, albeit with tree cover to the north of the site, is unlikely to have suited pigs, which were appropriately kept in small numbers. The dominance of pig bones in the Neolithic phase is notable, given that the environment was similarly open and dry, although, as noted by D Mullin above, this is likely to reflect a specialised feasting function associated with the Neolithic pits, rather than being representative of subsistence farming strategies. The late Iron Age and Roman landscape was good for horses. None of the horse bones from the site was found to have had evidence of butchery, and so were kept for uses other than food.

Data relating to age point to a trend for older sheep and younger cattle, suggesting that sheep were kept mainly for wool, but also meat, while cattle were reared for meat. Sheep and cattle also provided milk for human consumption. There was less importance placed on the use of cattle for traction, hinting that the communities living at the site were mainly pastoral.

Nevertheless, arable farming was practised (see Smith, Chapter 6, above), and the molluscan evidence, at least in the later Roman period, has identified fields set aside from crops to the south of the settlement (see Champness, Chapter 6, above). Wheat and barley were identified in middle and late Iron Age samples, and the recovery of a near-complete upper rotary quern from pit 8806 points to the processing of grain presumably grown locally at a subsistence level. The deposition of the quern itself was no doubt a special act for the late Iron Age inhabitants, resonating with the symbolism of food production and, ultimately, survival (Moore 2006, 123). But while cereals were grown, they were not the main crops. The abundance of wild species and grasses in the environmental samples raises the intriguing possibility that grasses, including brome and rye grass and species such as wild oat, were deliberately cultivated to provide animal fodder. To this list we may add the barley, which is well-known as an animal feed.

The evidence paints a picture of a pastoral landscape, with fields populated mainly by sheep, but also cattle and horses, with areas set aside for grassland and hay meadows and for crops to a lesser extent. The description of 16th-century Cirencester by the Tudor antiquary, John Leland, provides an interesting footnote. In observing that the stony fields around the town were more suitable for barley than wheat, and that there was not a great supply of wood (Chandler 1998, 190), Leland could equally have been describing the land around Kingshill North in the 1st century AD.

There was little evidence for other forms of economic activity. Hammerscale, the residue of iron smithing, and tiny spheres produced by high-temperature welding indicate that there was a small amount of ironworking on the site. A significant proportion of the material was recovered as intrusive occurrences in Neolithic pits and the ring-ditch of Beaker burial 8454, but otherwise was collected from features that dated almost exclusively to Phase 4c. However, the find-spots – within ditches 8413 and 8255 – give little focus to the location of the activity. Most of the pottery, particularly the calcareous and grog-tempered wares, would have been made locally, but there were no wasters or other forms of production waste to indicate manufacture on or close to the site.

Settlement and landscape

Taken together, the late Iron Age evidence represents successive phases of a farmstead set within an enclosure or field system. While the area encompassed by the ditches expanded with each phase, only one principal structure per phase, its position shifting with each development, was identified. The rectangular building of Phase 4a stands in obvious contrast to the roundhouses that replaced it, and, if occupied as a domestic structure, is unusual in the region. Six-poster rectangular structures are reasonably common, but these are likely to have served as storage buildings (Lambrick 2009, 271-2). Given the larger size of the Phase 4a building, this interpretation can be discounted. Rectangular structures of possible domestic function and late Iron Age date are known on sites along the Thames, but are confined to the lower and middle Thames Valley (Lambrick 2009, 151). While a structural function is favoured here, the possibility that the postholes represent parallel fence lines might also be considered. This seems especially pertinent given the five-metre gap at the west end of the structure and slight narrowing of the building's width towards the east end. If the west end were open, then we could envisage some sort of pen for livestock, holding sheep, perhaps, during wool clipping. If so, where the inhabitants of the Phase 4a settlement lived is not known, although the circular spread of occupation soil (8844) below the roundhouse of Phase 4b hints at earlier buildings existing on that site.

In broad terms, the site resembles other farming settlements in the region, although notably the closest parallels belong to the earlier Iron Age. A mid to late Iron Age settlement at Cotswold Community consisted of a large rectilinear enclosure – internally sparse in terms of features – and a small unenclosed area of domestic activity outside, comprising two roundhouses (Powell *et al.* 2010, fig. 3.5). Enclosures dating to the mid 1st century AD were recorded at Middle Duntisbourne (Mudd and Lupton 1999, fig. 3.34) and Duntisbourne Grove (Mudd and Lawrence 1999, fig. 3.41). None was associated with structures, but like Kingshill North was open on one or two sides and sparsely occupied within. The curving plan of the ditches at Kingshill North is obviously different from the rectangular enclosures of the Duntisbournes, but their function may have been similar. Parts of the middle to late Iron Age settlement complex at Mount Farm, Dorchester-on-Thames, Oxfordshire, particularly a curving enclosure ditch with possible roundhouses along its

length at the north-eastern end of the site, provide a better match for Kingshill North (Lambrick 2010, fig. 43b). The curving boundary ditch at Birdlip, potentially of middle Iron Age date (Parry 1998, fig. 3), recalls the form of ditch 8413 at Kingshill North. Another useful parallel was the early to middle Iron Age settlement at Groundwell Farm, Blunsdon St Andrew near Swindon, Wiltshire, which comprised a curvilinear enclosure which surrounded successive phases of a roundhouse. The excavator suggested that the farmstead was occupied by a single household (Gingell 1981, 73), an interpretation which might reasonably be applied to Kingshill North. Excavation at Groundwell Farm also uncovered parallel pairs or triplets of slots, usually with postholes inside, that represented structures up to 5 m square (Gingell 1981, 49). These are likely to be equivalent to the four-poster structures commonly recorded in the Thames Valley and typically interpreted as raised granaries or fodder storage (Lambrick 2009, 271; Powell *et al.* 2010, 72). The Phase 4c parallel slots at Kingshill North (9028 and 9076/8) lack the postholes, but can be viewed in similar terms. It is clear, therefore, that the late Iron Age settlement at Kingshill North is redolent of earlier Iron Age settlements, and takes the chronology of the settlement type into the 1st-century AD and beyond the Roman invasion of AD 43.

It is worth noting the sets of cropmarks that aerial photography has recorded to the south of Kingshill North (Fig. 1). Some of these have been investigated. The excavation by the Avon Archaeological Unit at the Beeches (Young 2001) has already been touched upon. An earlier excavation at the Beeches uncovered an enclosure and pits probably relating to a farmstead. Dating evidence was limited, but pointed to an Iron Age date (Reece 1990, 9-19). Cropmarks to the south-east of the town at Kingshill uncovered shallow ditches that were attributed to the 1st, and possibly the 2nd, century AD (Reece 1990, 39-40). How all these relate to each other and Kingshill North – it is possible, for example, that the cropmarks represent a sequence of settlement and relocation from the Bronze Age to the Roman period – cannot be addressed at present, and much of the investigation of the cropmarks is still to do. However, it is safe to assume that quite extensive areas of prehistoric and Roman land division, enclosures and settlement lay across the eastern side of Cirencester.

Funerary practice

What links the three burials belonging to Phase 4 is the fact that all were interred within ditches. Late Iron Age infant burial 1104 was deposited in ditch 8563. Inhumation 8724, though radiocarbon dated to the middle or late Iron Age, was placed in late Iron Age ditch 8918. This ditch also took early or mid Roman cremation burial 8227. The rites varied, but the type of burial location was unchanged for at least 100 years. While this is unsurprising in the context of the Iron Age – boundary locations are well known among archaeologically visible forms of burial – the continuity evident at Kingshill North, the use of boundaries extending well into the Roman period, adds to the perceived significance of ditches as landscape markers and liminal spaces separating the living and the dead (Moore 2006, 70).

This role of separating the realms seems particularly relevant at Kingshill North. Ditch 8563 not only formed an enclosure, but also surrounded and protected a home. A roundhouse was built next to ditch 8918. Here, then, the dead inhabited the same space as the living. Such treatment cannot have been accorded to all individuals, since the burials recorded here are unlikely to have represented the entire population of the farmstead, even if accommodating a single household. We might tentatively suggest that individuals 1104 and 8724 were deemed to be special. Potentially this presents a way of explaining the discrepant middle Iron Age date of 8724. If belonging to a socially high-ranking individual in life – a community leader, perhaps – the skeleton may have been re-buried to mark, say, the relocation of the farmstead. This does not explain the nature of the bones, which had a level of articulation consistent with a single episode of burial, but other mortuary rites before reburial – careful curation of the remains or a form of mummification – might be considered. However, the means by which preservation could have been achieved at the site cannot yet be suggested, returning us to the simpler explanation that the radiocarbon date was inaccurate. The association between infant burial 1104 and the structure enclosed by ditch 8563 might also identify the infant as special, and Eleanor Scott's discussion of the role of neonate and infant burials, which, she argues, serves to link life and death, the earthly world and domain of the gods and ancestors (Scott 1999), has its merits. Nevertheless, there is generally little to separate the treatment of children and adults in death in the Upper Thames Valley, as can be seen at Kingshill North, and that given infant burials in settlements was quite usual (Lambrick 2009, 321). The meanings imposed on both the adult and child burials need not be so different either.

Grave 8227 maintained the tradition of boundary burial into the Roman period. The choice of location, at a time when the settlement had been abandoned and formal cemeteries were established around Corinium – for example to the south of the town along Ermin Street immediately beyond Silchester Gate (Holbrook 1994, 83) – is curious. But if, as Moore (2006, 70) argues, boundary burials expressed the relationship between the land and its inhabitants, for instance defining territory and establishing or renewing ancestral tenure, then burial within ditch 8918 during a period of social and political upheaval and uncertainty is plausible. The former inhabitants of Kingshill North had moved into the town, but the land remained theirs,

at least in spirit if not the law. However, other interpretations are possible. The burial of the individual, otherwise unconnected with the Iron Age activity at the site, may have been a propitiatory act in prime farmland. What is less likely, though, is that the individual was a criminal or outcast, as his isolated position might suggest. The accompanying grave goods indicate that great care was taken with the cremation and the interment, and suggest that, like inhumation 8724, the individual was special, possibly a leader or otherwise of some social standing. The most obvious expression of that status is the deposition of over 1000 small nails within the grave. These belonged to a light structure, probably a litter or bier, which was used to carry the individual to the pyre. The structure was probably plain – there was no evidence for the sort of decorated and upholstered biers recorded, for example, in the Roman cemetery at Brougham, Cumbria (Cool 2004, 439-40) – but it brings a formality to the mortuary rite and, with its destruction on the pyre, implies relatively high expenditure by the estate of the deceased or through the contributions of the mourners. We can imagine the funeral procession or *pompa* winding its way from the town through Verulamium Gate and along Fosse Way before turning into the farmland exposed at Kingshill North.

If the body was cremated at the site, then there is no evidence for it. The grass or turves burnt as fuel in the pyre could have come from the meadowland around the site, but were not diagnostic of the site specifically. A shoe or pair of shoes was placed with the deceased on the pyre. Shoes were commonly deposited in graves (Philpott 1991, 168) and tend to be interpreted as an item necessary for the journey to the afterlife. The explanation is not altogether satisfactory when we consider the variation in the practice, for example the burial of one shoe or more than two in a single grave, and instead we might prefer to view the selection of shoes as a product of behaviours inherited from earlier generations or society more generally. The deceased in grave 8227 was accompanied by shoes because other individuals before him were accompanied with shoes; there need be no recourse to original meaning. Nevertheless, the shoes conform to standard Roman practice, and the deceased, carried on a litter, cremated, and wearing shoes, was for all appearances a Roman. But the location of the grave was Iron Age, and provides evidence for the survival of British burial traditions beyond the Roman conquest.

Status, function and identity

The farmstead at Kingshill North was established at the time that the enclosure at Ditches, some 8 km north of the site, was first occupied (Trow *et al.* 2009, 45). This enclosure appeared to represent the earliest activity of an extended 'oppidum' that was augmented in the mid 1st century by the earthworks at nearby Bagendon (Fig. 44). The oppidum was a sprawling complex that can be likened to Camulodunum (Colchester) and Verulamium (St Albans), whose earthworks define territory covering many square kilometres (Trow *et al.* 2009, 73). The territory of the Ditches/Bagendon complex encompassed settlements and farmsteads, among them Duntisbourne Grove and Middle Duntisbourne. This was the land of the Dobunni, and the Ditches/Bagendon complex served as a tribal centre. The distribution of Dobunnic coinage, some of it minted in the oppidum (Trow *et al.* 2009, 72), allows Kingshill North to be placed firmly within the tribal territory, which extended across Gloucestershire and Warwickshire, reaching areas south of the Thames, along the Avon Valley and west of the Severn (Jones and Mattingly 1990, 50; map 3.10).

Despite its proximity to the tribal centre, Kingshill North does not seem to have benefited materially. While the settlement may have supplied wool, meat, milk, fodder and, to a lesser extent, cereals, to neighbouring settlements, its catchment was limited, probably little more than a few kilometres around the site. It may have included an occupation site pre-dating the Leaholme fort, as represented by a stake circle (Wacher and McWhirr 1982, 28), but is unlikely to have included Ditches or Bagendon. Those sites saw to their own needs (Rielly 2009, 205-6). The absence of high-status goods, such as Gallo-Belgic finewares, which the inhabitants of Kingshill North might have received in exchange for agricultural produce, is telling. By contrast the Duntisbournes had similar ceramic assemblages to the site at the Ditches and benefited from closer contact or trade with the elite centre (see Figs 35 and 36). The Roman fort established during the third quarter of the 1st century (Darvill and Holbrook 1994, 53) was potentially another market for the farmers of Kingshill North. There is some support for this in the animal bone assemblage. It is evident from ageing data that wool production became more important after AD 43 (Phase 4d), and the relatively paucity of adult cattle (albeit based on a small sample) in the Phase 4c/4d assemblage hints at the trade of live animals (see Strid and Nicholson, above). Another potential product was the hay grown in the fields, which would have been a useful source of fodder for the horses stabled in the fort. But even the extent of this trade must have been limited. A measure of this is again provided by the pottery. The composition of the ceramic assemblage dating to the mid to late 1st century lacked the sorts of pottery, such as flagons, platters and imported finewares, attributed to the military levels (Cooper 1998, 325). If the farmers of Kingshill North were supplying the fort, then one might expect them to have received such goods in exchange or use the opportunity of the trade to acquire some choice pieces. This does not necessarily bring us to a deliberate rejection of, or resistance to, Roman culture on the part of Kingshill's inhabitants, simply that the farmers' cultural environment was not

susceptible to influence from the fort. Limited social contact and the ten years or so that the fort was occupied (Darvill and Holbrook 1994, 53) may not have been enough to create appreciable changes in the Iron Age lifestyles among the population of Kingshill North. However, we cannot dismiss the possibility that the site was abandoned when the Fosse Way was laid out and before the fort was established in *c* AD 55. This may explain the absence of a trackway to link Kingshill North with the Roman road.

If not by *c* AD 50/55, Kingshill North was certainly abandoned as a place of domestic occupation by *c* AD 75, the time when the fort was vacated and the civilian town of *Corinium Dobunnorum* established. The absence of occupation at the site from that time onwards indicates that the area was rural, and probably for the most part it provided pasture and arable land. There was some activity; a field ditch (8203) was cut in the 4th century, and the presence of highly fragmented and chronologically mixed animal bone and pottery is a product of agricultural activity such as manuring and ploughing. It is not clear whether this work was managed from Corinium or, say, a villa estate that had incorporated the land at Kingshill North, although the burial of cremated human remains in ditch 8913, as suggested above, could be cited as evidence that the inhabitants of Kingshill North or their descendants retained a degree of ownership over the site. Occupation immediately beyond the eastern side of the town did not cease altogether. Excavation of cropmarks on the Cirencester ring-road to the south-east of the town revealed an enclosure, possibly a farmstead dating to the 1st and 2nd century (see Fig. 1; Reece 1990, 39-40). What connection this had with the rectangular building and associated farm estate uncovered during excavations at Kingshill South by Oxford Archaeology in 2009-10 remains to be seen, but it is becoming clear that the extra-mural area continued to support a rural, if relatively high-ranking, population.

Building memories

It is worth considering the settlement's relationship with Beaker burial and ring-ditch 8454, which may have been visible to the late Iron Age inhabitants as a round barrow. If the barrow, whose location, as Mullin suggests (above), was determined by the late Neolithic pits, in turn served to locate the late Iron Age settlement, then the buried individuals may have been absorbed into the ancestry of the late Iron Age inhabitants and used to confer legal and spiritual ownership of the land. As discussed above, the later boundary burials may have maintained those rights. With the burial of cremation 8227, the inhabitants of Corinium who worked the land renewed a history that extended back almost 2500 years.

Potentially a connection exists between the late Iron Age settlement and the Tar Barrows, situated approximately 400 m to the west. The barrows may have reflected on the inhabitants of Kingshill North, strengthening their legitimacy as occupiers of the land. Unfortunately, the dating of the barrows is inconclusive, although it seems likely that the barrows were erected in the late Iron Age or early Roman period. One of the barrows has a conical profile more typical of Roman, rather than prehistoric date, and Roman coins, stonework and a 'pre-Roman cinerary pot' have been recorded during various openings of the barrows from the 18th century onwards (Holbrook 1994, 83; 2008c, 308). Reece (2003, 280) notes that Corinium, sited on a flood-prone gravel island surrounded by a marshy area, avoided, surely deliberately, the better ground occupied by the barrows, and suggests that the barrows marked an area of deep significance for the Dobunni, akin to the religious and high-status burial complexes of Stanway and Folly Lane in the

Catuvellaunian centres of Camulodumum and Verulamium respectively (Crummy *et al.* 2007; Niblett 1999; Creighton 2006). Further support for Reece's view is provided by cropmarks immediately adjacent to the barrows that take the form of a rectangular enclosure containing a masonry structure, and two conjoined enclosures that bring to mind the burial enclosures at Stanway (see Fig. 1; Holbrook 2008c, 310-11). This brings us back to the paucity of early Roman fine wares and other relatively high-status objects at Kingshill North. Just as the inhabitants derived no material benefit from military occupation in early Cirencester, they gained nothing from the special place on their doorstep. This suggests, as with the fort, that the settlement had been abandoned, and the Fosse Way laid out, before the Tar Barrow Hill site developed as an elite funerary or religious complex.

Bibliography

ABMAP, 2003 *Animal bone metrical archive project*, http://ads.ahds.ac.uk/catalogue/specColl/abmap/index.cfm?CFID=3073809&CFTOKEN=25669318

Albarella, U, 2006 Pig husbandry and pork consumption in medieval England, in *Food in medieval England: history and archaeology* (eds C Woolgar, D Serjeantson and T Waldron), Oxford University Press, Oxford, 72-87

Allen, J R L, 1998 Later Iron Age and earliest Roman calcite-tempered ware from sites on the Severn Estuary levels: character and distribution, *Studia Celtica* **32**, 27-41

Allen, T G, 1990 *An Iron Age and Romano-British enclosed settlement at Watkins Farm, Northmoor, Oxon.*, Oxford Archaeological Unit Thames Valley Landscapes Monograph: the Windrush Valley, vol **1**, Oxford

Allen, T G, Darvill, T C and Jones, M U, 1993 *Excavations at Roughground Farm, Lechlade, Gloucestershire: a prehistoric and Roman landscape*, Oxford Archaeological Unit Thames Valley Landscapes: the Cotswold Water Park, volume **1**, Oxford

Andrefsky, W, 1998 *Lithics: macroscopic approaches to analysis*, Cambridge University Press, Cambridge

Armitage, P, 1982 A system for ageing and sexing the horncores of cattle from British post-medieval sites (with special reference to unimproved British longhorn cattle), in Wilson *et al.* 1982, 37-54

Arthur, J R B and Pardine, P, 1975 *Seed i.d. of Neolithic Barrow, Nympsfield*, English Heritage Ancient Monuments Laboratory Report, Old Series **1784**, London

Ashbee, P, 1966 The Fussell's Lodge long barrow excavations, 1957, *Archaeologia* **100**, 1-80

Ashbee, P, 1978 Amesbury Barrow 51: excavation 1950, *Wiltshire Archaeol Mag* **70/71**, 1-60

Bacher, A, 1967 *Vergleichend morphologische Untersuchungen an Einzelknochen des postcranialen Skeletts in Mitteleuropa vorkommender Schwäne und Gänse*, unpubl. Inaugural-Dissertation, Ludwig-Maximilians-Universität, München

Baker, J and Brothwell, D, 1980 *Animal diseases in archaeology*, Academic Press, London

Bamford, H, 1985 *Briar Hill: excavation 1974-1978*, Northampton Development Corporation archaeological monogr **3**, Northampton:

Barclay, A, 1999 Grooved Ware from the Upper Thames Region, in Cleal and MacSween (eds) 1999, 9-22

Barclay, A, Glass, H and Parry, C, 1995 Excavations of Neolithic and Bronze Age ring ditches, Shorncote Quarry, Somerford Keynes, Gloucestershire, *Trans Bristol Gloucestershire Archaeol Soc* **113**, 21-60

Barclay, A and Halpin, C, 1999 *Excavations at Barrow Hills, Radley, Oxfordshire. Volume 1: the Neolithic and Bronze Age monument complex*, Oxford Archaeological Unit Thames Valley Landscapes Monograph **11**, Oxford

Barclay, A, Serjeantson, D and Wallis, J, 1999 Worked bone and antler, in Barclay and Halpin 1999, 235-236

Barrett, J C, Freeman, P W M and Woodward A, 2000 *Cadbury Castle, Somerset. The later prehistoric and early historic archaeology*, English Heritage Archaeol rep **20**, London

Barrett, R, 2004 *An archaeological evaluation of land off Bredon Road, Mitton, Tewkesbury, Gloucestershire*, unpublished report by Gloucestershire County Council Archaeological Service

Beek, G C van, 1983 *Dental morphology: an illustrated guide*, Elsevier, Boston

Bersu, G, 1940 Excavations at Little Woodbury, Wiltshire, *Proc Prehist Soc* **6(1)**, 30-111

Biddulph, E, 2010 LIA and Roman pottery, in Smith *et al.* (eds) 2010, 21-48

Boessneck, J, Müller, H-H and Teichert, M, 1964 *Osteologische Unterscheidungsmerkmale zwischen Schaf (Ovis aries Linné) und Ziege (Capra hircus Linné)*, Kühn-Archiv **78**

Booth, P, 2007 Pottery, in Miles *et al.* 2007, 77-80

Booth, P, nd *Oxford Archaeology Roman pottery recording system: an introduction* (revised June 2007), unpublished guidelines

Booth, P and Simmonds, A, 2009 *Appleford's Earliest Farmers: archaeological work at Appleford Sidings, Oxfordshire*, Oxford Archaeology Occasional Paper **17**, Oxford

Boyle, A, Jennings, D, Miles, D and Palmer, S, 1998 *The Anglo-Saxon cemetery at Butler's Field, Lechlade, Gloucestershire*, Oxford Archaeology Unit Thames Valley Landscapes Monograph **10**, Oxford

Bradley, P, 1999 Worked flint, in Barclay and Halpin 1999, 211-227

Bradley, R and Edmonds, M 1993 *Interpreting the axe trade: production and exchange in Neolithic Britain*, Cambridge University Press, Cambridge

Brickley, M and McKinley, J, 2004 *Guidelines to the standards for recording human remains*, IFA Paper **7**, Reading

Brossler, A, Gocher, M, Laws, G and Roberts, M, 2002 Shorncote Quarry: excavations of a late prehistoric landscape in the Upper Thames Valley 1997 and 1998, *Trans Bristol Gloucestershire Archaeol Soc* **120**, 37-87

Brothwell, D, 1981 *Digging up bones*, Oxford University Press, Oxford

Brown, D H, 2002 *Pottery in medieval Southampton c 1066-1510*, CBA Res Rep **133**, York

Brown, L and Mullin, D, 2010 Prehistoric pottery, in Smith *et al.* 2010, 1-20

Buikstra, J E and Ubelaker, D H, 1994 *Standards for data collection from human skeletal remains*, Arkansas

Bulleid, A and H St George Gray, 1911-1917 *The Glastonbury Lake Village: a full description of the excavations and the relics discovered, 1892-1907*, Glastonbury Antiquarian Society, Glastonbury

Burrow, E J, Knowles, W H, Paine, A E W and Gray J W, 1925 Excavations on Leckhampton Hill, Cheltenham, during the summer of 1925, *Trans Bristol Gloucestershire Archaeol Soc* **47**, 81-112

Butler, C, 2005 *Prehistoric flintwork*, Tempus, Stroud

Campbell, G, 2000 Plant utilization: the evidence from charred plant remains, in *The Danebury Environs Programme: the prehistory of a Wessex landscape. Volume 1: Introduction* (B Cunliffe), English Heritage and Oxford University Committee for Archaeology monogr **48**, Oxford, 45–59

Cappers, R T J, Bekker, R M and Jans, J E A, 2006 *Digital seed atlas of the Netherlands*, Barkhuis Publishing and Groningen University Library, Groningen

Case, H, 1982a Cassington 1950-2: Late Neolithic pits and the big enclosure, in Case and Whittle (eds) 1982, 118-151

Case, H, 1982b The Vicarage Field, Stanton Harcourt, in Case and Whittle (eds) 1982, 103-117

Case, H, 2001 The Beaker Culture in Britain and Ireland: groups, European contacts and chronology, in *Bell Beakers today: pottery, people, culture, symbols in prehistoric Europe* (ed. F Nicolis), Officio Beni Archeologici, Trento, 361-377

Case, H and Whittle, A (eds), 1982 *Settlement patterns in the Oxford Region: excavations at the Abingdon causewayed enclosure and other sites*, CBA Res Rep **44**, London

Chandler, J, 1998 *John Leland's itinerary: travels in Tudor England*, Sutton Publishing, Stroud

Chenery, C A, Müldner, G, Evans, J, Eckardt, H and Lewis, M, in press, Strontium and stable isotope evidence for diet and mobility in Roman Gloucester, UK, *J Archaeol Sci*

Chapman, J, 2000 *Fragmentation in archaeology: people, places and broken objects in the prehistory of south eastern Europe*, Routledge, London

Clark, J, 1960 Excavations at the Neolithic site at Hurst Fen, *Proc Prehist Soc* **26**, 214-245

Clarke, D L, 1970 *Beaker pottery of Great Britain and Ireland*, Cambridge University Press, Cambridge

Clarke, H H, 1970 Appendix III: Grain, in Frocester Court Roman Villa, Gloucestershire (H S Gracie), *Trans Bristol Gloucestershire Archaeol Soc* **89**, 81-2

Clarke, H H, 1971 The plant remains: analysis of vegetable matter from the corn-drier, in Archaeology and the M5: 1st report, 1969 (P J Fowler and C V Walthew), *Trans Bristol Gloucestershire Archaeol Soc* **90**, 48–9

Cleal, R, 1988 The occurrence of drilled holes in later Neolithic pottery, *Oxford J Archaeol* **7(2)**, 139-45

Cleal, R, 1991 Cranbourne Chase – the earlier prehistoric pottery, in *Papers on the prehistoric archaeology of Cranborne Chase* (eds J Barrett, R Bradley and M Hall), Oxbow monogr **11**, Oxford, 134-200

Cleal, R, 1994 Shells and sherds: identification of inclusions in Grooved Ware, with associated radiocarbon dates from Amesbury, Wiltshire, *Proc Prehist Soc* **60**, 445-448

Cleal, R, 1995 Pottery fabrics in Wessex in the Fourth to Second Millennia BC, in *'Unbaked urns of rudely shape': essays on British and Irish pottery for Ian Longworth* (eds I Kinnes and G Varndell), Oxbow monogr **55**, Oxford, 185-194

Cleal, R, 1999 The what, where and when of Grooved Ware, in Cleal and MacSween (eds) 1999, 1-8

Cleal, R and MacSween, A (eds), 1999 *Grooved Ware in Britain and Ireland*, Neolithic Studies Seminar Papers **3**, Oxbow Books, Oxford

Clifford, E M, 1930 A prehistoric and Roman site at Barnwood, near Gloucester, *Trans Bristol Gloucestershire Archaeol Soc* **52**, 202-254

Clifford, E M, 1937 The Beaker folk in the Cotswolds, *Proc Prehist Soc* **3**, 159-163

Clifford, E M, 1938a Beaker found at Prestbury, Glos., *Trans Bristol Gloucestershire Archaeol Soc* **60**, 348-9

Clifford, E M, 1938b The excavation of Nympsfield Long Barrow, Gloucestershire, *Proc Prehist Soc* **4**, 188-213

Clifford, E M, 1950 The Ivy Lodge Round Barrow, *Trans Bristol Gloucestershire Archaeol Soc* **69**, 59-77

Clifford, E M, 1964 Two finds of Beaker pottery from Gloucestershire, *Trans Bristol Gloucestershire Archaeol Soc* **83**, 34-9

Clough, T H McK and Cummins, W A, 1988 *Stone axe studies. Volume 2: The petrology of prehistoric stone implements from the British Isles*, CBA Res Rep **67**, London

Clutton-Brock J, 1982 *Neolithic antler picks from Grimes Graves, Norfolk and Durrington Walls, Wiltshire: a biometrical analysis. Excavations at Grimes Graves Norfolk 1972-1976, fasc. 1*, British Museum Press, London

Cohen, A and Serjeantson, D, 1996 *A manual for the identification of bird bones from archaeological sites*, Archetype, London

Coleman, L, Hancocks, A and Watts, M, 2006 *Excavations on the Wormington to Tirley Pipeline,*

2000, Cotswold Archaeology monogr **3**, Cirencester.

Coles, J M, 1987 *Meare Village East: the Excavations of A Bulleid and H St George Gray*, Somerset Levels Papers 13, Exeter

Conolly A P, 1982 Report on the plant macro-remains from Cirencester, in Wacher and McWhirr 1982, 228-31

Cool, H E M, 2004 *The Roman cemetery at Brougham, Cumbria: excavations 1966-67*, Britannia monogr. **21**, London

Cooper, N J, 1998 The supply of pottery to Roman Cirencester, in Holbrook (ed.) 1998, 239-82

Cotswold Archaeology, 2003 *Land south of Home Farm, Ebrington, Gloucestershire*, unpublished report

Crawford, O G S, 1925 *Long barrows of the Cotswolds*, Bellows, Gloucester

Creighton, J, 2006 *Britannia: the creation of a Roman province*, Routledge, London

Crummy, P, Benfield, S, Crummy, N, Rigby, V, and Shimmin, D, 2007 *Stanway: an élite burial site at Camulodunum*, Britannia Monogr. **24**, London

Cunliffe, B, 1984 *Danebury: an Iron Age hillfort in Hampshire. Volume 2: the excavations, 1969-1978 – the finds*, CBA Res Rep **52**, London

Cunliffe, B, 2003 *Danebury Hillfort*, 2 edn, Tempus, Stroud

Cunnington, M E, 1929 *Woodhenge: A description of the site as revealed by excavations carried out there by Mr and Mrs B H Cunnington 1926-7-8. Also of four circles and an earthwork enclosure south of Stonehenge.* Devizes, George Simpson and Co.

Curwen, E C, 1937 Querns, *Antiquity* **11**, 133-151

Dannell, G B, 1999 Decorated South Gaulish samian, in *Roman pottery from excavations in Colchester, 1971-86* (R P Symonds and S Wade), Colchester Archaeological Report **10**, Colchester, 13-74

Darvill, T, 1987 *Prehistoric Gloucestershire*, Alan Sutton, Stroud

Darvill, T, 2000 Early prehistoric settlement, in *Frocester, a Romano-British settlement and its antecedents and successors. Volume 1: the sites* (E Price), Gloucestershire and District Archaeological Research Group, Stonehouse, 193-220

Darvill, T, 2006 Early prehistory, in *Twenty-five years of archaeology in Gloucestershire: a review of new discoveries and new thinking in Gloucestershire, South Gloucestershire and Bristol, 1979-2004* (eds N Holbrook and J Jurica), Bristol Gloucestershire Archaeol Rep **3**, 5-60

Darvill, T and Gerrard, C, 1994 *Cirencester: Town and landscape*, Cotswold Archaeological Trust, Cirencester

Darvill, T, Hingley, R, Jones, M and Timby, J, 1986 A Neolithic and Iron Age site at the Loders, Lechlade, Gloucestershire, *Trans Bristol Gloucestershire Archaeol Soc* **104**, 27-48

Darvill, T and Holbrook, N, 1994 The Cirencester area in the prehistoric and early Roman periods, in Darvill and Gerrard 1994, 47-56

Darvill, T and Timby, J, 1986 Excavations at Saintbridge, Gloucester, 1981, *Trans Bristol Gloucestershire Archaeol Soc* **104**, 49-60

Davis, S, 1987 *The archaeology of animals*, Batsford, London

Degerbøl, M, 1970 *The Urus (Bos primigenius Bojanus) and Neolithic domesticated cattle (Bos taurus domesticus Linné) in Denmark, with a revision of Bos remains from the kitchen middens*, Biologiske Skrifter **17**, Munksgaard, København

Dixon, P, 1994 *Crickley Hill. Volume 1: the hillfort defences*, University of Nottingham, Nottingham

Dobney, K, 2001 A place at the table: the role of vertebrate zooarchaeology within a Roman research agenda for Britain, in *Britons and Romans: advancing an archaeological agenda* (eds S James and M Millett), CBA Res Rep **125**, York, 36-111

Driesch, A von den, 1976 *A guide to the measurement of animal bones from archaeological sites*, Harvard University

Dunning, G C, 1937 A Beaker from Bourton on the Water, Gloucestershire, *Proc Prehist Soc* **3**, 163-4

Ede, J, 2000 Carbonised plant remains, in Hearne and Adam 2000, 67-8

Edwards, E, 2007 Neolithic and Bronze Age pottery, in Mann and Jackson 2007

Ellison, A , 1984 Bronze Age Gloucestershire: artefacts and distributions, in *Archaeology in Gloucestershire* (ed. A Saville), Alan Sutton, Stroud.

Evans, D and McSloy, E, 2006 Some Beaker pottery from Station Road, Kemble, *Glevensis* **39**, 9-11

Evans, E-J, 2009 Animal bone, in Lamdin-Whymark *et al.* 2009, 108-112

Evans, J G, 1972 *Land snails in archaeology*, Seminar Press, London and New York

Evans J.G. 1984 Stonehenge – the environment in the Late Neolithic and Early Bronze Age and a Beaker burial. *Wiltshire Archaeol Mag* **78**, 7–30

Evans, J G, 1993 The influence of human communities on the English chalklands from the Mesolithic to the Iron Age: the molluscan evidence, in *Climate change and human impact on the landscape* (ed F M Chambers), Chapman and Hall, London, 147-154

Evans, J, Chenery, C, Fitzpatrick, A P, 2006 Bronze age childhood migration of individuals near Stonehenge, revealed by strontium and oxygen isotope tooth enamel analysis, *Archaeometry* **48 (2)**, 309-321

Faulkner, N, 1998 Urban stratigraphy and Roman history, in Holbrook (ed.) 1998, 371-388

Fell, C, 1952 A late Bronze Age urnfield and Grooved Ware occupation at Honington, Suffolk, *Proc Cambridge Antiq Soc* **45**, 30-41

Fell, C, 1961 Shenberrow Hill Camp, Stanton,

Gloucestershire, *Trans Bristol Gloucestershire Archaeol Soc* **80**, 16-41

Garrod, A and Heighway, C, 1984 *Garrod's Gloucester: archaeological observations, 1974-81*, Alan Sutton, Gloucester, 22-25

Garwood, P, 1999 Grooved Ware in southern Britain: chronology and interpretation, in Cleal and MacSween 1999, 145-176

Gibson, A, 2007 A Beaker veneer? Some evidence from the burial record, in From Stonehenge to the Baltic: living with cultural diversity in the third millennium BC (eds M Larsson and M Parker Pearson), BAR Brit Ser **1692**, Oxford, 47-64

Gingell, C, 1981 Excavation of an Iron Age enclosure at Groundwell Farm, Blunsden St Andrew, 1976-7, *Wiltshire Archaeol Mag* **76** (1982), 33-75

Giorgi, J A, 1998 Charred plant remains, in *Excavations at Kingscote and Wycomb, Gloucestershire: a Roman estate centre and small town in the Cotswolds, with notes on related settlements* (J R Timby), Cotswold Archaeological Trust, Cirencester, 273–274

Grant, A, 1982 The use of toothwear as a guide to the age of domestic ungulates, in Wilson *et al.* 1982, 91-108

Grant, A, 1989 Animals in Roman Britain, in *Research on Roman Britain: 1960-89* (ed. M Todd), Britannia monogr **11**, London, 135-146

Green, C.S, 1987 *Excavations at Poundbury, Dorchester, Dorset 1966-1982. Volume 1: the settlements*, Dorset Natur Hist Archaeol Soc monogr.7, Dorchester

Grigson, C, 1980 The animal bones in Robertson-Mackay 1980, 161-171

Grinsell, L V, 1961 Gloucestershire barrows. Part 2: north and east, *Somerset Archaeol Natur Hist* **115**, 43-137

Grinsell, L V, 1971 Somerset barrows, *Proc Bristol Gloucestershire Archaeol Soc* **79(i)**, 5-148

GSB Prospection, 2000 *London Road, Cirencester*, unpublished report ref 2000/11

GSB Prospection, 2006 *London Road, Cirencester*, unpublished report ref 2006/12

Guerra-Doce, E, 2006 Exploring the significance of Beaker pottery through residue analysis, *Oxford J Archaeol* **25(3)**, 247-259

Habermehl, K-H, 1975 *Die Altersbestimmung bei Haus- und Labortieren*, 2 edn, Berlin

Halstead, P, 1985 A study of mandibular teeth from Romano-British contexts at Maxey, in *Archaeology and environment in the Lower Welland Valley* (F Pryor), E Anglian Archaeol **27**, Cambridge, 219-224

Hambleton, E, 1999 *Animal husbandry regimes in Iron Age Britain: a comparative study of faunal assemblages from British Iron Age sites*, BAR Brit Ser **282**, Oxford

Hamiliakis, Y, 2000 Humans and animals *c* 450-270 cal BC, in *Prehistoric intertidal archaeology in the Welsh Severn estuary* (M Bell, A Caseldine and H Neumann), CBA Res Rep **120**, York, 276-281

Harcourt, R A, 1974 The dog in prehistoric and early historic Britain, *J Archaeol Sci* **1**, 151-175

Harcourt, R A, 1979 The animal bones, in *Gussage All Saints, an Iron Age settlement in Dorset.* (G. J. Wainwright) Department of Environment Report **10**, London, 150-60.

Harrison, E and Timby, J, 2004 Pottery, in *Iron Age and Roman settlement and landscape at Totterdown Lane, Horcott, near Fairford, Gloucestershire* (J Pine and S Preston), Thames Valley Archaeol Services monogr **6**, Reading, 55-68

Harrison, R, Jackson, R, and Napthan, M, 1999 A rich Bell Beaker burial from Wellington Quarry, Marden, Herefordshire, *Oxford J Archaeol* **18(1)**, 1-16

Hassall, T G, Halpin, C E and Mellor, M, 1984 Excavations in St Ebbe's, Oxford, 1967-1976. Part II: Post-medieval domestic tenements and the post-Dissolution site of the Greyfriars, *Oxoniensia* **49**, 153-276

Hawkes, C F C and Hull, M R, 1947 *Camulodunum*, Soc Antiq Res Rep **14**, London

Hazledine Warren, S, Piggott, S, Clark, D, Burkitt, M and Godwin, M, 1936 Archaeology of the submerged land-surface of the Essex coast, *Proc Prehist Society* **2**, 178-210

Healy, F, 1988 *The Anglo-Saxon cemetery at Spong Hill, North Elmham. Part VI: Occupation in the seventh to second millennia BC*, E Anglian Archaeol **39**, Gressenhall

Hearne, C M and Adam, N, 2000 Excavation of an extensive late Bronze Age settlement at Shorncote Quarry, near Cirencester, 1995-6, *Trans Bristol Gloucestershire Archaeol Soc* **117**, 35-73.

Hearne, C.M and Heaton, M J, 1994 Excavations at a late Bronze Age settlement in the Upper Thames valley at Shorncote Quarry, near Cirencester, 1992, *Trans Bristol Gloucestershire Archaeol Society* 112, 17-57

Hicks, D, 1999 *An archaeological evaluation at Cirencester Rugby Club, Cirencester, Gloucestershire*, unpublished report

Hill, J D, 1995 *Ritual and rubbish in the Iron Age of Wessex: a study of the formation of a specific archaeological record*, BAR Brit Ser **242**, Oxford

Hillson, S, 1992 *Mammal bones and teeth: an introductory guide to methods of identification*, UCL, London

Hillson, S, 1996 *Dental anthropology*, Cambridge University Press, Cambridge

Hodgson, J G, Halstead, P, Wilson, P J and Davis, S, 1999 Functional interpretation of archaeobotanical data: making hay in the archaeological record, *Vegetation History and Archaeobotany* **8**, 261–71

Holbrook, N, 1994 Corinium Dobunnorum: Roman civitas capital and provincial capital, in Darvill and Gerrard 1994, 57-86

Holbrook, N (ed.), 1998 *Cirencester: the Roman town defences, public buildings and shops*, Cirencester

Excavations **5**, Cotswold Archaeological Trust, Cirencester

Holbrook, N, 2008a Conclusions, in Holbrook 2008b, 137-9

Holbrook, N (ed.), 2008b *Excavations and observations in Roman Cirencester, 1998-2007*, Cirencester Excavations **6**, Cotswold Archaeology, Cirencester

Holbrook, N, 2008c Cirencester and the Cotswolds: the early Roman evolution of a town and rural landscape, *J Roman Archaeology* **21**, 305-323

Howell, L and Durden, T, 1996 A Grooved Ware pit on the Severn Barrows All Weather Gallop, Sparsholt, Oxfordshire, *Oxoniensia* **61**, 21-25

Hunt, L, 2006 Rotheley Lodge Farm (SK 592 140), in Archaeology in Leicestershire and Rutland (N J Cooper), *Trans Leicestershire Archaeol Hist Soc* **80**, 237-8

Hurst, H, 1972 Excavations at Gloucester 1968-1971: first interim report, *Antiq J* **52**, 24-69

Jay, M, Parker Pearson, M, Richards, O, Nehlich, J, Montgomery, A, Chamberlain, A and Sheridan, A, forthcoming, The Beaker People Project: an interim report on the progress of the isotopic analysis of the organic skeletal material, in *The British Chalcolithic: place and polity in the later 3rd millennium* (eds M J Allen, J Gardiner, A Sheridan and D McOmish), Prehistoric Society Research Papers **4**, Oxford

Jennings, D, Muir, J and Smith, A, 2004 Chapter 3: archaeological description, in *Thornhill Farm, Fairford, Gloucestershire: an Iron Age and Roman pastoral site in the Upper Thames Valley* (D Jennings, J Muir, S Palmer and A Smith), Oxford Archaeology Thames Valley Landscapes Monograph **23**, Oxford, 21-67

John Moore Heritage Services, 2001 *An archaeological evaluation at Leaze Farm, Kelmscott Road, Lechlade*, unpublished report

Jones, A M, 2005 *Cornish Bronze Age ceremonial landscapes, c 2500-1500 BC*, BAR Brit Ser **394**, Oxford

Jones, B and Mattingly, D, 1990 *An atlas of Roman Britain*, Blackwell, Oxford

JSAC, 2001 *A desk-based assessment on land north of London Road, Cirencester*, John Samuels Archaeological Consultants' report ref 592/01/002

JSAC, 2005 *An archaeological desk-based assessment of land at Kingshill North, Cirencester*, John Samuels Archaeological Consultants' report ref 1299/05/01

Kerney, M, 1999 *Atlas of land and freshwater molluscs of Britain and Ireland*, Harley Books, Colchester

King, A, 1991 Food production and consumption – meat, in *Britain in the Roman period: Recent trends* (ed. R F J Jones), J R Collis Publications, Sheffield, 15-20

King, R, Barber, A and Timby, J, 1996 Excavations at West Lane, Kemble: an Iron-Age, Roman and Saxon burial site and a medieval building, *Trans Bristol Gloucestershire Archaeol Soc* **114**, 15-54

Kinnes, I, Gibson, A, Ambers, J, Bowman, S, Leese, M and Boast, R, 1991 Radiocarbon dating and British Beakers: the British Museum programme, *Scottish Archaeol Rev* **8**, 35-68

Knight, S, 2007 The Iron Age and Romano-British animal bone from Ashton Keynes (59260), in *Excavations at an Iron Age and Romano-British settlement site at Cleveland Farm, Ashton Keynes, Wiltshire* (A Powell, G P Jones and L Mepham), Wessex Archaeology, http://ads.ahds.ac.uk/catalogue/archive/cleveland_eh_2007/downloads.cfm?archive=specialist

LAARC, 2007 *Post 1992 Museum of London code expansions: Post-Roman pottery*, http://www.museumoflondonarchaeology.org.uk/NR/rdonlyres/F0118AAF-EF24-4228-A07A-39F89E6F092E/0/post92mol_post_roman.pdf

Lambrick, G (with Robinson, M), 2009 *Thames through time: the archaeology of the gravel terraces of the Upper and Middle Thames Valley. Late prehistory: 1500 BC-AD 50*, Oxford Archaeology Thames Valley Monograph **29**, Oxford

Lambrick, G, 2010 *Neolithic to Saxon social and environmental change at Mount Farm, Berinsfield, Dorchester-on-Thames*, Oxford Archaeology occasional paper **19**, Oxford

Lambrick, G and Allen T, 2004 *Gravelly Guy, Stanton Harcourt: the development of a prehistoric and Romano-British community*, Oxford Archaeology Thames Valley Monograph **21**, Oxford

Lamdin-Whymark, H, 2008 *The residue of ritualised action: Neolithic deposition practices in the Middle Thames Valley*, BAR Brit Ser **466**, Oxford

Lamdin-Whymark, H, Brady, K and Smith, A, 2009 Excavation of a Neolithic to Roman landscape at Horcott Pit, near Fairford, Gloucestershire, 2002-3, *Trans Bristol Gloucestershire Archaeol Soc* **127**, 45-129

Lanting, J N and Waals, J D van der, 1972 British Beakers as seen from the Continent, *Helinium* **12**, 20-46

Leah, M and Young, C, 2001 A Bronze-Age burnt mound at Sandy Lane, Charlton Kings, Gloucestershire: Excavations in 1971, *Trans Bristol Gloucestershire Archaeol Soc* **119**, 59-82

Leech, R, 1977 *The Upper Thames Valley in Gloucestershire and Wiltshire*, CRAAGS, Bristol

Levinson, A A, Luz, B and Kolodny, Y, 1987 Variations in oxygen isotope compositions of human teeth and urinary stones, *Applied Geochemistry* **2**, 367-371

Lewis, J P and Mullin, D, forthcoming, Between the channel and the chalk: a regional perspective on the Chalcolithic from the Mendip Hills, Somerset

Locker, A, 2007 In piscibus diversis: the bone evidence for fish consumption in Roman Britain, *Britannia* **38**, 141-180

Longworth, I and Cleal, R, 1999 Grooved Ware gazetteer, in Cleal and MacSween (eds) 1999, 177-206

Lovejoy, C O, Meindl, R S, Pryzbeck, T R and Mensforth, R P, 1985 Chronological metamorphosis of the auricular surface of the illium: a new method for determination of adult skeletal age-at-death, *American Journal of Physical Anthropology* 68, 15-28

Lovell, J, Wakeham, G, Timby, J and Allen, M J, 2007 Iron-Age to Saxon farming settlement at Bishop's Cleeve, Gloucestershire: excavations south of Church Road, 1998-2004, *Trans Bristol Gloucestershire Archaeol Soc* **125**, 95-129

Lyman, R L, 1996 *Vertebrate taphonomy*, Cambridge University Press, Cambridge

Lynch, A H, Hamilton, J and Hedges, R E M, 2008 Where the wild things are: aurochs and cattle in England, *Antiquity* **82**, 1025-1039

Magnell, O, 2006 *Tracking wild boar and hunters: osteology of wild boar in Mesolithic South Scandinavia*, Studies in Osteology 1: Acta Archaeologica Lundensia Series in 8°, **51**, Lund

Maltby, M, 1996 The exploitation of animals in the Iron Age: the archaeozoological evidence, in *The Iron Age in Britain and Ireland: recent trends* (eds T C Champion and J R Collis), Sheffield Academic, Sheffield, 17-27

Maltby, M, 2007 Chop and change: specialist cattle carcass processing in Roman Britain, in *TRAC 2006: Proceedings of the sixteenth annual Theoretical Roman Archaeology Conference* (eds B Croxford, N Ray, R Roth and N White), Oxbow Books, Oxford, 59-76

Manby, T G, 1974 *Grooved Ware sites in Yorkshire*, BAR Brit Ser **9**, Oxford

Mann, A and Jackson, R, 2007 *Archaeological watching brief and contingency excavation at Clifton Quarry, Severn Stoke, Worcestershire (PNUM 5379)*, Worcestershire County Council Historic Environment and Archaeology Service report 1612, unpublished

Manning, W H, 1985 *Catalogue of the Romano-British iron tools, fittings and weapons in the British Museum*, British Museum Press, London

Mannermaa, K, 2008 Birds and burials at Ajvide (Gotland, Sweden) and Zvejnieki (Latvia) about 8000–3900 BP, *J Anthropological Archaeol* **27**, 201-225

McKinley, J, 1994 Bone fragment size in British cremation burials and its implications for pyre technology and ritual, *J Archaeol Sci* **21**, 339-342

McKinley, J, 1997 Bronze Age 'barrows' and the funerary rites and rituals of cremation, *Proc Prehist Soc* **63**, 129-145

McKinley, J, 2000 The analysis of cremated bone, in *Human osteology* (eds M Cox and S Mays), Greenwich Medical Media, London, 403-421

McKinley, J, 2004 Compiling a skeletal inventory: disarticulated and co-mingled remains, in Brickley and McKinley 2004, 14-17

McSloy, E R, 2008 The pottery, in Holbrook (ed.) 2008b, 98-101

Meindl, R S and Lovejoy, C O, 1985 Ectocranial suture closure: A revised method for the determination of skeletal age at death based on the lateral-anterior sutures, *American Journal of Physical Anthropology* 68, 29-45

Mellor, M, 1984 Hair and wig curlers, in Hassall *et al.* 1984, 262-3

Mellor, M, 1994 Oxfordshire Pottery: a synthesis of middle and late Saxon, medieval and early post-medieval pottery in the Oxford Region, *Oxoniensia* 59, 17-217

Mellor, M and Oakley, G, 1984 A summary of the key assemblages: a study of pottery, clay pipes, glass and other finds from fourteen pits, dating from the 16th to the mid 19th century, in Hassall *et al.* 1984, 181-219

Mennerich, G, 1968 *Römerzeitliche Tierknochen aus drei Fundorten des Niederrheingebiets*, unpublished dissertation, München

Miles, A, 1962 Assessment of age of a population of Anglo-Saxons from their dentition, *Proc Royal Society of Medicine* **55**, 881-886

Miles, D, Palmer, S, Smith, A and Jones G P, 2007 *Iron Age and Roman settlement in the upper Thames Valley: excavations at Claydon Pike and other sites within the Cotswold Water Park*, Oxford Archaeology Thames Valley Landscapes Monograph **26**, Oxford

Mithen, S, Finlay, N, Carruthers, W, Carter, S and Ashmore, P, 2001 Plant use in the Mesolithic: evidence from Staosnaig, Isle of Colonsay, Scotland, *J Archaeol Sci* **28**, 223-234.

Moffett, L, Robinson, M A and Straker, S, 1989 Cereals, fruit and nuts: charred plant remains from Neolithic sites in England and Wales and the Neolithic economy, in *The beginnings of agriculture* (eds A Milles, D Williams and N Gardner), BAR Int Ser **496**, Oxford, 243-61

Montague, R, 1995 Bone and antler small objects, in *Stonehenge in its landscape: twentieth century excavations* (R M J Cleal, K E Walker and R Montague), English Heritage, London, 407-14

Moore, T, 2006 *Iron age societies in the Severn-Cotswolds: developing narratives of social and landscape change*, BAR Brit Ser **421**, Oxford

Moore, T, 2009 The coarseware pottery, in Trow *et al.* 2009, 96-131

Morris, E L, 2005 Pottery and briquetage, in *Conderton Camp, Worcestershire: a small middle Iron Age hillfort on Bredon Hill* (N Thomas), CBA Res Rep **143**, London, 117-47; Appendix 3

Morris, J T, 2008 *Re-examining associated bone groups from southern England and Yorkshire, c 4000BC to AD1550*, unpubl. Ph.D. thesis, Bournemouth University

Mudd, A, 1999 The later prehistoric period, in Mudd *et al.* 1999b, 517-23

Mudd, A and Lawrence, S, 1999 Duntisbourne Grove, in Mudd *et al.* 1999b, 86-97

Mudd, A and Lupton, A, 1999 Highgate House, in Mudd *et al.* 1999b, 59-69

Mudd, A and Mortimer, S, 1999 Preston enclosure, in Mudd *et al.* 1999b, 42-59

Mudd, A and Muir, J, 1999 St Augustine's Farm and St Augustine's Lane, in Mudd *et al.* 1999a, 35-41

Mudd, A, Muir, J and Parkinson, A, 1999a Miscellaneous later prehistoric features, in Mudd *et al.* 1999a, 69-76

Mudd, A, Williams, R J and Lupton, A, 1999b *Excavations alongside Roman Ermin Street, Gloucestershire and Wiltshire: The archaeology of the A419/417 Swindon to Gloucester road scheme*, Oxford Archaeology Unit, Oxford

Mukherjee, A J, Gibson, A M and Evershed, R P, 2008 Trends in pig product processing at British Neolithic Grooved Ware sites traced through organic residues in potsherds, *J Archaeol Sci* **35(7)**, 2059-2073

Mullin, D, 2001 Remembering, forgetting and the invention of tradition: burial and natural places in the English early Bronze Age, *Antiquity* **75**, 533-7

Mullin, D, forthcoming, A round barrow cemetery in the Severn Vale: Richards Atkinson's excavations of five ring ditches at Netherhills, Frampton on Severn, 1948, and their archaeological context, *Trans Bristol Gloucestershire Archaeol Soc*

Mullin, D and Lewis, J P, forthcoming, *Between the Channel and the chalk: a regional perspective on Grooved Ware and Beaker pottery from the Mendip Hills, Somerset*, Festschrift in honour of Henrietta Quinnell

Needham, S, 2005 Transforming Beaker culture in north-west Europe: processes of fusion and fission, *Proc Prehist Soc* **71**, 171-217

Niblett, R, 1999 *The excavation of a ceremonial site at Folly Lane, Verulamium*, Britannia Monogr. **14**, London

Nichols, P, 2001 *An archaeological evaluation of land at Station Road, Kemble, Gloucestershire*, unpublished report by Gloucestershire County Council Archaeology Service

Nichols, P, 2004, *An archaeological evaluation at Cirencester Polo Club, Daglingworth, Gloucestershire*, unpublished report by Gloucestershire County Council Archaeology Service

OA, 2006 *Kingshill North, Cirencester: archaeological evaluation report*, unpublished report by Oxford Archaeology

OA, 2008 *Residential development site, Kingshill North, Cirencester, Gloucestershire. Archaeological investigation: written scheme of investigation*, unpublished report by Oxford Archaeology

OA, 2009 *Kingshill North, Cirencester, Gloucestershire: Post Excavation Assessment*, unpublished report by Oxford Archaeology

O'Connor, T, 1988 *Bones from the General Accident site, Tanner Row*, Archaeology of York **15/2**, York

O'Neil, H, 1966 Sale's Lot Long Barrow, Withington, Gloucestershire, 1962-1965, *Trans Bristol Gloucestershire Archaeol Soc* **85**, 5-35

O'Neil, H, 1967 Bevan's Quarry round barrow, Temple Guiting, 1964, *Trans Bristol Gloucestershire Archaeol Soc* **86**, 16-41

O'Neil, H and Bunt, J, 1966 A Beaker from Leckhampton, Cheltenham, Gloucestershire, *Trans Bristol Gloucestershire Archaeol Soc* **85**, 216-7

O'Neil, J R, Roe, L J, Reinhard, L and Blake, R E, 1994 A rapid and precise method of oxygen isotope analysis of biogenic phosphate, *Israel Journal of Earth Science* **43**, 203-212

Ogden, A, 2005 *Identifying and scoring periodontal disease in skeletal material*, paper given at the annual BABAO (British Association for Biological Anthropology and Osteoarchaeology) conference

Oswald, A, 1975 *Clay pipes for the archaeologist*, BAR Brit Ser **14**, Oxford

Parker Pearson, M, Chamberlain, A, Jay, M, Marshall, P, Pollard, J, Richards, C, Thomas, J, Tilley, C and Welham, K, 2009 Who was buried at Stonehenge?, *Antiquity* **83**, 23-39

Parry, C, 1998 Excavation near Birdlip, Cowley, Gloucestershire, 1987-8, *Trans Bristol Gloucestershire Archaeol Soc* **116**, 25-92

Parry, C, 1999 Iron-Age, Romano-British and medieval occupation at Bishop's Cleeve, Gloucestershire: excavations at Gilder's Paddock, 1989 and 1990-1, *Trans Bristol Gloucestershire Archaeol Soc* **117**, 89-118

Patrick Foster Associates, 2000, *Huntsmans Quarry (Phases 5-7). Excavations and Watching Briefs at Huntsmans Quarry, Naunton, Gloucestershire, 1994-1996*, unpublished report

Payne, S, 1973 Kill-off patterns in sheep and goats: the mandibles from Aswan Kale, *Anatolian Studies* **23**, 281-303

PCRG 1995 The Study of Later Prehistoric Pottery: General Policies and Guidelines for Analysis and Publication. PCRG.

PCRG, 1997 *The study of later prehistoric pottery: general policies and guidelines for publication*, Prehistoric Ceramics Research Group, Occasional papers nos 1 and 2 (revised)

Peacock, D P S, 1969 A petrological study of certain Iron Age pottery from Western England, *Proc Prehist Soc* **34**, 414-28

Pelling, R, 1999 Charred and waterlogged plant remains, in Mudd *et al.* 1999, 469-494

Pelling, R, 2000 The charred plant remains, in The excavations of early Iron Age and medieval remains on land to the west of Church View, Bampton.(A Mayes, A Hardy and J Blair), *Oxoniensia* **65** (2001), 286–87

Philpott, R, 1991 *Burial practices in Roman Britain: A survey of grave treatment and furnishing, AD 43-410*, BAR Brit Ser **219**, Oxford

Piggott, S, 1962 *The West Kennet long barrow excavations, 1955-56*, HMSO, London

Piggott, S, 1962 Heads and hoofs, *Antiquity* **36**, 110-178

Pine, J and Preston, S, 2004 *Iron Age and Roman settlement and landscape at Totterdown Lane, Horcott, near Fairford, Gloucestershire*, Thames Valley Archaeol Services monogr **6**, Reading

Pitts, M, 2008 Stonehenge: the Big Dig, *British Archaeology* **102**, 13-17

Pitts, M W and Jacobi, R M, 1979 Some aspects of change in flaked stone industries of the Mesolithic and Neolithic in southern Britain, *J Archaeol Sci* **6**, 163-177

Pollex, A, 1999 Comments on the interpretation of the so-called cattle burials of Neolithic Central Europe, *Antiquity* **73**, 542-550

Poole, C, 2010 Ceramic building material, in Smith *et al.* (eds) 2010, 153-65

Poole, K, 2009 The animal remains, in Powell *et al.* 2009, 98-104

Powell, A, 1999 Animal bone. Middle Duntisbourne and Duntisbourne Grove, in Mudd *et al.* 1999, 431-449

Powell, A, Jones, G P and Mepham, L, 2008 An Iron Age and Romano-British settlement at Cleveland Farm, Ashton Keynes, Wiltshire, *Wiltshire Archaeol Mag* **101**, 18-50

Powell, K, Laws, G and Brown, L, 2009 A late Neolithic/early Bronze Age enclosure and Iron Age and Romano-British settlement at Latton Lands, Wiltshire, *Wiltshire Archaeol Mag* **102**, 22-113

Powell, K, Smith, A and Laws, G, 2010 *Evolution of a farming community in the Upper Thames Valley: excavation of a prehistoric, Roman and post-Roman landscape at Cotswold Community, Gloucestershire and Wiltshire. Volume 1: site narrative and overview*, Oxford Archaeology Thames Valley Landscapes Monograph **31**, Oxford

Price, E, 2000 *Frocester, a Romano-British settlement, its antecedents and successors. Volume 2: the finds*, Gloucester and District Archaeological Research Group, Stonehouse

Prummel, W and Frisch, H-J, 1986 A guide for the distinction of species, sex and body side in bones of sheep and goat, *J Archaeol Sci* **13**, 567-577

Quinnell, H, 2003 Devon Beakers: new finds, new thoughts, *Proc Devon Archaeol Soc* **61**, 1-20

Rawes, B, 1991 A prehistoric and Romano-British settlement at Vineyards Farm, Charlton Kings, Gloucestershire, *Trans Bristol Gloucestershire Archaeol Soc* **109** 25-89

Reece, R, 1990 *Excavations, survey and records around Cirencester*, Cotswold Studies **2**, Cirencester

Reece, R, 2003 The siting of Roman Corinium, *Britannia* **34**, 276-80

Reimer, P J, Baillie, M G L, Bard, E, Bayliss, A, Beck, J W, Bertrand, C J H, Blackwell, P G, Buck, C E, Burr, G S, Cutler, K B, Damon, P E, Edwards, R L, Fairbanks, R G, Friedrich, M, Guilderson, T P, Hogg, A G, Hughen, K A, Kromer, B, McCormac, G, Manning, S, Ramsey, C B, Reimer, R W, Remmele, S, Southon, J R, Stuiver, M, Talamo, S, Taylor, F W, Plicht, Johannes van der, Weyhenmeyer, C E, 2004 IntCal04 terrestrial radiocarbon age calibration, 0–26 cal kyr BP, *Radiocarbon* **46(3)**, 1029-58

Reynolds, P J, 1979 *An Iron Age farm: the Butser experiment*, British Museum Publications, London

Rielly, K, 2009 Animal bone, in Trow *et al.* 2009, 187-209

Robertson-Mackay, M E, 1980 A 'head and hooves' burial beneath a round barrow, with other Neolithic and Bronze Age sites, on Hemp Knoll, near Avebury, Wiltshire, *Proc Prehist Soc* **46**, 123-176

Robinson, M, 1999 The land snails, in Barclay and Halpin 1999, 241-243

Roe, F, 1999 Stone axes, in Barclay and Halpin 1999, 228-33

Roe, F, 2001 The worked stone, in A prehistoric enclosure at Eynsham Abbey, Oxfordshire, (A Barclay, A Boyle and G D Keevill), *Oxoniensia* **66**, 140-144

Roe, F, 2003 Stone axe, in *Lines in the landscape: cursus monuments in the Upper Thames Valley* (A Barclay, G Lambrick, J Moore and M Robinson), Thames Valley Landscapes Monograph **15**, Oxford, 134-5

Roe, F, in prep a, Worked Stone, in Mann and Jackson in prep.

Roe, F, in prep b, From the Severn to Stonehenge: some new thoughts on stone axes found in Grooved Ware pits, in *Beyond the mundane: regional perspectives on Neolithic pit deposition* (eds H Lamdin-Wymark and J Thomas), Neolithic Studies Group seminar papers volume

Russell, M and Williams, D, 1998 Petrological examination and comparison of Beaker pottery from Bos Swallet and Gorsey Bigbury, *Proc University Bristol Spelaeological Soc* **21(2)**, 133-140

Ryder, M, 1964 The history of sheep breeds in Britain, *Agricultural History Review* **12**, 65-82

Saville, A, 1979 *Excavations at Guiting Power Iron Age site, Gloucestershire, 1974*, CRAAGS Occasional Paper **7**, Bristol

Saville, A, 1983 Excavations at Condicote henge monument, Gloucestershire, *Trans Bristol Gloucestershire Archaeol Soc* **101**, 21-47

Saville, A, 1990 *Hazleton North, Gloucestershire 1979-1982. The excavation of a Neolithic Long Cairn of the Cotswold-Severn Group*, English Heritage Archaeol Rep **13**, London

Scheuer, L and Black, D, 2000 *Developmental juvenile osteology*, Academic, London

Scheuer, L, Musgrave, J H and Evans, S P, 1980 The estimation of late fetal and perinatal age from limb bone length by linear and logarithmic regression, *Annals of Human Biology* **7**, 257-265

Schmid, E, 1972 *Atlas of animal bones for prehistorians, archaeologists and quaternary geologists*, Elsevier Pub. Co., Amsterdam, New York

Scott, E, 1999 *The archaeology of infancy and infant death*, BAR Int. Ser. **819**, Oxford

Sellwood, L, 1984 Objects of bone and antler, in Cunliffe 1984, 371-378

Serjeantson, D, 1996 The animal bones, in *Refuse and disposal at Area 16 East, Runnymede. Runnymede Bridge research excavations, volume 2* (S Needham and T Spence), British Museum Press, London, 194-253

Serjeantson, D, 2006 Food or feast at Neolithic Runnymede?, in *Animals in the Neolithic of Britain and Europe* (eds D Serjeantson and D Field), Oxbow Book, Oxford, 113-134

Serjeantson, D and Morris, J, 2011 Ravens and crows in Iron Age and Roman Britain, *Oxford J Archaeol* **30**, 85-107

Shaffrey, R, 2002 Worked stone, in Excavations at West Drive, Cheltenham, Gloucestershire, 1997-9 (T Catchpole), *Trans Bristol Gloucestershire Archaeol Soc* **102**, 99

Shaffrey, R, 2004 Worked stone, in *Thornhill Farm, Fairford, Gloucestershire: an Iron Age and Roman pastoral site in the Upper Thames Valley* (D Jennings, J Muir, S Palmer and A Smith), Oxford Archaeology Thames Valley Landscapes Monograph **23**, Oxford

Shaffrey, R, 2006 *Grinding and milling: a study of Romano-British rotary querns and millstones made from Old Red Sandstone*, BAR Brit Ser **409**, Oxford

Shaffrey, R, 2009 The worked stone, in Lamdin-Whymark *et al.* 2009, 103-4

Sharples, N M, 1991 *Maiden Castle: excavations and field survey, 1985-6*, English Heritage, London

Singh, S and Ernst, E, 2009 *Trick or treatment: alternative medicine on trial*, Transworld Publishers, London

Smith, A, Powell, K and Booth, P (eds), 2010 *Evolution of a farming community in the Upper Thames Valley: excavation of a prehistoric, Roman and post-Roman landscape at Cotswold Community, Gloucestershire and Wiltshire. Volume 2: The finds and environmental reports*, Oxford Archaeology, Oxford

Smith, I F and Simpson, D, 1966 Excavation of a round barrow on Overton Hill, North Wiltshire, *Proc Prehist Soc* **32**, 122-155

Smith, K, 2006 *Guides, guards and gifts to the gods: domesticated dogs in the art and archaeology of Iron Age and Roman Britain*, BAR Brit Ser **422**, Oxford

Smith, R and Cox, P, 1986 *The past in the pipeline: archaeology of the Esso midline*, Trust for Wessex Archaeology, Salisbury

Stace, C, 1997 *New flora of the British Isles*, 2 edn, Cambridge University Press, Cambridge

Straker, V, 1990 Plant and molluscan remains, in Saville 1990, 215–19

Stone, J F S, 1949 Some grooved ware pottery from the Woodhenge area, *Proc Prehistoric Soc* **15**, 122-27

Stone, J F S and Young, W E V, 1948 Two pits of Grooved Ware date near Woodhenge, *Wiltshire Archaeol Mag* **52**, 287-306

Strid, L, 2000 *To eat or not to eat? The significance of the cutmarks on the bones from wild canids, mustelids and felids from the Danish Ertebølle site Hjerk Nor*, unpubl. MA dissertation, University of Southampton

Strid, L, 2010 Animal bone, in Smith *et al.* (eds) 2010, 207-42

Sumbler, M G, Barron, A J M and Morigi A N, 2000 *Geology of the Cirencester district: memoir for 1:50,000 geological sheet 235 (England and Wales)*, HMSO, London

Swan, V, 1975 Oare reconsidered and the origins of Savernake ware in Wiltshire, *Britannia* **6**, 36-61

Sykes, N, 2007a The faunal remains from Longdoles Field, in Miles *et al.* 2007, http://ads.ahds.ac.uk/catalogue/adsdata/cwp_eh_2005/ahds/dissemination/eagle_in_the_landscape/home.htm

Sykes, N, 2007b The faunal remains from Warrens Field, in Miles *et al.* 2007, http://ads.ahds.ac.uk/catalogue/adsdata/cwp_eh_2005/ahds/dissemination/eagle_in_the_landscape/home.htm

Symmons, R, 2005 New density data for unfused and fused sheep bones, and a preliminary discussion on the modelling of taphonomic bias in archaeofaunal age profiles, *J Archaeol Sci* **32**,1691-1698

Thawley, C R, 1982 The animal remains, in Wacher and McWhirr 1982, 211-227

Thomas, A and Holbrook, N, 1998 Excavations at the Memorial Hall, Lechlade, 1995, in Boyle *et al.* 1998, 282-288

Thomas, A, Holbrook, N and Bateman, C, 2003 *Later prehistoric and Romano-British burial and settlement at Hucclecote, Gloucestershire*, Bristol Gloucestershire Archaeol Rep **2**, Cirencester

Thompson, I, 1982 *Grog-tempered 'Belgic' pottery of south-eastern England*, BAR Brit Ser **108**, Oxford

Thomas, J, 2010 The return of the Rinyo-Clacton folk? The cultural significance of the Grooved Ware complex in later Neolithic Britain, *Cambridge Archaeol J* **20 (1)**, 1-15

Timby, J, 1999 Later prehistoric and Roman pottery, in Mudd *et al.* 1999, 320-65

Timby, J, 2008 *Pottery from Eysey Manor Quarry*, unpublished report for Thames Valley Archaeological Services

Timby, J, 2010 *Pottery from Dryleaze Farm*, unpublished report for Thames Valley Archaeological Services

Tomber, R and Dore, J, 1998 *The national Roman fabric reference collection: a handbook*, MoLAS Monogr **2**, London

Tomek, T and Bocheński, Z M, 2000 *The comparative osteology of European corvids (Aves: Corvidae), with a key to the identification of their skeletal elements*,

Wydawnictwa Instytutu Systematyki i Ewolucji Zwierzat PAN, Kraków

Trow, S, James, S and Moore, T, 2009 *Becoming Roman, being Gallic, staying British: research and excavations at Ditches 'hillfort' and villa, 1984-2006*, Oxbow Books, Oxford

Veen, M van der, Livarda, A and Hill, A, 2007 The archaeobotany of Roman Britain: current state and identification of research priorities, *Britannia* **38**, 181-210

Vretemark, M, 1997 *Från ben till boskap. Kosthåll och djurhållning med utgångspunkt i medeltida benmaterial från Skara*, Skrifter från Länsmuseet Skara **25**

Wacher, J S and McWhirr, A D, 1982 *Early Roman occupation at Cirencester*, Cirencester excavations **1**, Cirencester

Wainwright, G, 1979 *Mount Pleasant, Dorset: Excavations 1970-1971*, Res Rep Comm Soc Antiq **37**, London

Wainwright, G J and Longworth, I H, 1971 *Durrington Walls: Excavations 1966-1968*, Rep Res Comm Soc Antiq **29**, Dorking

Wessex Archaeology, in prep, Report on earlier prehistoric sites at excavations at Boscombe Down, Wiltshire

Walker, G, Thomas, A and Bateman, C, 2004 Bronze Age and Romano-British sites south-east of Tewkesbury: evaluations and excavations, 1991-7, *Trans Bristol Gloucestershire Archaeol Soc* **122**, 29-94

Watkinson, D and Neal, V, 1998 *First aid for finds*, 3 edn, United Kingdom Institute for Conservation of Historic and Artistic Works (Archaeology Section), Southampton

Webster, P V, 1976 Severn Valley ware: a preliminary study, *Trans Bristol Gloucestershire Archaeol Soc* **94**, 18-46

Whimster, R, 1981 *Burial practices in Iron Age Britain: a discussion and gazetteer of the evidence, c 700 BC-AD 43*, BAR Brit Ser **90**, Oxford

Whittle, A, 1984 The pits, in *Danebury, an Iron Age hillfort in Hampshire. Vol. 1 – the excavations 1969-1978: the site* (B Cunliffe), CBA Res Rep **52**, London, 128-146

Wilkinson, D (ed.), 1992 *OAU fieldwork manual*, unpublished

Williams, A, 1948 Excavations in Barrow Hills Field, Radley, Berkshire, 1944, *Oxoniensia* **13**, -17

Williams, D F, 1982 Iron Age and Roman pottery from Cirencester and Bagendon, in *Early Roman occupation at Cirencester* (J Wacher and A McWhirr), Cirencester Excavations **1**, Cirencester, 201-2

Willis, S with Dannell, G, 2009 Catalogue of the samian: Trench E, in Trow *et al.* 2009, 80-2

Wilson, B, Grigson, C and Payne, S (eds), 1982 *Ageing and sexing animal bones from archaeological sites*, BAR Brit Ser **109**, Oxford

Wilson, B, Hamilton, J, Bramwell, D and Armitage, P, 1978 The animal bones, in *The excavation of an Iron Age settlement, Bronze Age ring-ditches and Roman features at Ashville trading estate, Abingdon (Oxfordshire), 1974-76* (M Parrington), CBA Res Rep **28**, London, 110-139

Wilson, B and Miles, D, 1986 Utilised bone, in *Archaeology at Barton Court Farm, Abingdon, Oxford* (D Miles), CBA Res Rep **50**, London, microfiche 3:B10-11

Woefle, E, 1967 *Vergleichend morphologische Untersuchungen an Einzelknochen des postcranialen Skelettes im Mitteleuropa vorkommender Enten, Halbgänse und Säger*, unpubl. Inaugural-Dissertation, Ludwig-Maximilians-Universität, München

Woodward, A, 2002 Beads and Beakers: heirlooms and relics in the British early Bronze Age, *Antiquity* **76**, 1040-47

Worley, F, forthcoming, Animal bone: Northfleet Roman villa, in *Settling the Ebbsfleet Valley: CTRL excavations at Springhead and Northfleet, Kent – the late Iron Age, Roman, Saxon and medieval landscape. Volume 3: Late Iron Age to Roman human remains and environmental reports* (P Andrews, E Biddulph and A Hardy), Oxford Wessex Archaeology, Oxford and Salisbury

Worssam, B C, Ellison, R A and Moorlock, B S P, 1989 *Geology of the country around Tewkesbury*, HMSO, London

Wymark, C, 2003 *Thames Water repairs to public sewers, Cirencester, Gloucestershire. Programme of archaeological recording*, Cotswold Archaeology CA 03140

Yates, D, 2007 *Land, power and prestige: Bronze Age field systems in southern England*, Oxbow Books, Oxford

Young, D, 2001 *Excavation of two prehistoric enclosures at the Beeches, London Road*, Cirencester. unpublished report by Avon Archaeological Unit

Zohary, D and Hopf, M, 2000 *Domestication of plants in the Old World: the origin and spread of cultivated plants in West Asia, Europe and the Nile Valley*, 3 edn, Clarendon Press, Oxford

Index